The Sea

The Sea is a comedy set in an East Coast village in 1907. The action centres round the drowning of a young man and the repercussions, emotional and political, it has on the tight, inward-looking village community. Eerie and funny by turns, *The Sea* is unlike Bond's earlier plays in many ways. But like all of them it bears the unmistakable stamp of a highly original imagination.

The photograph on the front of the cover shows a scene from the original Royal Court production. The photograph on the back of the cover is reproduced by courtesy of Mark Gerson.

Edward Bond

THE SEA

a Comedy

METHUEN · LONDON

A METHUEN PAPERBACK

First published 1973 by Eyre Methuen Ltd
11 New Fetter Lane London EC4P 4EE
Reprinted 1975, 1978 and 1980
Reprinted as a Methuen Paperback in
1982 by Methuen London Ltd
© 1973 by Edward Bond
Author's Note © 1975 by Edward Bond
Printed and bound in Great Britain by
Richard Clay (The Chaucer Press) Ltd,
Bungay, Suffolk

ISBN 0 413 30060 9 (Hardback)
ISBN 0 413 30070 6 (Paperback)

For
Bill Gaskill

The Sea was presented by the Royal Court Theatre and Michael Codron on 22 May 1973 with the following cast:

WILLY CARSON	Simon Rouse
EVENS	Alan Webb
HATCH	Ian Holm
HOLLARCUT	Mark McManus
VICAR	Jeremy Wilkin
CARTER	Anthony Langdon
THOMPSON	Simon Cord
LOUISE RAFI	Coral Browne
ROSE JONES	Diana Quick
JESSICA TILEHOUSE	Gillian Martell
MAFANWY PRICE	Susan Williamson
JILLY	Adrienne Byrne
RACHEL	Barbara Ogilvie
DAVIS	Margaret Lawley

Ladies and men.

Directed by William Gaskill
Designed by Deirdre Clancy

ONE	Beach
TWO	Shop
THREE	Beach
FOUR	House
FIVE	Shop
SIX	Beach
SEVEN	Cliff
EIGHT	Beach

There is an interval after Scene Five.

East Coast, 1907

SCENE ONE

Beach.

Empty stage. Darkness and thunder. Wind roars, whines, crashes and screams over the water. Masses of water swell up, rattle and churn, and crash back into the sea. Gravel and sand grind slowly. The earth trembles.

WILLY. Help. Aaahhh – (*The sound is drowned by water.*) Help. Colin. Shout. Oh, god, make him shout.

The tempest grows louder.

WILLY. Help – (*The sound is drowned by water again.*)

A drunken man comes on singing.

EVENS. I don't know why – I sing'ss song – 'Ss day'ss short – an' ss—
WILLY. Help. Help.
EVENS. Wha'?
WILLY. Here. In the water. A man's in the water.

Thunder.

EVENS. 'Ss too late f'ss thass. 'Ss sea 'sl finish all'ss thass. Have'ss drink. Lil'ss drink. Here'ss, take'ss bottle . . .
WILLY. Help me. Our boat turned over. I can't find him.
EVENS. I sing 'ss song – 'Ss day'ss short – an'ss —
WILLY. You bastard. Colin. Colin.
EVENS. Wah'? I don' know why'ss – 'Ssing'ss song – 'Ss some'ss in'ss wasser?

The storm is worse. Thunder. The wind screams. HATCH, *a middle-aged man, comes on with a torch.*

HATCH. What are you up to?

EVENS. Oh god, 'ss draper. Have'ss drink, ol' pal. Tha'ss bottle —
HATCH. Filthy beast.
EVENS. I'm off. (*Going*) Wha'ss night! Dear o' lor'.
HATCH. I know what's going on here.
WILLY. Help. Help.
HATCH. I know who you are. You thought you wouldn't be seen out here.
WILLY. Colin. For god's sake shout.

EVENS *goes out singing.*

EVENS. (*Going*) I ssing'ss my song – 'ss day'ss short –
WILLY. Oh god.

WILLY *comes out of the water. He is soaked. His hair and clothes are plastered down. He stands on the edge of the sea crying and pleading.* HATCH *catches him in his torch.* WILLY *is heard shouting above the storm.*

WILLY. Help us.
HATCH. Go back.
WILLY. Are you all mad? Where am I?
HATCH. I knew you were coming. We'll fight you, you filthy beast.

WILLY *turns and goes back into the sea.*

WILLY. Colin. Colin.

Heavy guns fire some way off.

HATCH. The guns! They've brought the guns up! Hurrah!
WILLY. What?
HATCH. Hurrah the guns! The army knows you're here. The whole country's turning out. We'll smash you.

HATCH *goes out with his torch. The storm grows.*

WILLY. Colin. Don't die. Not like this. Shout.

WILLY *runs through the water.*

SCENE TWO

Draper's Shop.

Counter. Shelves with rolls of material and piles of clothes. Two wicker chairs for customers. On the counter various haberdasheries, a wooden till, and a display dummy cut off at the waist and neck.

MRS RAFI *(ageing) and her companion* MRS TILEHOUSE *(forties, retiring but determined) are in the shop.* HATCH, *the draper, is serving them. He is fortyish, with oiled hair and a rather flat face. Very pale blue eyes.*

HATCH. Art serge is coming in now, Mrs Rafi. Very fashionable for winter curtains.

MRS RAFI *ignores him and goes on examining a specimen on the counter.*

MRS RAFI. Does this wear?

HATCH. Embosseds don't wear as well as Utrechts, of course.

MRS RAFI. Show me this in blue.

HATCH. We don't carry any blues, I'm afraid. I can show you a faded pink or the club green.

MRS RAFI *(to him as she looks through a bulky catalogue)*. Blue, blue.

HATCH. Have you seen the moquettes? *(He tries to show her a place in the catalogue.)*

MRS RAFI. Don't jolly me along. I wouldn't be comfortable with an artificial material. I want velvet.

HATCH. Velvet does hang best. It gives the wear and it keeps its lustre.

MRS RAFI. At that price it should.

HATCH *(to MRS TILEHOUSE)*. Have you seen our Indian Dhurries, Mrs Tilehouse? New in this week. You'll appreciate the superb colourings. You can carry them off.

MRS RAFI. I'm not interested in this new-fangled craze to support the trading efforts of the Empire by getting the east coast into native dress. I came to choose curtains, and I want Utrecht velvet – which I suppose comes from Birmingham. Your catalogue is full of interesting items but none of them are in your shop. You offer only shoddy! How can you attract a discriminating and rewarding class of client? Look, your catalogue lists blue – (*She hands him the catalogue.*) – at the bottom of page one three two one in the right hand column.

HATCH (*holding catalogue*). All you see here is available against special order, Mrs Rafi. Blue isn't asked for. (*To* MRS TILEHURST.) There isn't the demand for it. Not at the price, Mrs Tilehouse.

MRS TILEHOUSE (*nods sympathetically*). There wouldn't be.

MRS RAFI. I suppose it would be wholly optimistic of me to ask to see an example?

Silently HATCH *takes a blue sample from a drawer and hands it to her. She studies it.*

MRS RAFI. I take it delivery is appalling.

HATCH. The suppliers quote two weeks to the nearest railway station. Very reasonable, I think.

MRS RAFI. If you could rely on it.

MRS TILEHOUSE. My new work-basket came within the week.

MRS RAFI (*looking in the catalogue*). Nottingham lace, Guipure d'Art, Turkish carpets, Japanese Nainsooks: I suppose they all come in two weeks from the warehouse in Birmingham. The art has gone out of shopping. (*She sighs. She picks up the sample.*) Is this accurate?

HATCH. I believe so.

MRS RAFI. Most samples are sent out to deliberately deceive customers. I have no doubt about it, you could add it to the Articles of Religion. Well, it's a handsome material. I'll say that. It will look well at Park House. I want a hundred and sixty-two yards in three-yard lengths. I'll have it made up at

Forebeach. I can supervise the work there. (*She puts the sample in her bag.*) I'll take this piece of evidence.

MRS TILEHOUSE. Louise, would it be better to have one room made up first? So that you get the sight of it.

MRS RAFI. Why? The downstairs curtains are shabby, even you remarked on it. This material is suitable. I've already enlarged my impression of this small piece into the entire scene – and I can tell you it looks very well.

HATCH. I'll send a copy of the order up to Park House. (*A bit too firmly.*) Then you'll have your own reminder.

MRS RAFI. I'm obliged. Now gloves. What have you to offer me in that line?

HATCH. Only what you saw last week, Mrs Rafi.

MRS RAFI. Nothing new? But you undertook to obtain further examples for me to see.

HATCH. Not in yet.

MRS RAFI. I suppose on gloves they quote immediate delivery. Well, you'd better show me the ones I saw last week. I must have gloves and if that's all you offer I shall have to make do with them – until I can drive into Forebeach and select from a more convenient range.

HATCH *produces two boxes of gloves.*

MRS TILEHOUSE. I liked these on you, Louise. They go with anything.

MRS RAFI. Jessie, please don't try to hustle me into a purchase. You know it makes me cross. One uses one's hands to point and emphasize and gesture. People are judged by what they have on their hands. They're important.

HATCH. Gazelle. Five shillings and five and eleven. Buck. Close grained, hard wearing. Doe. Feel the softness, Mrs Rafi. Washable kid. Two and six. Natural beaver. These have white tips, which many ladies prefer for the few pence extra. Then we have the military style – that's coming in now. At three shillings.

MRS RAFI (*trying on a pair of gloves*). It says six and three-quarters in the cuff. Why can't I get into them?

HATCH. Perhaps if you tried a slender man's —

MRS RAFI. I've always worn a lady's habit. Seven at the most. And these come from Birmingham. Isn't that a centre of precision engineering? One should at least be entitled to expect them to manufacture gloves to size. (*She tries another pair.*) Six and three-quarters again and a completely different fit. (*She gets a glove on with difficulty.*) They support the hand comfortably, but will they stand wearing? (*She thumps her hand on the counter.*) No. Gone at the seams. There you are, they give under the slightest emphasis. (*Takes the glove off.*) I'm an emphatic woman and I must have gloves that accommodate themselves to my character. I'm not having those. Thank heavens I found out in time. (*She picks up another pair.*) Now these have style. I could wear this cuff. Tap on the window.

MRS TILEHOUSE. What?

MRS RAFI. Quickly.

MRS TILEHOUSE *taps on the window.*

MRS RAFI. Louder.

MRS TILEHOUSE *taps louder.* MRS RAFI *waves broadly but genteelly and calls by opening her mouth wide and whispering.*

MRS RAFI. A moment.

The doorbell clangs. WILLY *comes in.*

MRS RAFI. It is Mr Carson? I'm Mrs Rafi. Howdyoudo.

WILLY. Howdyoudo.

MRS RAFI. This is a terrible tragedy. Colin was engaged to my niece. My companion, Mrs Jessica Tilehouse.

WILLY. Howdyoudo.

MRS TILEHOUSE. Howdyoudo. Oh terrible. I knew Colin well.

So courteous. He always had a kind word, even for those in the background.

MRS RAFI. The coroner's wife called to tell me the details after breakfast. You must feel low. You can imagine the state my poor niece is in.

WILLY. I've just been at your house. I tried to see her but they told me to come back later.

MRS RAFI. Please treat my house as your home. I was devoted to Colin.

MRS TILEHOUSE. *He* was one for whom the future seemed all brightness. Oh dear.

MRS RAFI. Are you staying long?

WILLY. Till the inquest.

MRS TILEHOUSE. Oh dear.

MRS RAFI. You must tell me exactly what happened. I was going to complain to the Chief-of-Staff about the battery opening fire. But the coroner's wife tells me you'd strayed into their target area. How can that be? It's marked on the charts. Who was the navigator?

WILLY. Oh. We both looked after that. It was a small boat. The storm swept us off course. The guns didn't sink us. We'd already turned over.

MRS TILEHOUSE. Such a night. Thank heavens I didn't know you were out in it. I would have had no sleep. I assure you. I would have been tormented by the vision of – (*She stops in sudden realization and deep embarrassment. She almost panics.*) Not that my sufferings would have mattered. Of course. Compared to you. I would gladly, gladly have watched the whole night through if —

MRS RAFI (*drops a pair of gloves on the counter*). I shan't take these after all, Hatch. My umbrella handle lodges itself in the cuff. Send these others back to the manufacturers. Tell them they are not up to the standard one should be entitled to expect. Mr Carson, perhaps you'll drive back to Park House for luncheon. My pony and trap is outside.

WILLY. Will they find the body?

MRS TILEHOUSE. Oh dear. This terrible sea, this terrible life.

MRS RAFI. Everything is washed up. Our coast is known for it. You throw a handkerchief into the sea one day and pick it up the next. See Mr Evens. He's peculiar, but he knows the water round here. He'll tell you where anything will come out, and when. Jessie, you must walk. Pony can't manage three.

WILLY. I'll walk.

MRS RAFI. Come along.

MRS RAFI and WILLY go out. The doorbell clangs.

MRS TILEHOUSE. Mr Hatch, who was on coastguard duty last night?

HATCH. Why?

MRS TILEHOUSE. Surely it will come out at the inquest? Why was nothing seen by the town lookout?

HATCH. You'd need second sight to see anything last night. (*He is putting the gloves away.*) I was on duty.

MRS TILEHOUSE. Dear me, and the town pays you ten shillings a year to watch —

HATCH. I watch, Mrs Tilehouse. More than the town's ten shillings is worth.

The doorbell clangs. HOLLARCUT *comes in. He is a quiet, blond young man.*

HOLLARCUT. Oh.

HATCH. Morning, Billy. Wait out the back, lad.

HOLLARCUT *starts to go through behind the counter.*

MRS TILEHOUSE. Morning, Hollarcut. Were you on duty last night?

HOLLARCUT. No, Mrs Tilehouse.

MRS TILEHOUSE. Not? But surely on such a night? I thought all the coastguards would have gone to their posts.

HATCH. That's not in my copy of the Regulations, Mrs Tilehouse.

HOLLARCUT. An' I can't read mine.

HOLLARCUT *goes out behind the counter.*

HATCH. This material, Mrs Tilehouse. A hundred and sixty-two yards. Will she change her mind? Last time she ordered cushions she wouldn't even look at them. Now I have to send cash with every order, and they'll only take back against bona fide complaints. I've had a letter from the suppliers. It's signed by the managing director.

MRS TILEHOUSE. You're in business, Mr Hatch. You have to do what the customer wants.

HATCH (*goes to door*). Very good, Mrs Tilehouse. Good day.

MRS TILEHOUSE. I think I'll look at those Indian Dhurries.

HATCH. We're closed for lunch. Allow me. (*He opens the door for her.*) Good day, m'am. Much obliged.

MRS TILEHOUSE *goes out.* HATCH *locks the door behind her. He stands looking through the window.*

HATCH. Bit longer, lads. The old buzzard's still there . . . (*Turns back into the shop, smacking his hands together.*) She's gone.

HOLLARCUT, THOMPSON *and* CARTER *come out of the back of the shop.* THOMPSON *is a thinnish man with dark hair. Early middle age.* CARTER *is heavier and older.*

THOMPSON. My life. I was sweatin' back there. I was certain-shar Mrs Rafi'd come through. Juss the sort a notion she'd git took in her hid. She give me the sack doo she find me here.

HATCH. Did you follow him?

HOLLARCUT. I bin on his tail all mornin'. Then I seen him come here an goo off with that ol' bat. Tent no use followin' him now. She see you comin' afore yoo started.

HATCH. What did he do?

HOLLARCUT. Nothin' t' remark on.

HATCH. Clever.

THOMPSON. What yoo make on him then, Mr Hatch?

HATCH. Look at the facts. He lands in the middle of the storm when no one's going to see him. He arranges to meet that devil Evens out on the beach.

HOLLARCUT. Right.

HATCH. And Mr Bentham's dead. They've started with murder and they'll do worse.

THOMPSON. Oh lor'.

HATCH. That boat didn't go down by accident.

HOLLARCUT. You may depend on it.

CARTER. We must take this to the magistrates, lads. It's too big for us.

HATCH. They wouldn't believe us, Mr Carter. You coastguards don't believe me half the time, in spite of all my warnings.

THOMPSON. Thass a rum ol' do.

CARTER. You hear tell a such queer ol' gooins on. Tell the truth, I on't know what I doo believe n'more . . .

HOLLARCUT (to HATCH). They do believe sometime. (To THOMPSON.) Don't yoo, Wad?

THOMPSON. Oh I believe sometime right enough. Oh ah.

HATCH. They come from space. Beyond our world. Their world's threatened by disaster. If they think we're a crowd of weak fools they'll all come here. By the million. They'll take our jobs and our homes. Everything. We'll be slaves working all our lives to make goods for sale on other planets.

THOMPSON. An' the women folk? They after that?

HATCH. No. They come from a higher stage of progress. Their intellects run more on science and meditation. They build formal gardens for a hobby.

THOMPSON. Chriss.

HATCH. Listen, where's the world's weak spot? Here. (HOLLARCUT and THOMPSON grunt assent.) They know there's no leadership, no authority, no discipline in this town. So it's up to us. All these ships in distress are really secret landings

from space. We won't go out to help them, we'll go and drive
them off. Run them down.

CARTER. What if they're sailors in distress?

HATCH. They aren't sailors, they aren't even real storms. These
people come millions of miles – they know how to whip up
a storm when they get here. We might lose a few innocent
men. (*Shrugs.*) That's a risk, but *they're* guilty, not us. Now
go and wait outside Park House, Billy. Follow him when he
leaves.

HOLLARCUT. Right.

HATCH. They'll have arranged times to hover overhead invisibly.
You watch and you'll see him make signs in a prearranged
code. It could be anything: a scratch, a wave, or he'll pretend
to tie his shoe. Keep it all in your head. I'll go through it
with you later.

HOLLARCUT, THOMPSON *and* CARTER *go out. The doorbell
clangs.* HATCH *bolts the door behind them. He goes to the till, takes
out the money and puts it into a little canvas bank-bag. He looks up
into the air and makes a small ritualised gesture of defiance. He
speaks in an almost business-like voice.*

HATCH. St George for England.

SCENE THREE

Beach.
*An old hut with an old bike leaning against it. An empty shopping
bag hangs from the handle bars. A few washed up wooden spars and
boxes smoothed by water.*

Bright, sunny, fresh. A wind from the sea. WILLY *is just coming on.
His jacket collar is turned up and his hands are in his pockets. He
looks round, goes to the hut and taps on the door. No answer. It is
padlocked. He tries the padlock.* EVENS *comes on behind him and
watches. He is old, weathered and bearded.*

EVENS. It's locked.

WILLY. Oh. Hello. I'm a friend of Mrs Rafi.

EVENS. Yes.

WILLY. I was on the boat that turned over last night.

EVENS. A boat?

WILLY. Yes.

EVENS. Last night?

WILLY. Yes.

EVENS. It was rough.

WILLY. My friend drowned.

EVENS. Oh. You want to know where he'll come up.

WILLY. Well yes.

EVENS (*shrugs wearily*). Depends where he went down.

EVENS *goes into the hut.* WILLY *stands silently. When* EVENS *comes out again he is surprised to see* WILLY *still there.*

EVENS. Oh. I'll think about it. (*He is turning to go back into the hut.*) I'm sorry about the accident.

WILLY. You live here?

EVENS. Yes.

WILLY. It must be nice.

EVENS. . . . Sometimes. It gets cold. The wind.

WILLY *sits down on a box and starts to cry into his hands.* EVENS *looks at him for a moment and then goes slowly into the hut.* WILLY *cries a bit longer before he speaks.*

WILLY (*trying to stop*). So stupid – doing this – coming here and . . .

EVENS (*inside the hut*). Is there a proper place?

WILLY (*trying to stop*). . . . last night . . .

HATCH *comes on.* HOLLARCUT *follows a little way behind and stands watching.*

HATCH. It didn't take you long to get out here. You've got to get rid of the body before anyone sees the marks. Wait till it comes in and tow it out to sea or bury it in the sand. I'm watching you —

EVENS *comes out of the hut.*

HATCH. – yes, and you, Evens. You're both under surveillance. (*Yells back to* HOLLARCUT.) Did you see him cry, Billy?

HOLLARCUT. Ay.

HATCH. That was a sign. Crying: bad news. That's us. Those devils are up there watching. He's telling them we're onto him.

WILLY (*trying to stop crying*). What's the matter with him?

EVENS. He's harmless.

HATCH. Oh, we know how to handle you, Evens. This isn't your sort of sea. This is real sea where you drown. It's not governed by your fancy, twisted laws of gravity. You'll find out. (*Yells back to* HOLLARCUT.) They're afraid of our sea, Billy. They're not immune to wetness. It soaks in and melts their insides. You watch: they're terrorized of it.

HOLLARCUT. They en't worth a sermon, Mr Hatch. Give the word an' I'll kick their bloody hids off.

HATCH. Not yet. We'll make a study of them first. Learn their ways. Break their code. You keep the watching going. Goodbye, Mr Evens. We'll settle our account shortly.

HATCH *and* HOLLARCUT *go out.*

EVENS (*normally*). It's nice now. I hope the weather lasts.

WILLY. Do they often come here?

EVENS. No. They're as timid as mice. You coming, the storm, the boat – they're excited.

WILLY. Aren't they dangerous?

EVENS (*shrugs*). Yes, to themselves.

WILLY. Why d'you live here?

EVENS. Isn't it what everyone wants?

WILLY. No.

EVENS. Perhaps not. We're into the spring tides now. He'll be

washed up where the coast turns in. (*Points*.) You see?
People are cruel and boring and obsessed. If he goes past that
point you've lost him. He should come in. He's hanging
round out there now. He could see us if he wasn't dead.
My wife died in hospital. She had something quite
minor. I sold up. They hate each other. Force. Make. Use.
Push. Burn. Sell. For what? A heap of rubbish. Don't
believe what they say: I don't understand the water. I
know the main currents, but luck and chance come into it.
It doesn't matter how clear the main currents are, you have to
live through the details. It's always the details that make the
tragedy. Not anything larger. They used to say tragedy
purified, helped you to let go. Now it only embarrasses.
They'll make a law against it. He should come out in the
middle of next week. Don't count on it. There might be a
flood. Then everything goes by the board. A man was drowned
at sea and the next day a flood washed him miles inland and
left him in his own garden hanging up in the apple tree. All
the apples were washed off and went bobbing away in the
water. His wife and children were stranded up on the roof
watching him. They sat there three days.

HOLLARCUT *throws a lump of driftwood against the side of the
house.*

HOLLARCUT (*off*). Let yoo know I'm still watchin'.
WILLY. Couldn't you have him certified?
EVENS. The town doctor's madder than he is.

EVENS *takes out a half-bottle of whisky. He removes the cap and
holds the bottle out towards* HOLLARCUT.

EVENS. Drink?
HOLLARCUT (*off*). Is it poisoned?
EVENS. Yes.
HOLLARCUT. No ta then.

EVENS *drinks from the bottle. He holds it towards* WILLY.

EVENS (*looks round*). I don't have a cup.
WILLY. No thanks.
EVENS (*calls to* HOLLARCUT). Come and sit by the house, lad. Out of the wind.

HOLLARCUT *comes and sits down by the house.*

HOLLARCUT. Juss so's I see yoo better.
EVENS. What's old Hatch been telling you?
HOLLARCUT. Thass right, he say yood start in with yoor questions. On't took you long, hev it!
EVENS. You know he's mad.
HOLLARCUT (*evenly*). So you say.
EVENS. You're not that stupid, lad.
HOLLARCUT. He on't normal like me, or Wad, or my ma. But how'd I know he can't fathom out things I can't? Thass a rum ol' world. Yoo hev t'be a bit daft in the hid to know what doo goo on in en. Ask me it on't pay t'be too level-hided. I know it on't pay *me*.
EVENS. It's hard work talking to you.
HOLLARCUT (*contentedly*). I never ask yoo t' start. I on't interfere. I'm quite content sittin' here listenin'. You think I'm soft in the hid. Well there on't much goo' by I miss. I'll surprise the lot on yer one day.
EVENS (*drinks*). It keeps the wind out.

EVENS *puts the whisky bottle down on a box.*

WILLY. I met you on the beach last night.
EVENS. Oh?
HOLLARCUT. Thass right, when yoo was up t'yoor tricks in the water.
WILLY. You were drunk.
EVENS. Was I? I am sometimes.
HOLLARCUT. If they put yoo through a wringer they could start a brewery.

WILLY. You had a lantern.

HOLLARCUT. Signal for yoo t' come ashore.

EVENS (*sudden irritation*). You said you wouldn't talk.

HOLLARCUT. Juss let yoo know I'm listenin'.

WILLY (*calmly*). Why were you drunk?

HOLLARCUT. Cause he drunk too much. (*Laughs.*) There, I told yoo: I hev a sharp wit when I like. I hev em in stitches in our kitchen some nights when I hev my sprits up. My ma doo laugh. She hev all the neighbours in. She goo hollerin' arter 'em down the road. That make me laugh even more. We doo enjoy ourselves. Then we hev a singsong.

EVENS. I drink to keep sane. There's no harm in the little I drink. Li Po: you who are sated with life, now drink the dregs.

HOLLARCUT. Ah, code-talk now. We're on to that.

EVENS. Who drowned?

WILLY. From this town. Colin Bentham.

EVENS. Oh.

WILLY. He was going to marry Mrs Rafi's niece.

EVENS. I knew him. He came here when he was a boy. All the time. He used to play by the hut and swim. I remember the sea last night.

> Mad woman in a grey bed
> She struggles under the sheets
> Threshing her grey hair.

WILLY. If you hadn't been drunk.

EVENS. I answered that question long ago: *if* he hadn't gone to sea.

WILLY. He wanted to get here quickly, not go round on land.

EVENS. Why?

Silence. WILLY *stands.*

HOLLARCUT. Where yoo gooin?

EVENS. Hatch told you to watch us both, didn't he. Now you're for it.

WILLY *goes out.*

HOLLARCUT. I'll stay put an' watch you. I'm settled down now.

EVENS. You'll miss something.

HOLLARCUT (*contentedly*). 'S obvious yoo want a get rid a me. So I'll stay. I can work that out, boy.

EVENS *screws the cap onto the whisky bottle and goes towards the house.*

EVENS. Go and watch the vicar's girls swimming.

HOLLARCUT. Thass right: Mr Hatch say yoo come t' corrupt our manhood. What yoo get up to in there?

EVENS. I shrink little men and put them into bottles. Then the Martians stand them over the mantlepiece.

EVENS *goes into the hut and shuts the door behind him.* HOLLARCUT *settles down more comfortably against the side of the house.*

HOLLARCUT (*contentedly*). I on't believe that. Thass a tall story, I *doo* know.

SCENE FOUR

Park House.

Drawing room. Upper middle-class furniture. Comfortable, hard-wearing, good. Round table. Bookcase.

MRS RAFI, MRS TILEHOUSE, MAFANWY PRICE (*thirtyish, bun*), JILLY (*eighteen, bright cheeks and eyes*), RACHEL (*slightly plump, and neat and capable*). *The* VICAR (*about forty-three but looks younger. Wears a grey, summer suit*). ROSE *has just come in. She is pale and tired. The others are staring at her in surprise.*

MRS RAFI. Go back to your room, Rose. We'll manage without you.

ROSE. I'll stay.

MAFANWY. Poor thing.

MRS RAFI. You'll bring yourself down.
ROSE. I can see the sea through the windows.

A hushed moan from the LADIES

JILLY. How awful.
MAFANWY. In this town you can't get away from the sea.
MRS RAFI. Pull the curtains.
ROSE. O no.
MRS RAFI. The curtains. The curtains. Shut it out.

LADIES *hurry to close the curtains.*

MRS RAFI. Lights.

Some of the LADIES *change direction and hurry to fetch lights.*

MRS RAFI. Yes, stay with us. We understand. We've all known
    pain in our time. Bereavements, lost hopes. All our lives
    pass through the shadows. Jessica, hand out the books. I
    hope we've all got up our lines.
LADIES. Yes. Oh dear.
MRS RAFI. We shall see.
MRS TILEHOUSE (*to* ROSE). How brave of you to challenge your
    despair. You are right. We dare not fall back under the
    blows.
MRS RAFI. Jessica, stop trying to sound like a woman with an
    interesting past. Nothing has ever happened to you. That
    is a tragedy. But it hardly qualifies you to give advice. Hand
    out the books. Act one, scene three. Enter Orpheus.

A flurry of nervous anticipation.

I have lost my Eurydice. You all have the place? Over-
whelmed with misery I set out on the journey down the
steep rocky path to hell. On either side rise terrible bottom-
less pits blazing with smoky darkness. The rocky cavern
arches over my head. Maddened bats fly through its black-

ened vaults. I reach the river that lies before hell. Wearily I sit down on a rock and survey the dismal scene. I take out my lute and sing 'There's no place like home'.

MRS TILEHOUSE. Louise, dear. Is that the right song?

MRS RAFI. The right song? I always sing 'There's no place like home'. The town expects it of me.

MRS TILEHOUSE. Yes.

MRS RAFI. Then am I to disappoint them? I will not break the stage's unwritten law and comment on my fellow artistes' performance, but I will say, with confidence that comes from many tributes, that my performance of 'There's no place like home' will be one of the highlights of the evening.

RACHEL. We always enjoy it.

MRS TILEHOUSE. Well we'd better get on.

MRS RAFI. Get on, she says – as if we were drawing a glass of water from a tap. I do not know on what level you would find your inspiration – had you been entrusted with a part – but I cannot jump in and out of my part like a lady athlete. (*Silence. She sings.*) 'Bait havver sah hoobull hahs noo-hoo place lake hoo . . . (*She cuts quickly to the end of the song.*) dum-di-dum-di – *Ya*-ho-hoo place lake hoo.' Moved by the atmosphere I have created, I cry – together with a large part of the audience, if things go as usual. The sound of my torment attracts Cerberus, the watch dog of hell. He comes swimming over the dark water towards me.

MAFANWY. Louise, couldn't I already be on your side of the river?

MRS RAFI. Would you sit quietly by while I sang? Not at all. You would want to join in the chorus.

MAFANWY. It's so difficult to pretend I'm swimming when I am in fact walking.

MRS RAFI. Act, Miss Price. Remember your audience will do most of the work for you. They have already been set up by the poetry that has gone before.

MAFANWY (*sudden temper*). I can't I can't!

MRS RAFI. Every year the same. One sympathizes with god when he struggled to breathe life into the intractable clay. Do you not wish to support the coastguard fund? Has it no meaning for you?

MAFANWY. How cruel, Louise.

MRS RAFI. Then act. Give yourself to the part and it will carry you through.

MAFANWY. Why must I be a dog? Last year I was the monkey. If we did a pantomime you'd make me be the cat. I want to be one of the floral maids-of-honour who greet Orpheus with rose petals and song when he comes out of hell.

MRS RAFI. You'll be a dog. You collect for your Save the Animals Fund every year and you never go away till we've given twice as much as we can afford. Now you have the chance to earn some more gratitude from your little friends. (*Sighs.*) I know you need all the help you can get. I have foreseen it. Therefore two auxiliary ladies will hold a sheet across the stage. It will be decorated with dolphins, starfish and other sea emblems, and the ladies will be clad in bathing attire. You swim on behind the sheet. Only your head, arms and chest will show.

The LADIES *exclaim happy approval.*

MAFANWY. Oh thank you, thank you, Louise. You have such an inspiration.

MRS RAFI. At the same time – Mrs Tilehouse will crawl along in the dark under the stage and splash water round in a basin.

MRS TILEHOUSE. I can't. There isn't room.

MRS RAFI. Then create room. Don't you aspire to be an artist? Think of the miners who spend their lives crawling through darkness so that you may have light. That also, in its way, is the task of art.

The LADIES *murmur fervent agreement,* MRS RAFI *picks up a loose cover decorated with flowers, stems and leaves.* JILLY *and* RACHEL *hold it shoulder high across the stage.* MAFANWY *swims along behind it, as if the top of her body were coming out of the waves.*

MAFANWY. I come along, spitting water out of my mouth . . .
MRS RAFI. Not the dog paddle, I think. It's too obvious. Eurydice, are you for ever lost? No, no, I cannot bear it.

Normally MAFANWY *manages an acceptable middle-class accent, but the effort to act makes the dog very Welsh.*

MAFANWY. Who calls? What terrible shouts sound through these halls of death? Is that all right?
MRS RAFI. Don't be afraid to attack your part. I start up crazily at the sound of your voice. I cry: Eurydice, is it you?
MAFANWY. I step from the water and shake myself.
MRS RAFI. Shake yourself?
MAFANWY. All dogs shake themselves when they leave the water. I've been studying our Roger very carefully for the part.

MAFANWY *shakes herself.*

JILLY. It's so real, Fanny. I can feel the water. I want to dry myself, Mrs Rafi. I want to put on my overshoes and open my umbrella.
MRS RAFI. Yes, dear. Describe your reactions later over tea. They sound so interesting and fresh.
MAFANWY. From whence this voice of terror? It is the voice of a living man. The dead are spared such sufferings. Oh mortal, do not disturb these shades of darkness.

A knock on the door.

MRS RAFI. Never more shall I be silent. Lo, I tamed the wild beasts, but I cannot tame the torments of my breast —

DAVIS, *the maid, puts her head round the door.*

What is it, Davis?

DAVIS. Begpardonmam. Mr Carson. You said to show him in anytime.

MRS RAFI (*nods to* DAVIS). Ladies, you don't mind?

DAVIS *goes.*

For a few moments they stand and fidget nervously. Then WILLY *comes in. He looks round at the darkness.*

MRS RAFI. Come in, Mr Carson. We're rehearsing a performance.

WILLY. Ah, I'm sorry. Let me come back at —

MRS RAFI. No, no. Do come in. Here is my niece. Rose.

WILLY. Miss Jones. Howdyoudo. I wish our meeting was different. I can only tell you —

MRS RAFI. Hush, hush. Not now, children.

ROSE *shakes* WILLY'*s hand. Then she goes back to her place.*

MRS RAFI. Sit down, Mr Carson. Your presence might shame our ladies into some efforts at creativity. I'm about to cross the Styx by ferry. The Styx is made from the tears of the penitent and suffering, which is interesting. Do sit down. There – you'll see everything there.

MAFANWY. Do not disturb these shades of darkness. I use the special tone, Mr Carson, because I am portraying a dog.

MRS RAFI. Eurydice, let me clasp your marble bosom to my panting breast and warm it with my heart.

JILLY *starts to cry.*

JILLY. Oh dear. So sorry. It's so moving. So sad.

MRS RAFI. Let it flow, dear. Be moved. It's to be expected.

JILLY. How awful!

JILLY *runs crying from the room.*

MRS RAFI. I hope you'll all act like that on the night.

RACHEL. I'll go after her.

MRS RAFI. Leave her. Never show any interest in the passions of
the young, it makes them grow up selfish. Davis will pat her
and give her some tea and a slice of cake. Eurydice, oh speak.
(*She embraces* MAFANWY.)

MAFANWY. Away, distracted man. I am a dog.

MRS TILEHOUSE. Shouldn't she get down on all fours?

MRS RAFI. Jessica, I am directing this production. Your job is to
sell programmes and assist the stage carpenter. Eurydice, oh
speak.

MAFANWY. Alas, you have awakened old Pluto, the god of
this place. Now I shall be well thrashed.

Slight pause.

MRS RAFI (*loudly*). Pluto comes. (*Nothing happens. Louder.*) The
god of hell. (*Calls.*) Vicar.

VICAR. Oh, dear, I thought I was being summoned by Gabriel.
Pardon me, fellow Thespians. I was admiring your biblio-
graphic splendours, Mrs Rafi. A true delight.

MRS RAFI. Never mind books now, Vicar. We're struggling with
life.

VICAR. Quite so. I await direction.

MRS RAFI. You come on on the far side of Styx.

VICAR. Like so? Good. Now where are these excellent lines?
What is this dreadful wailing? By-the-by, Mrs Rafi. In the
interest of light relief might I at this juncture add a reference
– a sly reference, ladies – to a certain church choir of my
acquaintance?

MRS RAFI. No.

VICAR. I feared not. I do lend myself to these ribald interjections,
Mrs Rafi. However. Bad dog, come to your master.

MRS RAFI. Try: bad dog, come to your master.

VICAR. Dear me, if I were Cerberus I would run straight back to hell. However. Down, sir.

MRS RAFI. On your knees, dog.

VICAR. Ah yes. On your knees, dog. Oh excellent, Miss Price. Our Ajax lies just so before the hearth when he comes home from his walk on winter evenings.

MAFANWY. Thank you, Vicar. I've been noting the mannerisms of our Roger in a little book.

MRS RAFI. Ah! Eurydice.

VICAR. The excellent Roger. Yes. I'm sorry to tell you, Miss Price, that Roger has been chasing Ajax. I should explain, ladies, that I've always wanted an Ajax and I had bestowed that name on my dog before I noticed that she was of an altogether inappropriate gender. However, Roger noticed. Yes. I wonder, Miss Price, if I might ask you to —

MRS RAFI. Vicar.

VICAR. Indeed the subject is somewhat delicate. (*To* MAFANWY.) A few whispered words after choir practice will suffice.

MRS RAFI. Ah! Eurydice.

VICAR. Who calls my wife.

MRS RAFI. Ah horror.

VICAR. Yes, she is mine. Oh man, in this cold place of hell I lost my heart to her.

MRS RAFI. Ah horror. Ah horror.

MRS TILEHOUSE. That's only written down once. I hope I shan't be told I can't read – or count.

MRS RAFI. You can say what you like as long as you can carry it off. Ah horror. Ah horror. You shall not come out of hell to fetch that which is not thine or all women shall live in fear of Pluto's lust.

VICAR. He sounds like Roger. I cannot let her go.

MRS RAFI. Then defiance and resistance are my lot.

VICAR. Rise, my sleeping furies. Mrs Rafi, might I here make

reference to a certain local congregation toward the end of
sermon time?

MRS RAFI. No, Vicar.

VICAR. Furies, up!

LADIES *surround the* VICAR *gesturing and grimacing.*

VICAR. Be warned, oh vain and foolish man. That way lies
madness and despair. Oh man, a god pleads with you. You
may not put your hand into the iron sea to pluck out the
glittering thing. Behold, my ferryman. Think well before
you step into my ferryboat.

RACHEL *picks up a punting pole and a straw boater.* LADIES *lay
the loose cover flat on the floor.*

RACHEL. I'm sure Mr Carson will think I row like a chump. Here
goes.

RACHEL *steps onto the cover. She speaks her part very timidly and
can't remember the lines.* MRS TILEHOUSE *whispers prompts to her
all the time she speaks.*

RACHEL. I am . . . the ferryman of hell. I . . . come to . . . take
you over the black . . . water.

MRS RAFI *is about to step into the boat. She stops and peers down
into the water.*

MRS RAFI. I see a white thing shining down in the darkness.

RACHEL. That is the . . . reflection . . . of . . . Narcissus. It is
condemned to haunt these . . . waters for ever —

MRS RAFI. Ah horror. *Ah horror.*

RACHEL. – and . . . stare . . . up at the tormented and harrowed
. . . faces of those who . . . pass to death. Look, and turn . . .
back.

MRS RAFI. I cannot.

MRS RAFI *steps onto the cover.* RACHEL *starts to punt rhythmically.*
MRS RAFI *poses on an imaginary prow and stares at the distant
far shore of Styx. The rest of the cast softly hum the* 'Eton Boating

Song'. ROSE *slowly comes into the space on the shore and stands by Pluto.*

MRS RAFI *(ecstatic)*. Eurydice. Beloved. I see you.

ROSE. I am queen of this dark place. My heart burns with a new cold fire. Your love, your fear, your hope – what are they to me now? Dust scattered over the sea.

MRS RAFI *(stretching both arms towards Eurydice)*. Eurydice I cannot hear you. The wind blows your words over this cold river, I only see you calling me.

ROSE. Go back.

MRS RAFI *(ecstatic)*. Beloved, I come.

ROSE. Go back.

MRS RAFI. Yes, I come.

The rumble of very distant guns. The people in the room are silent for a moment. Then they make a low moan of annoyance and regret.

MRS TILEHOUSE. The battery.

RACHEL. Such a sad sound.

MRS RAFI. They practice all day and night! Someone should write to the War Office.

MAFANWY. They have their job.

MRS TILEHOUSE. I gladly embrace the inconvenience. The soldiers are our defenders.

VICAR. Just so, ladies. One reads the newspapers. The continental balance of power is threatened. Then there's the naval question . . .

MRS RAFI. I hope I'm a patriot. But an army belongs in the battlefield or the barracks. Not at the bottom of one's garden rattling the windows. Open the curtains. (*The* LADIES *sigh with relief.*) The mood of art has been pounded away. If I were doing Lear I could rise to it. But one can't play lutes to the sound of gunfire.

VICAR. What a pity. I do enjoy our clash on the bleak strand. Two mighty Titans locked in mortal battle.

RACHEL. I've laid out the designs on the table.

They go up to the round table to look at the designs. ROSE *crosses to* WILLY. *He sits alone on a chair. While they talk the others are admiring and giggling at the designs.*

ROSE. What is the matter, Mr Carson. You're white.

WILLY. It's nothing.

ROSE. Surely you're ill.

WILLY. The guns.

WILLY. They fired when our boat turned over.

ROSE. Can I get you something?

WILLY. No, no. That's very kind. I'm all right.

ROSE. It's an ordeal for you.

WILLY. We'd been friends so long.

ROSE. Yes.

WILLY. I can't say how sorry I am. There's nothing I can do.

ROSE (*nods*). No. There's nothing.

VICAR (*looking at a design; frightened*). Oh Mrs Rafi, do I approve? Is it proper to wear tights in front of one's parishioners? I must have a vestry ruling.

MRS RAFI (*at the round table*). They can't object. I designed them.

WILLY. They say his body will be washed up.

VICAR (*as before*). And the trident?

MRS RAFI. Pitchfork.

WILLY. I know he's dead, but when there's no body there's still a chance he might be . . .

ROSE. Mr Carson, you must go home.

WILLY. No. I sat in that hotel all yesterday. No. And what has been happening here this afternoon, I noticed nothing till the guns . . .? There were people on the beach when the boat turned over.

ROSE. Who?

WILLY. One was drunk and the other stood and shouted at me.

ROSE. Shouted?

WILLY. The man who runs the draper's on the front.

ROSE. Surely you're mistaken.

WILLY. No, no. He swore at me.

ROSE. Swore?

WILLY. Waved his arms. I thought he was mad. Or I was.

The VICAR *has come down to them.*

VICAR. We've shocked you, Mr Carson.

WILLY. How?

VICAR. Rehearsing a play when an inquest is about to take place
in our town. You see, it's for our yearly evening in aid of the
coastguard fund. Under the circumstances . . .

WILLY. Of course.

VICAR. Yet I feel some guilt. (*To* ROSE *as she is about to speak.*)
Yes, my dear, pardon me, but I do. I'd be happier on my
knees praying for our dead friend. And I would pray for
guidance and understanding. He was so very young. God
asks much of us. I christened him. I was hardly more than a
boy myself, you know. Quite new here. And now he's gone.
If the body is found I shall read the burial service. That
is always – well, particularly moving, you find, when you
bury someone you baptised. (*He starts to mumble some tears.*)
Now you must forgive me . . . One comes to live the life
of the parish. The births and deaths are in part one's
own.

The VICAR *goes away.*

WILLY. We were so near the shore. If only I'd been able to get
to him. It was so dark. I went back in the water. I think I
went in four times. More.

ROSE (*frightened*). Please go home, Mr Carson.

JILLY *comes into the room.*

JILLY. I'm sorry. Aren't I a silly? But I'm better now. I helped
   them to set tea. It's all ready in the conservatory.
MRS RAFI. Shall we go through?

WILLY *stands. Everyone moves towards the door.*

SCENE FIVE

Draper's Shop.

HOLLARCUT, THOMPSON, CARTER *and* HATCH.

HATCH. Read the papers between the lines. It says preparations
   against continental powers. Now what does that mean? Space
   travellers. But London can't say that.
THOMPSON. Count a they'd start up a rare ol' panic?
HATCH. Right. Imagine it, Wad, the enemy from another world!
   People would lose hope. They wouldn't even try to fight.
CARTER. Some on us would.
HATCH. *You* would. But would they at Forebeach?
CARTER. Wouldn't bet on that, true. But how'd yoo know he
   come from space?
HATCH. The guns. You can't get round that. They opened
   up the moment he came. Oh the army knows what's going
   on. That new range's not for practice. They mean business.
THOMPSON. Oh lor'. 'S plain as a baptist's funeral.
CARTER. Well why'd he drown young Bentham?
HATCH. That's obvious. Mr Bentham was about to marry. We
   may hope, he and his lady being nice, clean, well-brought
   up members of the gentry, they'd provide offspring.
THOMPSON (*knowingly*). Oh ah.
HATCH. And that's just what *they* don't want. The fewer we are
   the easier we're overcome.

THOMPSON. What? You mean everytime a chap's thinkin' a gooin' t' church he's liable to be done in?

HATCH. 'Fraid so, Mr Thompson.

THOMPSON. An' every time yoo tak' a gal back of a hedge they're watchin' an' . . . my life.

HATCH. If you only knew the half of it. There's no end to their cunning.

HOLLARCUT. Bet even yoo don't know, Mr Hatch – meanin' no disrespect.

HATCH. I know you don't, Billy. Still, I do know they've got more than one friend in this town.

THOMPSON. ⎱ (together). Who?
CARTER. ⎰ Not just Evens, then?

HATCH. Oh no. You soon spot them behind this counter. You get a fair indication from the way they pay their bill. That shows if they respect our way of life, or if they're just out to make trouble by running people into debt. Oh, some of them don't even know themselves. Their brains are taken out at night, bit by bit, and replaced by artificial material brought here in airships. Course, that's a slow method, it can take years —

HOLLARCUT. Oh you hadn't ought 'a say that, Mr Hatch. That worries a man. I hope there on't no particle a me I warn't born with.

HATCH. Not you, Billy. They wouldn't try it on you. You've led a clean life and now you see your reward. They tried to bribe me, you know.

THOMPSON. Goo on.

HATCH. Oh yes. Leave notes. I found one in the jam. Took the lid off and there it was.

THOMPSON. The devils!

HATCH. Write on a steamy window. That's another of their tricks. By the time you've brought someone to see it it's gone.

CARTER. How much did they offer yer?

HATCH. I didn't read the exact sum. I was too disgusted.

The doorbell clangs. MRS RAFI *and* MRS TILEHOUSE *come in.*

HATCH. Thank you for coming lads. I'll gladly help raise money
for new instruments for the town band. That's a worthy
cause. Ah, Mrs Rafi, ma'am. I was hoping you'd call. Good
day, Mrs Tilehouse. Right lads, out through the back.

MRS RAFI. Thompson, what are you doing here?

THOMPSON. Mornin', missus. I juss come down t' get some
seedlin' off the market —

MRS RAFI. Get back to the house. I pay you to work in my
garden, not come here and idle and gossip. See me in the
morning.

THOMPSON. Missus.

MRS RAFI. Mr Hatch, will you explain why you're holding a mass
meeting in secret at eleven o'clock in the morning on a
working day? Has the whole town gone on strike?

HATCH. Now, Mrs Rafi, your curtainings have come. Mr Hollarcut was just running up to the house with a message. (*To
the men.*) Off you go, there's good lads.

The three men go out behind the counter. HATCH *goes to two large
rolls of velvet on the counter and pats them.*

HATCH. Not many houses in these parts can afford to hang this
quality at the window, Mrs Rafi. I congratulate you on an
excellent choice. That's very like the sample, I think you'll
agree. Identical.

MRS RAFI. Mr Hatch, I've been speaking to Mr Carson.

HATCH. Ah yes, and I hope the young gentleman's as well as
circumstances allow.

MRS RAFI. Mr Carson tells me that on the night of the drowning
he met you on the beach. That he called on you for help.
And that you refused – in a language not merely abusive but
callous.

HATCH. Ah.

MRS RAFI (*taps the material*). Send it back.

HATCH. What?

MRS RAFI. Mr Hatch, you cannot expect me to patronize a
     tradesman who ignores his duty as a coastguard —

HATCH. But you must take it!

MRS RAFI. – for which he is paid ten shillings, and who allows
     his fellow man —

MRS TILEHOUSE. And your duty as a Christian!

HATCH. Did you see the storm? What could I do – Christian or
     not! – calm the waters, Mrs Rafi?

MRS TILEHOUSE. Oh.

MRS RAFI. Hatch, it's all of a piece. I'd expect you to blaspheme.
     Mr Carson tells me you raved and swore at him.

HATCH. He's a liar!

MRS RAFI. A liar?

HATCH. And a scoundrel!

MRS TILEHOUSE. Oh dear.

MRS RAFI (*taps material*). Send it back.

HATCH. Not a liar. No. But he was half drowned. He couldn't
     understand me. How could you expect it? The gentleman
     was hallucinated. Shocked. I shouted instructions to him. I
     tried to help.

MRS RAFI. You let an innocent man drown.

HATCH. I've sent back so many things for you, Mrs Rafi. The
     calico. The Irish muslin. The set of renaissance chair
     covers, with those wonderful embroidered hunting scenes.
     The manufacturers won't deal with me any more.

MRS RAFI. Nor will I.

HATCH. I'm in a *small* way of business, Mrs Rafi. I'm on the
     black list. I had to pay for all this before they sent it. And
     I made such a fuss about delivery. All my capital has gone
     into it.

MRS RAFI. You should have thought of that before. I won't have
     it in the house. I'd be afraid to have the curtains drawn.
     They'd remind me of the tragedy.

HATCH. I tried to help. I've never seen such a storm. You didn't see it. You were safely tucked up in bed. My name, my goodwill, my whole life's work is at stake. I'm on the edge of a terrible disaster.

MRS RAFI. It goes back. (*Prepares to go.*)

HATCH. I see. You're acting on his instructions already then? What's he said to you? Has he told you to break me? You're his first victim, you've been corrupted.

MRS RAFI (*turning to go*). Good day.

HATCH (*standing between her and the door, some way from her*). I must speak out, Mrs Rafi. Mr Carson is a spy. He murdered Mr Bentham. He's here on a mission. He's sowing the wind of discord. He'll reap the whirlwind.

MRS TILEHOUSE. Mrs Rafi corrupted? Oh! What else did he say? A spy? Murder? Oh dear, I must go home immediately. (*She sits.*)

MRS RAFI. Of course I shall not take your allegations seriously. You always were over-imaginative for a draper. No doubt you should have taken up something more artistic. Certainly you haven't found your proper place in our community. It would be better if you were to close your shop and leave.

HATCH. Yes, yes, I am more in the creative line. They always said that at school. I was head scholar in bible class. You will take the material, Mrs Rafi? This whole shop's tied up in it. The little I've put by – not much, there's no big buyers here. I couldn't set up in the larger towns. No capital. But I've worked hard, much of it against the grain – my inclinations being elsewhere, as you so rightly pointed out. D'you want me to crawl, Mrs Rafi? Feel the stuff, ma'am. Really, an educated person of your taste can't resist a product as beautiful as – (*Crying.*) but oh the pity of it is you don't see the whole community's threatened by that swine, yes swine, bastard, the welfare and livelihood of this whole town! He's tricked you. Only I spotted him. Well I've warned the coastguards. We don't let anyone land here now. They'll drown. I'll kick them under with my boot.

THOMPSON, CARTER *and* HOLLARCUT *come out from the back of the shop.*

MRS RAFI. Thompson, are you still here?

THOMPSON. Missus, missus —

CARTER. Can't you keep your snout clean, Hatch? Now there'll be the devil to pay.

THOMPSON. Don't mind Mr Hatch, missus. He likes t' spout a lot a ol' rot. We coastguards well's we can. We on't put town money in our pocket till we earn en —

HOLLARCUT. Doo watch that stuff, Mr Hatch. Yoo dutty en with yoor cryin'.

MRS RAFI *takes hold of* THOMPSON's *ear.*

MRS RAFI. Just as you earn money in my garden! Now get back to work.

THOMPSON. Ouch, missus. Yoo'll hev my hid off.

MRS RAFI. I've had enough of this tomfoolery.

MRS TILEHOUSE. Careful, Louise. He's too heavy for you.

MRS RAFI *leads* THOMPSON *out by the ear. The doorbell clangs.* CARTER, HOLLARCUT *and* MRS TILEHOUSE *go out after her.* HATCH *is left alone.*

HATCH. I took an order and there's a copy in the order book. (*He picks up his draper's shears.*) So she'll take delivery and pay. And she can collect – I'm damned if I'll deliver to the door. Pieces of three yards. (*He starts cutting three-yard lengths from the rolls.*) This is the moment that tests and proves. Events are moving and I must act. Three yards. I'll disclose it all at the inquest. Yes, that's my public pulpit. Oh god, what can I do? They'll never believe me. The fools. The swine. (*Cutting.*) Careful. Three yards. Don't let your hand shake. Stop that! No trembling. No complaints. Three yards. I'll take my shears to that little swine. I'll snip him. I'll improve his outline. Send me to the workhouse! Begging like a skivvy-worker. Picking rags. Cleaning drains. 'Here's a crust, my man, here's a mug. Draw yourself some water from the pump.' No! Three yards: one, two, three.

HOLLARCUT *appears in the doorway. He is looking down the street. The doorbell clangs all the while he talks.*

HOLLARCUT. She's leadin' him along the front by the ear. They're comin' out a shops t' gawk. Ol' Mrs Tilehouse's tannin' his arse with her brolly. The ol' tarter. He'll be blacker'n a nigger on a dark night. Hev you ever seen the like? Ho up, lads. Here she come!

HOLLARCUT *runs into the shop. The doorbell stops clanging.* HOLLARCUT *stops when he sees* HATCH. HATCH *is still cutting the material – slashing and tearing at it when the shears stick. The material unrolls over the floor.*

HOLLARCUT. Whatever yoo up to, Mr Hatch?

HATCH (*points to the pieces he has cut*). Roll them up, Billy. Nice and neat. You can't drop high-class goods in the bottom of a cart like a sack of sprouts. That's the makings of the good draper: finesse, industry, and an understanding of the feminine temperament. They stamp on you but they wipe their little boots first.

HOLLARCUT. I on't touchin' nothin', Mr Hatch. Folks've got their dander up. You must fend for yoorself now.

HATCH. I'll start on the other roll. Bit off each. Three yards. The moment for action, Billy. Time draws near. An army can't watch the grass grow round it. It's out in the open now. People will rally round the truth. You'll see many signs and wonders in the days to come.

HATCH *goes on cutting.* MRS RAFI *comes in. The doorbell clangs.* HOLLARCUT *goes behind the counter and watches.*

MRS RAFI. Hatch, I'll report this morning's outrage to the constable and the town doctor. I shall certainly see that no one under my influence ever uses *any* shop of yours again.

MRS TILEHOUSE *appears in the doorway behind* MRS RAFI. *Until she comes into the shop later on, the doorbell makes isolated, spasmodic clangs.*

HATCH. Come in, Mrs Rafi. Your order is being attended to.

MRS TILEHOUSE. Louise, don't go in.

MRS RAFI *comes further into the shop.*

MRS RAFI. Hatch, pull yourself together.

HATCH (*still cutting*). The cutting's nearly done. You see I cut it all myself. You have to know cloth. There's an art to this. That's why I don't hire an assistant. They'll never stop long enough to learn the trade. Oh it's not that I can't afford one. Look at that edge. I could have ten assistants. Open departments. Haberdasheries. Riding habits. Liveries. A sporting counter. I could attract the towns to *me*. But no one stays long enough to learn the trade. It takes a life time, Mrs Rafi. Three yards. Always move. Why? Don't they take to me? Am I so hard to . . . They must be off. What do they ever see, what are they looking for, what do they ever find? The trade is a respectable vocation. Sons of the gentry haven't been above it. (*In tears.*) I walked my life away on this floor. Up and down . . . Three yards . . . Why isn't the floor worn through . . . Thirty years . . . I'm worn through . . . (*He goes on cutting, tearing, ripping and slashing.*)

MRS RAFI. Mr Hatch. You're hacking it to pieces. No one can take the material now.

MRS TILEHOUSE. Hollarcut, take his collar.

HOLLARCUT. I on't touch him.

HOLLARCUT *ducks down out of sight behind the counter.*

HATCH (*smiles and cuts*). These shears are part of my hand. Watch how the cloth leads them. That's the gesture of my soul, Mrs Rafi, there's a whole way of life in that . . .

MRS RAFI. Mr Hatch, listen to your friends. You make it hard for me to help you.

HATCH. There, Mrs Rafi. Some lengths to be getting on with. Will you take them with you now?

MRS RAFI. No.

MRS TILEHOUSE. Don't beard him, Louise.

HATCH (*cunningly*). Ah, but it must be taken. You see, it's cut. According to the customer's requirement. It's in pieces.

MRS RAFI. No.

MRS TILEHOUSE. What foolishness to bait the unchained lion.

MRS RAFI *turns to go.* HATCH *stops her by cutting off her path.*

HATCH. Are you paying now? Pay the bill and tidy it away. Of course! Don't let these things hang over you.

MRS RAFI. Hollarcut.

HOLLARCUT *looks over the top of the counter.*

HOLLARCUT. Don't antagonize him, missus.

HOLLARCUT *goes down out of sight.* HATCH *holds one end of* MRS RAFI'S *bag and she holds the other.*

HATCH. You've brought the money. Are you too shy to take it out? The company of men? I understand all that. Don't look away, m'am. Each one has his failings. I never put a lady to shame. Let me. I do it all in a nice, clean way. A lady can't be soiled with money.

MRS RAFI. Take it. (*She gives him her bag and turns away. Weakly.*) My legs . . .

MRS TILEHOUSE *hurries into the room. The doorbell clangs and stops.*

MRS TILEHOUSE. Louise, your bag.

MRS RAFI. Nonsense, Mrs Tilehouse. Farthings. Shout in the street. Mr Hatch has made me a prisoner.

MRS TILEHOUSE *collapses in a chair.* HATCH *is struggling with*

MRS RAFI. HOLLARCUT *looks up from behind the counter, yells and runs out. The doorbell clangs.*

HATCH. Farthings! Farthings! All that money under your bed and you won't pay your debts!

MRS RAFI. Mr Hatch, remember who we are.

HATCH. Mr Carson keeps your money now! You're all liars, swindlers, frauds, bankrupts —

HATCH *hits* MRS RAFI *with the shears. She is cut. They stand in silence for half a second.*

MRS RAFI. Hatch, you're a fool.

CARTER *comes in. The doorbell clangs.* HATCH *goes behind the counter.*

MRS RAFI. See to Mr Hatch. He's very poorly. I have only a slight cut.

HATCH. Well, well. How did that happen? She tried to grab my shears, Jack. She must be a lady burglar. She interfered with work on the premises. You know they come in here and whisper, ask for intimate garments. Could I try this on, Hatch. Then they're off to the fitting room before you can stop them and leave the curtain open. All the intimate things. Wriggling into this and that. Is it too tight, Mr Hatch? Is this gusset in order?

CARTER. Thass enough a that, Hatch. You howd yoor noise an' come with me like a good man.

CARTER *goes cautiously towards* HATCH. HATCH *dodges round him and goes out of the shop. The doorbell clangs. As he goes he points to* MRS TILEHOUSE. *She is sitting unconscious in a chair.*

HATCH (*going*). There's the worst. Leaves the curtain open and turns the mirror – brazen! – so you see the darkness underneath.

MRS RAFI *takes a piece of material from the display dummy on the counter and wraps it round her wrist while she talks. She is frightened and angry.*

MRS RAFI. I don't know what you've been up to amongst yourselves. Have you no respect for public opinion —

CARTER. Yes, m'am.

MRS RAFI. Will your wives and children hold their heads up for years? And your superiors, they'll certainly be pained by these excesses?

CARTER. Yes, m'am. Please don't goo on, m'am.

MRS RAFI. Put your finger on this knot. (CARTER *holds the knot while she fastens the material on her wrist.*) You've plunged the town into scandal. What will they say in Forebeach?

CARTER. Yes, m'am.

MRS RAFI. Thank you. I shall go and alert the town constable. As it's only midday I suppose he's still in bed. That is, if he's as conscientious as the rest of the town. I hardly know if I dare approach a representative of the law. In this state of anarchy one might find oneself inside. See to my companion – another sentry asleep at her post.

MRS RAFI *goes out. The doorbell clangs.* CARTER *goes quietly to* MRS TILEHOUSE.

CARTER. Mrs Tilehouse, m'am.

MRS TILEHOUSE (*jumping to her feet*). Help! I am about to be attacked by a large man.

CARTER. Mrs Rafi tol' me t' say —

MRS TILEHOUSE. Louise is dead! What were her last words? She apologised to me for it all! I forgive her! I hold no grudge, however justified —

CARTER. No, no. She's gone for the officer.

MRS TILEHOUSE. Thank god. The town is relieved! We're saved!

CARTER. She said I'm to see yoo home.

MRS TILEHOUSE. Ah, thank you, Carter. I don't think I could

walk there unassisted, I shall require your arm – in the
less public places. (*She sees the shears on the counter.*) Ah! The
murderer's shears.

CARTER. Look the other way, ma'am.

MRS TILEHOUSE. Yes. After this I shall regard Gomorrah as a
spa resort.

CARTER *leads* MRS TILEHOUSE *out. The doorbell clangs. Immediately* HOLLARCUT *comes on through the back of the shop. He
calls softly.*

HOLLARCUT. Mr Hatch . . . Where yoo hidin', Mr Hatch? . . .
I'll put some bread an' cheese on the window ledge out the
back for yoo, an' a bottle a sweet tea . . . Don't you run out
without yoor coat . . .

SCENE SIX

Beach.
*The stage is empty except for a body upstage. It is covered with
trousers, socks, vest and jersey – all dark. There are no shoes. The
jersey is pulled up over the head and the arms, which are lifted up
and bent at the elbows in the act of removing the jersey – so the jersey
forms a hood covering the head, neck, shoulders, arms and hands.
The dark vest covers the trunk. The top half of the body is on the
beach and the rest in the water.*

ROSE *comes on. She is looking ahead at someone who has gone on in
front of her.*

ROSE (*calling ahead*). I must sit down. (*She sits.*)

WILLY *comes on from the direction in which she shouted.*

WILLY. Are you all right?
ROSE. Yes.

WILLY. Shall I leave you alone?

ROSE. Yes.

WILLY (*nods. Slight pause*). I don't like to. You haven't been out here since he drowned.

ROSE (*remotely*). I'll see you back at the house.

WILLY. All right.

Pause. WILLY *doesn't move.*

ROSE. This stupid inquest.

WILLY. Why?

Pause.

ROSE. The coroner will say he's sorry and decide why he died. Why? You might as well have an inquest on birth. They're afraid of me. I'm touched by death. Perhaps you are. I see it when they call to say they're sorry. They look at me as if I'm a dangerous animal they have to pat . . .

WILLY. You're supposed to forget what they look like very soon. It comes as a shock. But it's hard to forget the voice. You suddenly hear that twenty years later.

ROSE. Really they come to be calmed and assured. I have to find some of my pain to share with them. A taste. Then they know that if I can bear it so can they when it comes.

WILLY. He knew more about sailing than I do. But we both knew it was wrong to be out. He wanted to get here quickly. To see you. Perhaps he wanted to show something. I mean: prove. (*Shrugs.*) I said let's go back. I kept asking, 'How close is the land?' He didn't answer. He went on working. Pulling ropes. And he baled water in a bucket. He knew we'd made a mistake. It was dangerous to be there.

ROSE. What did he say?

WILLY. Nothing. Then the boat turned over. I saw the bottom

coming up out of the water. It looked very ugly. It was wet and suddenly smooth in all that chaos. I yelled but I couldn't hear him. He was gone.

Pause.

WILLY. Did you love him . . . a great deal?

ROSE. What?

WILLY. I thought perhaps he wasn't sure. I mean about what you felt. It was clear what he felt.

ROSE. Why are you saying this?

WILLY. Somehow, he was afraid. That was so unnatural for him. He was sure and firm about everything else. It seems terrible that he could be afraid . . . I think that would have destroyed him. A hero's fear.

ROSE. Fear?

WILLY. You were brought up together. Your aunt wanted you to marry. Everyone knew you would. It was too easy. He was afraid one day you'd meet another man – perhaps even a weaker man – and he'd lose you. A hero must be afraid of weaker men.

ROSE. Why?

WILLY. He never talked of you. No photographs. I didn't know what you looked like. Sometimes he said he'd written or you'd been somewhere. Of course I'd formed my own picture of you.

ROSE. How long did you know him?

WILLY. Seven years. I'm twenty-one. We were the same age.

Silence.

ROSE. If I'd seen him die it would be easier to forget him. I can see him working and not saying anything. Wet to the skin. And the noisy sea. But I can't see him when he dies. (*Pause.*) He was very beautiful. He had dark eyes. I think of him as a fire.

WILLY. Why?

ROSE. A fire that doesn't die out. I've seen it burn in the sea.

WILLY. What d'you mean?

ROSE. When we were young we lit fires on the beach. At night. The fire shone on his face. I saw it reflected in the sea. It danced because both the flames and the water moved.

WILLY. D'you feel anything wrong?

ROSE. You mean guilty?

WILLY. Yes. When someone dies people sometimes —

ROSE. No. I was always happy with him. There was nothing mean and selfish in it. It seemed perfect. Now I have nothing to live for. There's nothing to look forward to. I don't know what I shall do. I can't think of anything to make one day pass. Yet I have most of my life to live. I don't know how I shall get through it. He was the only person who could understand me now.

WILLY. I understand you a little.

ROSE. Yes, but what does that matter to me?

WILLY. All people matter to each other.

ROSE. That isn't true, of course.

WILLY. No.

Silence.

ROSE. I can't bear to lose him. I don't think I can live without him.

WILLY (*quiet anger*). I think that love can be a terrible disaster. And hope is sometimes pride and ambition. When I'm lost in darkness I'll shut my eyes and feel my way forward, grope like an animal, not be guided by some distant light.

ROSE. How can you escape from yourself, or what's happened to you, or the future? It's a silly question. It's better out here where he died. At home there's so much to do. People coming and going. Why? What does it matter to them? How can I escape from *that*?

WILLY. If you look at life closely it is unbearable. What people suffer, what they do to each other, how they hate themselves, anything good is cut down and trodden on, the innocent and the victims are like dogs digging rats from a hole, or an owl starving to death in a city. It is all unbearable but that is where you have to find your strength. Where else is there?

ROSE. An owl starving in a city.

WILLY. To death. Yes. Wherever you turn. So you should never turn away. If you do you lose everything. Turn back and look into the fire. Listen to the howl of the flames. The rest is lies.

ROSE. How just. How sane.

WILLY *stands and looks upstage.*

ROSE. What is it?

WILLY. He's on the beach. There.

ROSE *and* WILLY *go up to the body.*

ROSE. Why is he like that?

WILLY. He tried to pull the jumper over his head. So he could swim.

ROSE. He drowned.

WILLY. Yes.

They stare silently for a moment.

ROSE. Is it him?

WILLY. Yes. I know his clothes. Go and fetch Mr Evens. I'll keep watch.

ROSE. Yes.

ROSE *hurries out. After a moment* WILLY *crouches down by the body.*

WILLY (*coldly*). How will they get you into the box? You're a corpse and they'll break your arms. They'll cut your clothes and fold you up like a dummy. What's on your face now? Is it quiet, or swollen, or scratched?

A sound in the distance. Not a tune, but a high, inarticulate, sing-song whining, mad, with the note of a hunter in it. WILLY *looks at something offstage. He comes quickly downstage and crouches out of sight. The sound comes closer. He waits.* HATCH *comes on. He carries a knife.* WILLY *crouches lower.*

HATCH. More prints. And still someone with him. Always back to the beach. He can't keep away. What drags him back time after time? Obsession. You must get him, Mr Hatch. The fools in this town think they're safe. No, life's being worn away. Their bodies are crunched underfoot like sand. This long beach is a stream trickling through god's hands. Their bones are ground down and fall through the hour-glass. Time runs and the enemy is closer. Quiet, Hatch. Hold your noise. Stop your rant. Follow your victim. (HATCH *takes a few steps towards the body. He stops and looks round.*) Mr Carson asleep on the beach. Where's the head? In his hands. That's it! What confidence. Insolence. Sleeping while he waits for his friends to come out of the sea. This is the quiet place where the sea monsters breed and play and lie in the sun. Mr Hatch, you have him. Careful. (*He creeps towards the body. He still holds the knife.*) A sound and he's gone ... (HATCH *reaches the body. He falls on it and knives it in a frenzy.*) Kill it! Kill it! Kill it! At last! What's this? Water! Look, water! Water not blood? (*Stabbing.*) Kill it! Kill it! (*He stops.*) More water? (*Stabs.*) The filthy beast!

WILLY (*to himself*). Hit it. That's an innocent murder.

HATCH. No blood. Only water. How do I know he's dead? Surely, surely! (*Stabs.*) There, that's hard enough. Hack his throat. Cut it! Tear it! Rip it! Slash it! (*Stops stabbing. Rambles on quickly to himself.*) Still no blood! Oh who would have thought of this? Surely they die? Why come here, why do anything, if you're not afraid of death? Yes. Their worlds' dying and they'll die if they stay – they know, they know! Of course they die! Yes – watch and see if they bury him! You can't bury something that's still alive. (*Looks offstage.*) Hide, Mr Hatch. They're after you.

HATCH *hurries out.* WILLY *is sitting downstage with his back to the body.* ROSE *and* EVENS *hurry on.* EVENS *brings a folded blanket.*

ROSE. We saw the draper.
EVENS. The town's out looking for him.
ROSE. Are you all right?
WILLY. Yes. (*To* EVENS.) The body's up there.

EVENS *stares offstage after* HATCH. *Then he goes upstage to the body.*

ROSE. He's cut. Look. His clothes. His arms.
WILLY. Hatch. He went for him with a knife.
ROSE. How terrible.
WILLY. He thought it was me.
ROSE. How terrible. How terrible.
WILLY. Why? What does it matter? You can't hurt the dead. How can you desecrate dust? (*Shrugs.*) He's just dead bait for a mad man.
ROSE. But it seems so violent.

EVENS *covers the body with the old blanket. It is pale green or faded, dirty white. He lays it out like a square and doesn't tuck it in. The body makes a bump in the middle.*

EVENS (*to* ROSE). Go into town and fetch a horse and cart. Go quietly or they'll come out to gape. There's no need for that. We'll watch.
ROSE. Yes.

ROSE *goes out.* EVENS *and* WILLY *stand some way apart. They face half upstage and wait in silence. The body lies upstage.*

SCENE SEVEN

Clifftop.

Open, windy, sunny morning. An upright piano has been carried up on to the cliffs. When it is played the sound is hollow and spread. A chair stands in front of it. MAFANWY *and* JILLY *are alone. They arrange sheet music on the piano.*

MAFANWY. The wind.

JILLY. When *I'm* dead I'll be brought up here to the cliff tops.

MAFANWY. How can you even think about it!

JILLY (*looking off*). They're coming. Why don't you play?

MAFANWY. Mrs Rafi wants to enter to silence.

JILLY (*looking offstage*). Oh isn't she marvellous? Look how she holds the urn. Oh, isn't it small.

MAFANWY. How disgraceful.

JILLY. Whatever is it, Fanny?

MAFANWY. They've brought Mr Evens.

JILLY. Oh where?

MAFANWY. He's lower than a tramp. Louise only does it to annoy.

JILLY. Oh, is that what he looks like? Oh dear. You must let me stand by you. I feel quite afraid. How silly. Are those stories true?

MAFANWY. I haven't listened to them.

JILLY. The girls say that if you go by his hut at night —

MAFANWY (*sharply*). Sh-sh! What is the matter with you? Your neck's gone quite red.

JILLY. Oh dear.

MAFANWY *and* JILLY *stand with bowed heads. Their hands are crossed in their laps. The procession comes on.* MRS RAFI, MRS TILEHOUSE, ROSE, RACHEL, WILLY, EVENS, VICAR, CARTER, THOMPSON *and other* MEN *and* LADIES. MRS RAFI *carries a small urn. Two of the* MEN *carry the town banner. It is a red strip stretched between two poles. It is heavily embroidered with gold-coloured wire and silk. Everyone goes to their place in silence.*

VICAR (*low and considerate*). You'll be more comfortable over there, Mrs Rafi. A trifle more sheltered from the blast.

MRS RAFI *goes silently to her place. The group settles down.*

VICAR. Dearly beloved, we the friends of this poor departed soul in god remember today, as we cast his ashes about this favourite walk, the faithful townsman who has gone before us on the great journey that leads to that home where there is always peace. Let us pray, each in the silence of his heart (*They bow their heads and clasp their hands. A short silence.*) Amen.

ALL. Amen.

VICAR. I heard a voice from heaven saying unto me, write. From henceforth happy are the dead, for they rest from their labours. The first hymn, Miss Price, thank you. Page 432.

Some of the people use hymn books, others know the words. As they sing a rivalry for the most elaborate descant develops between MRS RAFI *and* MRS TILEHOUSE. MRS TILEHOUSE *becomes operatic.* MAFANWY *stamps out the proper rhythm at the piano.*

> Eternal father, strong to save
> Whose arm doth bind the restless wave
> Who bidst the mighty ocean deep
> Its own appointed limits keep
> O hear us when we cry to thee
> For those in peril on the sea
>
> O Saviour, whose almighty word
> The winds and waves submissive heard
> Who walkedst on the foaming deep

And calm amid its rage didst sleep
O hear us when we cry to thee
For those in peril on the sea

ALL ⎫   Amen.
MRS TILEHOUSE ⎬ (*sing*) A-a-a-a-a-a-a-a-meeeeeeeen.
MRS RAFI ⎭   A-a-a-a-

MRS RAFI (*sung*). -men.

VICAR. Colin's goodness speaks for him. I will not tarnish that sound with my foolish words. One incident I cannot forbear to relate. Yesterday I went to the battery commander at Forebeach and asked if, during the brief moments of our ceremony here today, his guns might be silent. Without prompting he lifted up his martial voice and said '*Yes*. Mr Bentham was a good man, Padre. He goes before the Almighty with a clean record. He is destined for high rank among the heavenly hosts. Would that I had numbered him amongst my own officers.' Saying which this soldier, so reminiscent of some fine hero of the ancient world, raised his sherry glass and sang the opening lines of the Regimental —

In the distance the battery starts to fire. There is an embarrassed silence.

VICAR. Miss Price, perhaps we might go on to the next hymn.

They sing the 'Old One hundredth'. MRS TILEHOUSE *again delays the tune with her descant.* MRS RAFI *glares at her angrily and unconsciously beats time against the urn.*

All people that on earth do dwell
Sing to the lord with hopeful voice
Him serve with fear, his praise forth tell
Come ye before him and rejoice

O enter then his gates with praise
Approach with joy his courts unto
Praise laud and bless his name always
For it is seemly so to do.

MRS TILEHOUSE *begins to sing* 'amen', MAFANWY *doesn't accompany her.* MRS TILEHOUSE *stops. During the singing the* VICAR *has gone upstage to the edge of the cliff. The guns have stopped.*

VICAR. We commit this body to the air over the deep waters; to be turned to corruption; and we look to the resurrection of the body when the sea shall give up her dead. Amen.

ALL. Amen.

VICAR. I believe you have prepared a few words, Mrs Rafi.

MRS RAFI *goes towards the edge of the cliff. She still carries the urn.*

VICAR. Not too near the edge, dear lady.

MRS RAFI. Be not afraid, Vicar.

MRS RAFI *turns to the congregation and recites. While she does so she mimes to her words. The effect suggests* 'Under the spreading chestnut tree'.

At the same time MRS TILEHOUSE *starts to search in her large handbag. She can't find what she is searching for. She speaks to herself in a sweet, patient, chiding voice, lower than* MRS RAFI's, *but loud enough to be heard, especially in* MRS RAFI's *dramatic pauses. She hands things from her handbag to those next to her to hold.*

MRS TILEHOUSE. Smelling salts. Smelling salts. Dear me, where are you? Did I leave you in my trinkets box? Under this distress I may perchance have left the top off. What misfortune! – the mixture is so volatile . . .

MRS RAFI. Like dust and ash all men become
Broken and old when they reach home

(*She reacts to a sudden idea.*)

I'll throw his ash into the heartless sea
The waves will calm, like water under lee
And in that water that is always night

(*She dramatically gropes a few steps towards the edge. The spectators gasp.*)

His ashes fall, sparkling as light!
There they will drift through ages yet to come
Lighting the deep with dreams of home!

(*She unscrews the top of the urn.* MRS TILEHOUSE *has stood her handbag on the ground and is rummaging in it.*)

Men who live out their little year

(*She stares dramatically into the urn as if she discovers something in it.*)

Are diamonds polished by their labours here!
Fire has burned! It gives no ashes grey!
Diamonds only from this mortal clay!

She snatches out a handful of ashes and holds them up triumphantly. The spectators gasp.

MRS TILEHOUSE. Or might I indeed have lent them to the cook?

MRS RAFI. Arise ye dust, and take the air on wings!
Pale spirit rise! For hark! the angel —
Mrs Tilehouse, perhaps you would like to go down and cut the sandwiches for our tea?

MRS TILEHOUSE. I beg your pardon.

MRS RAFI. I only wish to spare you your little upset.

MRS TILEHOUSE (*plaintively*). Louise, how can you? I cannot help it if my feelings make the use of salts necessary —

MRS RAFI. Feelings!

VICAR. Ladies, let us pray.

MRS RAFI. Is this an exhibition of feelings?

MRS TILEHOUSE (*angrily*). You would not understand, Louise. No one has feelings except you, of course.

MRS RAFI. Most people would say it is an exhibition of hysteria. It seems to me to be quite close to insanity!

VICAR. Our father which art —

MRS RAFI. Oh do be quiet, Vicar!

MRS RAFI *crosses to* MRS TILEHOUSE. *She still carries a handful of ashes. As she passes* JILLY *she gives them to her.*

MRS RAFI. Hold these for a moment.

JILLY. Ah! (*She bursts into tears.*)

MRS RAFI. You've deliberately destroyed this occasion. (*She holds up the urn.*) Now what are my last memories of this poor dead boy? Your absurd singing. Your absurd histrionics. Oh, I know what's behind this, madam. (*Going back to her place.*) It's because she didn't get a part in the play.

EVENS *goes to help* JILLY. *He puts his hand on her shoulder.*

EVENS. Allow me, my dear.

JILLY *turns and sees him. She screams. He tries to take her hand.*

EVENS. But I want to help —

JILLY. You beast! You beast!

JILLY *faints and drops the ashes on the ground.*

MRS TILEHOUSE. Look at this poor girl. Another of your victims.

VICAR. Miss Price, the next hymn.

MAFANWY *starts to play* 'Eternal Father'. *She switches to* 'All people'. *She stops in confusion and starts to cry.* MRS TILEHOUSE *is trying to sweep up the ashes in her handkerchief.*

MRS RAFI. Wallow, Mrs Tilehouse. Look at her. Snatch and grab! That's what she wanted all along. She wants to scatter them. Well let her. I won't!

MRS TILEHOUSE. I'll never forgive you. You've gone too far this day, madam.

HATCH *comes in in a frenzy of excitement and triumph.*

HATCH. He's dead! He's dead! The first one's chalked up!

VICAR. The devil's come.

HATCH. Put him in a hole at the crossroads. (*He dodges about. The others try to catch him.*) Put him in quicklime. There's a place for him in the prison wall. The little green where the hangman grows flowers for Buckingham Palace.

MRS RAFI. Ruffian, have you no respect for the dead?

MRS TILEHOUSE. Anarchist!

HATCH (*dancing*). Witches! Hussies!

MRS RAFI. Silence before your betters.

HATCH *attacks them.* HOLLARCUT *runs on.*

HATCH. Push them over the top, Billy. That's where the swine go!

RACHEL *starts to beat* HOLLARCUT *with the sheet music.* LADIES *surround* HOLLARCUT *and* HATCH *and hit them. The* VICAR *kneels.*

VICAR. Page seventy-eight in your prayer books. A prayer in time of war and tumult. Save and deliver us, confound their devices —

MRS RAFI (*throwing handfuls of ashes at* HATCH). Have you no respect for the dead?

HATCH. Billy, save me!

HOLLARCUT. Mr Hatch, help!

CARTER. I'll larrup yoo, lad. I'll bang yoo. I'll knock 'em into next week, Mrs Rafi.

HATCH (*throwing his arms open.*) Take me to my end. My work is done.

Suddenly HATCH *steps in front of* WILLY. WILLY *is taking the empty urn from* MRS RAFI. *He holds it awkwardly upside down. He stares at* HATCH. *The silence spreads.*

HATCH. Alive? (*He half reaches out to touch* WILLY.) Alive? (*He begins crying.*) No. No. No. No. He's still alive. (*He falls to his hands and knees.*)

WILLY. Touch me. I won't hurt you. No one will hurt you here.

HOLLARCUT. Mr Hatch ... Don't yoo cry. 'Tis better so. (*He goes to* HATCH *and crouches beside him.*) Stop that ... (*He looks at the others.*) Why yoo do this to Mr Hatch? He on't done yoo no harm.

MRS RAFI. No harm! D'you know what you're saying?

HOLLARCUT. He only stopped yoor spoutin' for a little while.

Not even so much. Take more'n a few whacks t' shut her up.
How hev the likes a him ever harmed yoo? Look on him
now, if yoo can.

MRS TILEHOUSE. He wounded Mrs Rafi's arm.

HOLLARCUT. She on't die a no scratch. She come nearer dyin'
every time she stick her ol' hat pin in.

VICAR. Hollarcut, I have failed. Week after week I laboured at
your side in the heat of Sunday School. For hours I struggled
with your soul. I fought with your rational mind to instil some
order into it. Did you not understand one word?

HOLLARCUT. No.

VICAR. Oh. Excuse me, I must go down and prepare myself. The
time of the great beast cannot be far off.

The VICAR *goes out.* MRS RAFI *shouts after him.*

MRS RAFI. Remember, Vicar: the Lord moves in a mysterious
way. The poor man's gone. (*To* HOLLARCUT.) You bully!
Surely you know it's your duty to look after him? He's
weaker than you!

MAFANWY *fusses round* MRS RAFI *with a shawl.*

MAFANWY. Oh Mrs Rafi, I'm so sorry. You tried so hard to make
everything nice today.

MRS RAFI. Carter, take Hatch down to the town lock up.

CARTER *and* THOMPSON *are holding* HATCH.

HATCH (*afraid*). I don't know if you're all ghosts or if you still
have time to save yourselves. (*He cries to himself.*) I'm out
of touch. I tried to save you from your foolishness and
selfishness ... (*Cries.*) Now someone else will come and take
my place and no one will help you ... no one can help you
now ...

CARTER *and* THOMPSON *take* HATCH *out.*

MRS RAFI. Mafanwy, stop fussing and put your shawl on.

Whenever you catch a cold you behave as if you'd taken the sins of the world on your shoulders and we should all be grateful. You'll be snivelling round self-righteously for half the year.

MAFANWY (*turns away in tears*). How can you be so hard . . .

MAFANWY *starts to collect the scattered sheet music.*

MRS RAFI (*making an announcement*). Ladies, attention. I think I may say that everything was going very well today until Mr Hatch came on with his lunacy. Our behaviour was as usual an example to the town.

LADIES. Yes.

MRS RAFI. No doubt some of us had been moved by the high emotionalism of the occasion —

MRS TILEHOUSE. Ah yes, how true.

MRS RAFI. – but that is only proper. (*A murmur of agreement.*) Indeed it shows the depths of our feelings. (*A few claps from the* LADIES.) No more will be said about that. By anyone. Of course, it was unfortunate that the wind blew some of our articles about – (*She takes the urn from* WILLY.) – but you expect it in these high, exposed places. (*She gives the urn to* EVENS.) Mr Evens, kindly see that is returned to my study. Perhaps you will help me to choose a niche. Our work is done – (*She dusts a speck from herself.*) – and we may safely say the ashes have been well scattered. Where's Rose?

They look round. She is not there.

MRS TILEHOUSE. Something terrible is going to happen. I know it. A thing brushed past me through the air.

MRS RAFI. Nonsense, Jessica. Rose is a sensible girl. She's gone off for a few moments' peace away from this madhouse. Hollarcut, can I trust you to go quietly down to the town with at least the outward show of decorum?

HOLLARCUT. I on't give yoo n'more chance to pin nothin' on me, if thass what yoo mean.

MRS RAFI. You can come and work *hard* in my garden every
     evening for the next two months. There's a lot of especially
     hard digging you can do. That, or I must take up this matter
     with the local magistrates. Which?
HOLLARCUT (*grumbling*). Diggin', I suppose.
MRS RAFI. I'm glad you've got some wits left. I shall assume
     Hatch led you astray – an easy assumption. Present yourself
     at my back door tomorrow at five-thirty sharp.
HOLLARCUT. Mornin' or evenin'?
MRS RAFI. Both.

HOLLARCUT *goes out grumbling to himself.*

     Ladies, you can go down now.
RACHEL   ⎰ But are you all right —
MRS TILEHOUSE ⎱ Oh no, my dear. I won't leave you out here
     unattended —
MRS RAFI. You'll be safe, Jessica. Carter won't let Hatch slip
     away.

The LADIES *and the others go out.* MRS RAFI *and* WILLY *are left
alone. She is downstage and he is upstage. The empty chair still
stands in front of the piano. It has not moved.*

MRS RAFI. Fetch me the chair. Willy.

WILLY *fetches her the chair. He sets it downstage. She sits on it.
He stands a little way from her.*

MRS RAFI. I'm afraid of getting old. I've always been a forceful
     woman. I was brought up to be. People expect my class to
     shout at them. Bully them. They're disappointed if you
     don't. It gives them something to gossip about in their bars.
     When they turn you into an eccentric, it's their form of
     admiration. Sometimes I think I'm like a lighthouse in their
     world. I give them a sense of order and security. My glares
     mark out a channel to the safe harbour. I'm so tired of them.
     I'm tired of being a side-show in their little world. Nothing

else was open to me. If I were a Catholic – (*She looks round.*)
– it's all right, the vicar's gone – I'd have been an abbess.
I'd have terrified the nuns. They'd have loved it. Like living
next door to the devil. But the grand old faith didn't allow
me even that consolation. Of course I have my theatricals –
(*She looks round as before.*) – yes, the ladies have gone – none
of them can act, you know. Oh no. I'm surrounded by
mediocrities. A flaming torch and no path to shine on . . .
I'll grow old and shout at them from a wheel-chair. That's
what they're waiting for. They get their own back for all the
years I bullied them. They wheel you where they like. 'Take
me there.' 'You went there yesterday. We want to go the
other way.' 'Take me down to the beach. I want to see the
sea.' 'You don't want to see the sea. You saw the sea yesterday.
The wind's bad for your head. If you misbehave and catch
a cold we'll shut you up in bed. You'll stay there for good this
time.' Subtle. Jessica would probably stick matchsticks under
my nails. I'll see she's pensioned off. She is one of those ladies
who are meant to die alone in a small room. You give up
shouting. You close your eyes and the tears dribble down your
ugly old face and you can't even wipe it clean – they won't give
you your hanky. 'Don't let her have it. She gets into a tizzy
and tears it to shreds.' There you are: old, ugly, whimpering,
dirty, pushed about on wheels and threatened. I can't love
them. How could I? But that's a terrible state in which to
move towards the end of your life: to have no love. Has
anything been worth while? No. I've thrown my life away.
(*She sees someone offstage.*) Come along. They've gone.

ROSE *comes on. She walks calmly towards them.*

MRS RAFI. Go away, Rose. Don't stay in the town and marry the
solicitor or doctor or parson. You can't breathe here.

ROSE. Where shall I go?

MRS RAFI. Colin would have taken you away. He'd never settle
down in this ditch. Oh no. But they've got him now. He's

up on these cliffs for ever. A ghost haunting the sea. Till
that goes – even the sea must go sometime. Even the ghosts.
Ha, ha. You take her, Willy.

WILLY. Will she come?

MRS RAFI. If she's got any sense.

ROSE (*to* MRS RAFI). You didn't go.

MRS RAFI. No. (*She stands.*) I've arranged a burying tea. These
little things break the monotony of their lives. There'll be
chaos if I don't go and rule the tea room. They'll hack
themselves to pieces on the cake knives and empty the
tea pot over the sandwiches. But I shall be thinking of the
sea and dead Colin, and how the world is full of things
that have always been far away from me. Don't come
down – it'll disgust you. Stay up here and shock them.
They'll have a good gossip and it'll help them to get over
the funeral.

MRS RAFI *goes out.*

WILLY. Are you all right?

ROSE. Yes.

WILLY. Shall we go away?

ROSE (*calmly*). Would you like to?

WILLY. . . . Yes.

ROSE. Oh yes, but then I could go away with anyone.

WILLY. Who?

ROSE. Any sailor from the port. I don't mind having my life
messed up. Or I could go to London and work. Don't feel
sorry for aunt Louise. She's such a coward. Haven't you
noticed? It's safer to stay in the garden and shout over
the wall. Don't feel sorry for her. She's a bully and only the
weak ones like being bullied. The town's full of her cripples.
They're the ones she's nicest to.

WILLY. I know.

ROSE (*shrugs slightly*). When are you going?

WILLY. Soon. Everything's done here.

ROSE. If you'd drowned I'd be married to Colin now.

WILLY. I suppose it was a near thing.

ROSE. You missed drowning. You missed the draper's knife. Does living excite you?

WILLY. Shall I kiss you?

WILLY *kisses her in silence.*

ROSE. In a dead man's shoes.

WILLY. The dead don't matter.

ROSE. I'm not sure.

WILLY. Then you're like your aunt. You talk and have no courage.

ROSE. Look, they've left the cover off the piano. Damp spoils the strings. (ROSE *covers the piano with a green or faded dirty white sheet.*) Aunt will order two strong men with a barrow to bring it back. (*She stands the chair in front of the piano.*)

WILLY *turns to go.*

ROSE. Where are you going?

WILLY. For a swim.

ROSE. Today?

WILLY. Yes.

ROSE. In the sea?

WILLY. Yes.

ROSE. Where's your towel?

WILLY. I don't need one.

ROSE. Will you?

WILLY. Oh yes.

He looks at her for a moment and then turns again to go.

ROSE. Wait. (*He stops.*) I'll come down and hold your clothes . . .

WILLY *nods at her and starts to go.* ROSE *follows him off. The stage is empty except for the covered piano and the empty chair.*

SCENE EIGHT

Beach.

EVENS's *hut. Bright, clear morning with some wind.* EVENS *sits on a box. He has a small whisky flask in his hand but he doesn't drink. After a moment he shouts offstage.*

EVENS. You've been hanging round there all morning!

HOLLARCUT (*off*). Oh ay?

EVENS. What's the big stick for?

After a few moments HOLLARCUT *comes in. He looks tired and unshaved. His collar is open. He is exhausted but has the energy of anger.*

HOLLARCUT (*flatly*). What, scum?

EVENS. Come to batter me to death, have you? Batter me with your big stick?

HOLLARCUT (*flatly*). What if I have?

EVENS. You won't.

HOLLARCUT (*flatly*). Oh ay?

EVENS. You haven't got it in you.

HOLLARCUT (*flatly*). No?

EVENS. Not now Hatch is inside.

HOLLARCUT. Don't you dutty his name with yoor foul ol' snout.

EVENS. You don't believe the stories he told you? D'you believe I ride on a broomstick?

HOLLARCUT (*flatly*). What if I don't?

EVENS. Then why d'you come to batter me with your big stick? (*He takes a drink.*)

HOLLARCUT. Who drove him wrong in the hid? Why'd he take up all they daft notions? I don't know no one doo that if that weren't yoo. (*He hits a box with the stick. It breaks.*)

EVENS. Probably.

HOLLARCUT. He allus treat me right. Who else talked t' me

'cept t' say goo here, fetch that, yoo en't got this in yoo, yoo
can't doo that? He on't ashamed t' talk t' me, or listen. He
on't used me like that ol' bitch an' the rest on yer. He wanted
me with him.

EVENS. Yes, I see.

HOLLARCUT. I count in the end. Yoo may not like it but mostly
I'm like yoo an' I count. He knew that. That on't so mad.
Thass all I'll say for today.

EVENS. All right, Billy. But don't do mad things. Drop your
stick on the ground.

HOLLARCUT. Mr Hollarcut.

EVENS. Drop your stick Mr Hollarcut.

HOLLARCUT. No. I'll howd on to en now I got en. That remind
yoo I'm here.

WILLY *comes in.*

WILLY. Hello. I thought I'd walk out this way.

EVENS (*nods*). They had their inquest this morning.

WILLY. Yes.

EVENS. It's all wrapped up.

WILLY. Death by drowning.

EVENS. Satisfied?

WILLY. And the coroner mentioned careless people who go to
sea in bad weather and put the coastguard at risk.

EVENS. When are you going?

WILLY. Now. Morning, Billy. I see Mrs Rafi's got you digging
in her garden.

HOLLARCUT. Mr Hollarcut.

WILLY. Ah yes.

HOLLARCUT. Thass all right – Carson on't it? I'll tell you
something you ought a know, boy. I dig for her – (*He lays
the side of his index finger against the side of his nose and looks
crafty.*) – but will anything grow? . . . Mornin'.

HOLLARCUT *goes out.* WILLY *sits on a box.*

EVENS. Have you come to kill me?

WILLY. I don't believe so.

EVENS. He had.

WILLY. Oh dear. Should we take it seriously?

EVENS (*shrugs*). God knows.

WILLY. Perhaps you'd better move back into town. For a while anyway.

EVENS. I'd rather be battered to death.

WILLY. Tch tch.

Silence.

WILLY. The draper thought there were more people up there. Other worlds.

EVENS. There are countless millions of suns, so there must be more planets. Millions and millions of living worlds.

WILLY. But would they come all this way to visit us even if they could?

EVENS. No, hardly worth the trip.

WILLY. Perhaps they're all busy killing each other and killing other things. But what if they've killed everything up there? Then they might come here to kill us. I mean, that would make the long trip worth while. A space safari. Perhaps we're just violent little vermin to them. Not to be taken seriously. Just sport.

EVENS. Yes.

WILLY. D'you think they kill each other?

EVENS. Must do. Where there's life it kills, after all.

WILLY. But up there. Out there. When I look up into the sky there are things dying and bleeding and groaning?

EVENS. Oh yes. The music of the spheres.

WILLY. How can you bear to live?

EVENS. I really don't know. I don't know why I'm not mad.

Silence.

WILLY. I'm not sure if I can bear it.

EVENS. You don't have to bear it long. The years go very quickly and you seem to be spared the minutes. Have faith.

WILLY. In what?

EVENS (*shrugs*). Well. (*Looks round.*) Would you like some tea?

WILLY. No.

EVENS. It's no trouble. It's already made. I fill two flasks every morning and that sees me through the day.

WILLY. No thanks.

In silence EVENS *takes two flasks from a box. He unscrews one flask and pours tea. He lets it stand in the cup. He takes the small whisky flask from his pocket and drinks. He puts it away again. He picks up the tea and warms his hands on the cup. The two flasks stand on a box beside him. The silence lasts a moment longer.*

EVENS. I believe in the rat. What's the worst thing you can imagine? The universe is lived in by things that kill and this has gone on for all time. Sometimes the universe is crowded with killing things. Or at any rate there are great pools of them in space. Perhaps that's so now. At other times it falls out that they've killed everything off, including each other of course, and the universe is almost deserted. But not quite. Somewhere on a star a rat will hide under a stone. It will look out on the broken desert and from time to time it will scatter out to feed on the debris. A sham-bolling, lolloping great rat – like a fat woman with shopping bags running for a bus. Then it scuttles back to its nest and breeds. Because rats build nests. And in time it will change into things that fly and swim and crawl and run. And one day it will change into the rat catcher. I believe in the rat because he has the seeds of the rat catcher in him. I believe in the rat catcher. I believe in sand and stone and water because the wind stirs them into a dirty sea and it gives birth to living things. The universe lives. It teems with life. Men take themselves to be very strong and cunning. But who can kill space or time or dust? They destroy everything but they only make the materials of life. All destruction is finally petty and in the end life laughs at death.

WILLY. Then it goes on and on. But if it fails in the end? If it always goes back to the rat.

EVENS. I also believe in the wise rat catcher. He can bear to live in the minutes as well as the years, and he understands the voice of the thing he is going to kill. Suffering is a universal language and everything that has a voice is human. We sit here and the world changes. When your life's over everything will be changed or have started to change. Our brains won't be big enough. They'll plug into bigger brains. They'll get rid of this body. It's too liable to get ill and break. They'll transplant the essential things into a better container. An unbreakable glass bottle on steel stilts. Men will look at each other's viscera as they pass in the street. There'll be no more grass. Why? What's it for? There'll be no more tragedy. There's no tragedy without grass for you to play it on. Well, without tragedy no one can laugh, there's only discipline and madness. You see why the draper's afraid. Not of things from space, of us. We're becoming the strange visitors to this world.

WILLY. Perhaps a better world.

EVENS. Then why will they fill it with bombs and germs and gas? You'll live in a time when that happens and people will do nothing. They'll sit on the ground and say perhaps a better world.

WILLY. What should I do? Come and live here? Work hard? Make money? Become mayor?

EVENS. No.

WILLY. You sound so sure.

EVENS. I'm a wreck rotting on the beach. Past help. That's why I live here out of people's way. It wouldn't help *them* if they lived here. We all have to end differently. . . . Don't trust the wise fool too much. What he knows matters and you die without it. But he never knows enough. No. Go away. You won't find any more answers here. Go away and find them. Don't give up hope. That's always silly. The truth's waiting for you, it's very patient, and you'll find it. Remember, I've told you these things so that you won't despair. But you must still change the world.

ROSE *comes on.*

ROSE. I followed you. We mustn't miss our train. What were you saying?

WILLY. I came to say goodbye, and I'm glad you —

END

The Author's Note for Programmes

The sea could be a negative image. It washes everything away and stands for nothing itself. The tide washes out everything written on the shore. You can't shape it with your hands yet it wears down rocks. It lets nothing be permanent and so makes nonsense of human effort.

But I see it another way. Living involves failure. Evolution is the record of failure at the same time as it's the record of success. So is history. So is moral action. No action is wholly pure. No action except death is final. So there are no supernatural guarantees for the strength and endurance of moral actions, and no actions that protect our sanity except our own. This idea depressed the nineteenth century. They called it god being dead. They thought of human beings as dwarfs isolated in an empty world, and human action as morally meaningless and fundamentally irrational. They saw the universe as a coffin. In our time that becomes the commonplace idea that life is absurd, that we can't prevent suffering except of the most elementary sort – and then only if the economics of charity don't disrupt our own security. In the play Evens argues against this pessimism. The universe spontaneously produces life. It's said there are many other inhabited worlds. We may never contact them, but at least we're not biologically freaks cowering in the corner of a vast and otherwise empty lunatic asylum. It suggests we're not the only world in which moral problems arise. The universe produces minds with moral consciousness. When we look at the night sky there are other moral beings, an infinity of space and time away, looking at the night sky in our direction and asking the questions we ask.

Moral actions have meaning because we give them meaning. We act morally because we're concerned for others' happiness. Or if that's too ambitious for our society, at least for their freedom from obvious pain and need. What gives living a meaning and stops it being absurd?: our happiness and pain, the happiness we feel when others are happy, the pain we feel when others despair. It's a natural human reflex to smile when others smile. It's also naturally human to shudder when they suffer – only we're taught not to, it costs too much. Happiness and pain are the things that give social life meaning, and it's wrong to ignore this and say: No, life is absurd. We can't avoid our moral element. People who live by the sea never get away from its sound. It murmurs, roars, soothes, threatens, and shifts like an unanswered question. And we, who live with other men and women, never get away from moral involvement with them. Some try. But you deny the humanity of others only by destroying your own. And when you destroy your humanity you destroy the most characteristic mark of your species. You cripple yourself. And then – because when you subvert moral concern you subvert your own intelligence – you end by asking why your life is empty and trivial, and why you've created a society threatened by political gangsters.

The sea also stands for hope. It doesn't accept error. It's always new. It washes itself – just as in us the act of consciousness purifies consciousness. The surface of the sea changes as much as anything except the human face. When we despair it's as if the sea dried up. When we're cynical it's as if whole oceans turned sour. So the sea is a symbol of our strength and resourcefulness, as well as a description of our lives as moral animals. It describes the solution as well as the problem. Evolution proceeds by solving problems. You could almost say moral evolution proceeds by making mistakes. Without problems our species would stagnate and probably regress. The act of solving is almost as important as the solution itself – because it means we keep the ability to grow. In a scientific age we should remember that we may reach a time when science will make more problems than it solves. I'm not denying the value of science and technology. But scientists work in a society which includes politicians, sick people, rabid militarists and commercial imperatives. These impose their own characteristics on the social use of science. And because our institutions were evolved by pastoral communities there are no democratic institutions for the control of science and technology – even though they change our lives more than anything else. There is no pure science because all science takes place in a social context, no such thing as the abstract search for knowledge because knowledge becomes technology and so changes our lives. Science for science's sake is as misleading (and unobtainable) as art for art's sake. When scientists talk of pure science, or knowledge for its own sake, they're asking to be allowed to act like apes. Apes make H-bombs. Being human is a matter of choosing to be human.

Our species doesn't have to avoid problems. We have to make our problems fruitful. Human beings mustn't be reduced to two dimensional cut-outs for politicians to tinker with. The danger of science is that it makes politicians too powerful. They can start to dream of final solutions, and under pressure of economic and social crises begin to create the people they need to make their systems work – instead of people choosing the governments they want to make them happy and which will respect human dignity. Our species is open-ended. No man is god-like enough to lay down its final goals.

We even need a sense of tragedy. No democracy can exist without that. But tragedy as something to use in our lives, that gives us sympathy and understanding of other people. Only a moron wants to grin all the time, and even he weeps with rage in the night. Tragedy in this sense is necessary for moral maturity, it doesn't lead to despair, and it certainly has nothing to do with a catharsis that makes us accept abominations to which there should be political solutions. It leads to knowledge and action.

So the sea is a symbol of hope justified by constant new chances and opportunities. Life becomes meaningless when you stop *acting* on the thing that concerns you most: your moral involvement in society. Indifference and cynicism, and pseudo-philosophy (we're all animals), pseudo-psychology (we're all basically selfish) and pseudo-science (we all have a need to act aggressively) add up to that pseudo-profundity: life is absurd.

If I had to name my theatre I would call it a rational theatre.

Edward Bond, 1974.

Methuen's Modern Plays

Jean Anouilh	*Antigone*
	Becket
	The Lark
John Arden	*Serjeant Musgrave's Dance*
	The Workhouse Donkey
	Armstrong's Last Goodnight
John Arden and	*The Business of Good Government*
Margaretta D'Arcy	*The Royal Pardon*
	The Hero Rises Up
	The Island of the Mighty
	Vandaleur's Folly
Wolfgang Bauer,	*Shakespeare the Sadist*
Rainer Werner	
Fassbinder,	*Bremen Coffee,*
Peter Handke,	*My Foot My Tutor,*
Frank Xaver Kroetz	*Stallerhof*
Brendan Behan	*The Quare Fellow*
	The Hostage
	Richard's Cork Leg
Edward Bond	*A-A-America!* and *Stone*
	Saved
	Narrow Road to the Deep North
	The Pope's Wedding
	Lear
	The Sea
	Bingo
	The Fool and *We Come to the River*
	Theatre Poems and Songs
	The Bundle
	The Woman
	The Worlds with *The Activists Papers*
	Restoration and *The Cat*
	Summer
Bertolt Brecht	*Mother Courage and Her Children*
	The Caucasian Chalk Circle
	The Good Person of Szechwan
	The Life of Galileo
	The Threepenny Opera
	Saint Joan of the Stockyards
	The Resistible Rise of Arturo Ui
	The Mother
	Mr Puntila and His Man Matti
	The Measures Taken and other Lehrstücke
	The Days of the Commune

	The Messingkauf Dialogues
	Man Equals Man and *The Elephant Calf*
	The Rise and Fall of the City of Mahagonny and *The Seven Deadly Sins*
	Baal
	A Respectable Wedding and other one act plays
	Drums in the Night
	In the Jungle of Cities
Howard Brenton	*The Churchill Play*
	Weapons of Happiness
	Epsom Downs
	The Romans in Britain
	Plays for the Poor Theatre
	Magnificence
	Revenge
	Hitler Dances
Howard Brenton and	
David Hare	*Brassneck*
Shelagh Delaney	*A Taste of Honey*
	The Lion in Love
David Edgar	*Destiny*
	Mary Barnes
Michael Frayn	*Clouds*
	Alphabetical Order and *Donkey's Years*
	Make and Break
	Noises Off
Max Frisch	*The Fire Raisers*
	Andorra
	Triptych
Simon Gray	*Butley*
	Otherwise Engaged and other plays
	Dog Days
	The Rear Column and other plays
	Close of Play and *Pig in a Poke*
	Stage Struck
	Quartermaine's Terms
Peter Handke	*Offending the Audience* and *Self-Accusation*
	Kasper
	The Ride Across Lake Constance
	They Are Dying Out
Barrie Keeffe	*Gimme Shelter (Gem, Gotcha, Getaway)*
	Barbarians (Killing Time, Abide With Me, In the City
	A Mad World, My Masters
Arthur Kopit	*Indians*
	Wings

John McGrath	*The Cheviot, the Stag and the Black, Black Oil*
David Mercer	*After Haggerty*
	The Bankrupt and other plays
	Cousin Vladimir and *Shooting the Chandelier*
	Duck Song
	The Monster of Karlovy Vary and *Then and Now*
	No Limits To Love
Peter Nichols	*Passion Play*
	Poppy
Joe Orton	*Loot*
	What the Butler Saw
	Funeral Games and *The Good and Faithful Servant*
	Entertaining Mr Sloane
	Up Against It
Harold Pinter	*The Birthday Party*
	The Room and *The Dumb Waiter*
	The Caretaker
	A Slight Ache and other plays
	The Collection and *The Lover*
	The Homecoming
	Tea Party and other plays
	Landscape and *Silence*
	Old Times
	No Man's Land
	Betrayal
	The Hothouse
Luigi Pirandello	*Henry IV*
	Six Characters in Search of an Author
Stephen Poliakoff	*Hitting Town* and *City Sugar*
David Rudkin	*The Sons of Light*
	The Triumph of Death
Jean-Paul Sartre	*Crime Passionnel*
Wole Soyinka	*Madmen and Specialists*
	The Jero Plays
	Death and the King's Horseman
C.P. Taylor	*And a Nightingale Sang . . .*
Nigel Williams	*Line 'Em*
	Class Enemy
Charles Wood	*Veterans*
Theatre Workshop	*Oh What a Lovely War!*

Methuen's Theatre Classics

gentleman realized that he had an opponent! If he had started earlier, he would've won. I won by less than 51 percent. He didn't do much of anything, and we had worked our heads off.

Did you have a campaign manager and a campaign plan?

Oh, we had everything and everybody. Anybody who was kind to me was on my campaign committee. We had a large committee instead of one campaign manager. I did have a campaign manager, but everyone talked strategy and tried to raise a few dollars for newspaper ads and radio. It was just a lot of fun. Nobody thought that we could win. We were just out having fun and working.

We didn't raise that much money, but I had a good friend, one of these early day admitted Republicans, named Payton Anderson who had been on the State Republican Executive Committee and who was well placed within the community. He buttonholed some of these Republicans and got some money out of them.

Did you have a problem with the idea of a woman being county judge?

Yes. The beautiful thing was that being a Republican was so much worse. They got off of being a female pretty quickly.

We ran an issue-oriented campaign. We had to go on the offensive. His dockets were a bit behind. We made a lot of points on what could be done with juveniles. We talked about the county budget and how to spend it—all of the issues pertaining to the office. A candidate should be focused on the issues.

How did you get recruited to run for state legislature in 1962?

MARJORIE ARSHT, HOUSTON
They called me up before the vacancy committee. I enjoyed it a great deal because I was a curiosity. Here was a Jewish woman from Yoakum, Texas. I was such an enigma. They had such limited perspective, with yes-or-no answers. They would ask questions like, "Are you for or against capital punishment?" I would say, "Well, until our system is geared so that really serious criminals can be kept behind bars for life without parole, we have no choice." The

answer wasn't on their paper. One of them who was a friend of mine called me one day and said, "I think it is hysterical they don't know what to do with you." Because I was such a curiosity, I really attracted a crowd. Mostly they wanted to ask how I could be Jewish and not a Communist. My husband, Raymond, would say, "I'd love to come along, but I'm sick of the Jewish question." Then I started asking them how many Jewish people did they think were in Houston, and I got answers like a million. Houston's population was about 400,000 people. I said there are 25,000 men, women, and children, which means there might be 5,000 to 7,000 votes in metropolitan Houston. From the back of the room a man called out and said, "Marjorie, are you sure? They must all live around me." That's one of millions of things that happened.

I had $8,000. I had no district—that was part of my problem—because there were nineteen legislators running around Harris County. So I went to the newspapers, and I knew I would have no problem with George Carmack of the *Houston Press* and the Negro newspaper. I went to the *Houston Chronicle*. I interviewed with the political editor, and he said to me. "Who is your opponent?" I said, "Don't you know who Wally Miller is? You endorsed him last time." With that, I went all the way up to John Jones, the newspaper owner. I said, "Your political editor doesn't even know whom you're endorsing just because he is a Democrat, and that is not worthy of this paper. If you want decent people to run for office, then you ought to know them." He knew my family, who was well known in Houston. They waited until the last day, and they endorsed me. So I had every endorsement.

I beat the gubernatorial candidate, who was Jack Cox, on the west side of Houston. But I had to stay on the west side to convince the Republicans that were there that I was not Communist. I went day and night. If I had only had enough time to spend in the black community. Later, I had a lot of blacks say to me, "We had no idea. Why didn't you come?" I just didn't have time. I appeared before the labor unions, which no Republican had ever done. Of course, Wally Miller didn't go. He was a conservative Democrat. Somebody in the audience said to me, "How could someone of your nationality support somebody like Goldwater?" I said, "Wait a minute. I am an American." Well, the Mexicans just rose to their feet and cheered. Somebody said to me, "Are you a Goldwater Republican?" I said, "No, a Marjorie Arsht Republican." They all just clapped. When I got through, the labor union man said, "You got a lot of votes in this hall tonight." It really was an exciting thing.

LOIS WHITE, SAN ANTONIO

In 1966, they [*the Bexar County Republican Party*] said, "We want you to run for state representative." It was Brotherhood Week, which was February 7 through 12. Black History Month has kind of taken over now. A young man at Republican headquarters asked me to come to his youth group on a Sunday afternoon and talk about the race problem. It went off very well. I think that was probably to see if I could handle myself and make a speech. My husband and I talked about it. I said, "I will still teach, whether I go to Austin or not." That just turned out to be a shot heard around the county. A black woman running for state legislature on the Republican ticket?

I had people that were supporting me, but they weren't going to cross the line and be called Republicans. We never had more than ten blacks that would admit to being Republicans. I had the best teachers in the world. They took me step-by-step. The Republican Party had a fantastic esprit de corps and a fantastic structure. Joci Straus and Mary Lou Grier were our committeewomen. I learned very early that volunteers did much of what was done here. I found out what I was supposed to do. I got people to help me. I got friends who volunteered to do this for free.

What we ran into was the East Side was galvanized during district-wide political campaigns. Lots of people were dangling money in front of these people to get workers for this candidate or that candidate. These people would do a little work for a nice bit of money coming in to their households for grocery money. I got these friends, some of them were teachers, and they would work for free. We didn't have money to pay people. At the end, I had six people that volunteered, and we paid three. My campaign manager was Mary Johns. She contacted the churches and saw how many would let me come and speak. I found that they were very reluctant. What I did was, I said to people, "I don't want to offend you, but it is time that you woke up, and if you don't have any attachment to anybody come hear what I have to say." I seemed like a threat to some of them. There were a number that did support me. I got some contributions. What I wanted to do was give blacks a chance to have something besides one party to vote for. I had a fundraiser. The East Side had never had something like that. The attendance was quite good. Kids volunteered to help me at headquarters. I opened my little headquarters, and one night the boys helped me and one night the girls helped me because I didn't want to be suborning romance. Kids made their parents come out and help. Mrs. Johns kept the place open for me during the day.

I walked the East Side area. In a barbershop, an elderly white gentleman getting his haircut said, "We've got to help her." A younger man in a pawnshop said, "You've got that much nerve, I just might vote for you."

When people asked me to come, I would go to speak at night. There were picnics and things with Republicans all over the county. My principal asked me, "Well, how is it going?" The night before I had been out at a very good meeting. I said to myself quickly, "What does he really want to hear?" I said, "I don't think I'm going to make it." The man looked so relieved. The expression on his face was such that I almost died laughing. I turned and ran into one of my friend's classroom and started laughing. He said, "What is going on?" and I told him. Of course, if I had told the principal things were really going well, he would've found something for me to do. I was free for another week.

SITTY WILKES, AUSTIN

Charlotte Ferris, Beryl Milburn, and Yvonne Gardner talked me into running for the school board. They kept saying, "It is a nonpartisan race. You can win." Somehow or another they talked me into it. I cannot imagine, looking back, why I did it because I knew I didn't have a prayer even though it was a nonpartisan race. There was a guy here, Mark Yancey. He was with the highway department. He was brilliant, and he would brief me on the issues and on how to make speeches. So I went down and registered as a candidate and ran. It was in a field of about five, and you had to have a majority vote to win. I campaigned and won, if you can believe. But I went to one of my husband's furniture manufacturing business clients, Louis Shanks, who was an LBJ man, and asked him if he would get his friends to support me. He said, "Why are you running? What is in it for you? Are you going to sell furniture to the school district?" That motivation had never occurred to me. I said, "Oh, no, we make upholstered furniture. We would never be able to sell to the schools." I got a few people like that to help me. Then there was a woman named Mitchell, she was one of the past presidents of the Republican Women's Clubs. It was her idea to get up call sheets to call the voters. I had never seen that done before. She got call sheets for everybody and gave them a list of thirty people to call that day to see if they had gone and voted. I ran in '67 and was elected in '68.

MARY LOU GRIER, SAN ANTONIO & BOERNE

In '74, we had a full ticket statewide. It was something we had wanted to do for a long time. I ran for Texas Land Commissioner and traveled all over the state. We had a motor home. I'd say, 90 percent of the time all the candidates were on board. We'd stop at night at motels. The next morning we'd head out again. Sometimes we'd get out and walk down Main Street, go to a luncheon, or talk to a Republican Women's Club or some other group. There'd usually be a barbecue or something in the evening. We'd stop here and there in different cities. We got good press. The media were always there. We had some of the major city press traveling with us. TV and radio showed up. Everybody likes to be asked for their vote, even though they don't plan to vote for you. So we were pretty well received. We covered a lot of the state. Everybody got along real well. We had camaraderie. Even though most of the men thought they were going to win.

You didn't think you were going to win?

No. I didn't think I would win. But I thought I had a better chance than I did in '62 when I ran for Bexar County District Clerk.

Why didn't you win in 1974?
Well, I think it was too early [*laughing*].

Too early for a Republican or too early for a woman?

Nobody seemed to say you couldn't win because you're a woman. But it was still too early. You know, we just had the problem with Nixon and Watergate.

How do you think that your run for office in 1962 helped your future run for office?

I made a great number of speeches, and I was pretty articulate. I think that was a great deal of the reason behind the Party recruiting me, because they figured I could get up and talk on my feet, which I could do. I think that's why I was recruited. They didn't think I'd be an embarrassment. I could hold my own.

I had been involved in campaigns, so it wasn't as though I didn't know how they were run or what you did in a campaign. I guess I had been involved in almost every aspect of it, other than being a candidate, so there weren't any surprises.

When she ran for land commissioner in 1974, was Mary Lou Grier the first woman to run for statewide office since former governor Ma Ferguson?

CATHERINE SMYTH COLGAN, DALLAS
That's right.

How did people react to having a modern woman candidate?

I never saw a bit of problem. Of course she was such a capable, excellent person, excellent speaker. She was a stronger spokesman than some of the men. I did not see in that particular tour any discrimination because of her wearing a skirt. She could truly communicate with her audience. They were fascinated because of her demeanor and her presence. Had she been another type of female, perhaps it would have been different. She was a strong candidate that just happened to be a woman. That to me is important. Through the years, from what I have seen, the Texas Republican Party really was an open arena for women candidates. I never saw any discrimination. A close friend in Dallas once said the Republican Party in Texas is never going to achieve its place in history until the caliber of the men equals that of the women. You know what, that was correct. As the Party grew in strength, it became socially and professionally acceptable for a man to jump in the ranks.

> *Did your run for Congress in 1982 and also your run for state*
> *treasurer in 1990 affect how you put your campaign together*
> *when you ran for the Senate in 1993?*

KAY BAILEY HUTCHISON, HOUSTON & DALLAS

I ran for the legislature in 1972 and was elected and served from 1973 to 1976. The legislative campaign was very grassroots oriented. The congressional campaign certainly was, too. I learned a lot from that because it was my only loss, and you learn as much or more from losses as you do from wins. Then in the state treasurer's race, everyone said you couldn't run a statewide race grassroots. It takes too much time. It takes money. It takes effort away from what you have to do to win, and don't do it. I said, "No, that is my strength, and it is the only way I know to run. It's the only way that we can elect a candidate at the down ballot level, because I will never have enough money to be on TV so that people will know who I am. If I don't have a grassroots organization, I don't see how I win against a Democrat in a Democrat state." So I did. I learned grassroots and I stuck to grassroots and it was all very much a stair-step effort. But I never forgot my base and that grassroots effort.

> *Why would advisors think that it is more expensive than*
> *running a standard media-based campaign?*

Because they thought to have a volunteer organization, you had to feed it, and you had to have a staff person to make contact and keep generating enthusiasm. People would expect you, if you had a grassroots organization, to communicate with it, and therefore the thought was, you don't have enough effort to do it. But my grassroots effort was mostly volunteers. My whole campaign for state treasurer had only three paid staffers in the beginning and four in the end. I had a campaign manager, a finance director, and a scheduler, who were paid. I had a volunteer press secretary and a volunteer volunteer coordinator, and that was all. I didn't even have a travel aide. I traveled by myself. Later, I traveled with my volunteer press secretary. Then, right at the end, I gave her a nominal salary, nothing like what she was worth. That was it. I won with grassroots. In 1990, the governor of our Party was not elected. Nobody else was either except for myself and Rick Perry [*as agriculture commissioner*]. I believe that the only reason I was in the leading role to be Senator is because I was the highest ranking statewide elected official in Texas. I was a natural, with the grassroots-based organization, to be the nominee for the Senate because we didn't have anyone else.

ANITA HILL, GARLAND

It was a summer election for an open seat in the legislature. People don't think about elections during the summer. My husband insisted that I do it. I had never planned to run. Finally, I agreed. In 1972, my husband had been asked to run for the legislature. He said, "I can't think of a better thing to do to ruin your reputation." Then five years later, I ran. Now, I wouldn't take anything for it.

You ran as a Democrat?

Right. It really didn't come down to party affiliation but being known in the community. It was a three-person race, and we had a runoff. It was real tight. My husband and I had been very active in Democratic Party politics. After I was elected in 1977, one of the questions the Dallas County media asked was, "Are you going to support the candidate of your party in the presidential election?" At that time, it was either going to be Ted Kennedy or Jimmy Carter. I knew I wasn't going to vote for the Democrat. I always voted for the Republican in November. Democrats in Dallas County were having a fight between the established faction and the George Wallace faction. My husband usually was the chairman of the district convention. We saw a little of everything and a lot of hatred. When I decided to change parties, my husband was the secretary of the Dallas County Democratic Party. He resigned the day I made the announcement. They found somebody to run against me. A lot of people thought I should resign my seat. I didn't see it that way because I had been representing my district.

What was the reaction of the Democrats when you switched?

Some anger, but there weren't that many Democrats in Garland. Most of them were very nice about it. I still get along with them. John Bryant, a Congressman who was sort of the Democratic leader for Dallas County, made a statement that if you don't like Democratic Party politics then just get out. Now I am an avid Republican.

What was the reaction of the Republicans when you switched parties?

Enthusiasm! Soon after that, the Republican men's club started. The Garland Republican Women already existed.

When you switched and ran in your first election as a Republican, was there a difference between how you campaigned as a Republican and as a Democrat?

No, not really, but it was harder. My son took a leave from law school for one semester and came home and ran my campaign. The Republican Women from Dallas came up two or three nights to do telephone polls. It showed then that I would win with 65 percent. I actually won with 62 percent. When I ran the first time, I had never made a public speech. My mouth would get very dry. I would always have to go first. Finally, I would say, "I don't want to take advantage of my gender. Let Mike go first." Then I would say, "You have heard the sublime; here is the ridiculous." There are not many people who are very good speakers, so you get a lot more sympathy if you do that.

When I ran as a Republican, my opponent's family was very active in the Democratic Party. It was rough. I do not blame the woman who ran against me. One time they stole my yard signs. A man called and said, "Are you the Anita Hill that has all of these signs out on the lake shore?" Supporters who had my bumper stickers were forced off the road.

LEON RICHARDSON, NEDERLAND

In '76, we were able to get redistricted and thought we might be able to elect a state representative. No one would run. After we fought to get the redistricting, somebody had to do it. So I put a lot into it. Of course, I lost, but I got more votes than anybody ever had before. If I had had a real bad opponent I probably could have won, but he was real popular and I liked him myself. It's terrible to like your opponent.

Who managed your campaign?

One of the extreme right wing [*laughing*]. I have a letter, and she said, "Leon, it's getting hard to dislike you." One of the presidents of the bank was my finance manager. [*Senator*] John Tower came down for my announcement, and he went door-to-door in Nederland with me. He volunteered. Our relationship was platonic. We were buddies. He was here for the whole weekend. We went door-to-door one day, and we went to a high school football game. We had a luncheon and coffees.

How did people react when they opened the door and saw you and the Senator?

Their mouths dropped open. We stopped after a dog chased us.

MARJORIE VICKERY, COPPER CANYON

In the early '70s, I complained to my husband about our children's school. He said, "If you feel that strongly why don't you run for the board?" I never thought of that. I ran and won that election, and I became the first woman ever elected to the Lewisville school board. That was great preparation for me to serve on the state board of education.

After I went off the Lewisville school board, I decided I wanted to run for the state board of education. So I filed. Lots of people in the school system and, in fact, the whole community got behind me. The boundaries for the state board of education at that time were the same as the congressional boundaries. I grew up in Dallas, so I was familiar with a lot of people in North Dallas, and they were very, very supportive of me. In the primary, I had two opponents, both of whom were men. One of them was the former school superintendent in Irving. The other one had been a president of a school board in a parochial school system. When the election came, I almost won. We had to have a runoff. I started immediately getting on the telephone and calling the people who had helped me. I started early and told them that this was going to be the only runoff for the whole Republican Party in the Third Congressional District, so it was really vital that, if they would like for me to be their representative, they should take the time to put it on their calendars and vote one more time. They said that they would. The next time I won with like 70 percent. I had opponents in the general election, and I won.

How were you able to build your core of supporters?

First of all, my husband's company had a gentleman who had run many, many political campaigns. He offered to help me in my campaign. He gave invaluable advice and information on how to run a campaign and promote name recognition. He said it starts with your brochure. It has to be concise and, of course, all truthful. It was. It also had to describe my qualifications for the job. We mailed them out at bulk rate. To do that all over the district was very expensive but very worthwhile.

Because I had grown up in the Park Cities and graduated from high school there and graduated from SMU [*Southern Methodist University in Dallas*], I knew a lot of people in North Dallas and Park Cities that helped me to become known. I didn't have to start from scratch, so to speak. I relied on the Republican Women's Clubs. After I filed, they immediately started extending invitations to me to speak at their meetings.

SHAROLYN WOOD, HOUSTON

I had to make it clear very early on, because a lot of people want you to take political stands. Every time I got questionnaires from people, I sent them back a letter trying to be courteous, telling them, you go elect the legislators and congressmen who will enact the laws that you think are important. As a judge, I will keep my oath to uphold those laws. Of course, that means I uphold laws that I may not personally agree with.

My husband's office manager, Joyce Streeter, had run Jack Kemp's first two congressional campaigns. She had run Republican gubernatorial campaigns. She grew up politically in California with Lynn Nofzinger and all of the Reagan crew. I had Joyce as a secret weapon. She told me the first thing you do is you get a card that says you are a candidate. Next thing, you get some Monarch stationery and you put your name on it and the fact that you're a candidate. Then write a letter to every elected Republican and tell them that you're running. She said to get a list of the Republican clubs and start calling the presidents. They were so appreciative of candidates that wanted to run. The Republican Women's Clubs very quickly understood what judges were about and knew that judges couldn't get involved in the politics. They just wanted people. That's why I encouraged so many people to run as Republicans when they came to me about running for judge. I said, "The Republican Women are wonderful. They are just looking for good, honest, hardworking people. They just want a commitment from you that you're going to be a good judge." That's what they did for me.

When I spent $40,000, I thought that was a fortune. By 1984, I had had a contested primary, a contested runoff, and a contested general [election] in '80; a contested primary in '82; a contested general in '82; and a contested general in '84—six elections in two and a half years. You had better believe that for my husband and me and our two older boys—my sons were four and one—those were very tough years. From 1980 to 1984 was basically one continuous election, one continuous race. It was very difficult to be a judge and a Republican in those days. You had to really work for it. It was much easier to just be a Democrat. You were assured a big block of votes just from the lever—the straight-ticket voters. Republicans were so proud of picking who they knew and only voting for people they knew well. That's because for many years they could only vote for Democrats and had to be very careful about which Democrat they voted for. If the Republicans did not support all the candidates, we couldn't win. By 1984, we got that message across, and we elected our entire slate. It helped to have the president. Running with Ronald Reagan was wonderful. That was the turning point. We knew it was safe to be a Republican.

BARBARA CULVER CLACK, MIDLAND

Governor Clements called me and said, "Barbara, I want to appoint you to the Texas Supreme Court to fill a vacated seat." I said okay. That was a great experience. It was a year like the supreme court has never had and never will have again. Remember that justice had been for sale in Texas. We had had a very liberal court. Tom Phillips was getting situated as chief justice, and I came on.

Then, after a year, there were the normal people that were running. There were six vacancies on the supreme court in 1988, all of us out groveling for money and all of us with opponents. It was just the most unnatural year. I'd work Sunday night until whenever. Go Monday, Tuesday, Wednesday, leave Wednesday afternoon and hit the campaign trail. You must do fundraising to run for statewide office. I raised over $550,000.

Jack Hightower was my opponent. Of course, I had known him for years. He was a former state senator, a former congressman, a lobbyist in Austin, and he was an original good old boy. He campaigned pretty hard. All of the lobbyists really helped him. They felt so virtuous because they backed Phillips and they backed the others and then they backed Hightower. That did not make them look like they were just backing Republicans because they were backing a Democrat. He trounced me.

What did you learn about campaigning for statewide office?

It's hard work, and it is a lot of fun. You meet a lot of wonderful people, but the whole point of your going out is usually to raise funds. How in the world can anybody meet many voters when you catch yourself going back to Dallas or San Antonio, and you see the same twenty people every time you go there? Loyal Republicans come out, but you know that you are not reaching the man on street, the voters, and the people. You have to raise millions of dollars to do enough TV to really reach people. You can't run an ad in Dallas at 5:30 in the afternoon and think that you have won many voters. You have to run lots of them. You have to do mailouts. You have to do some radio. It was hard to get any identity when there were six Republicans running—twelve people when you considered the opponents. They were all vying for media attention, plus you've got governors and senators and congressman and everything else in there. It's terrible.

If you haven't got the stomach for it, you shouldn't get into politics. This is what I tell people all the time. If you can't stand the thought of losing, don't do it because you've got a 50 percent chance of losing. If you can't take that, then don't do it. You see a lot of these people just crushed and humiliated for life because they lost. You've just got to grow up. You have to be prepared to take a win or a loss. You don't know what is going to affect the voters. You don't know what makes them stay home or go to the polls.

Those lobbyists, bless their hearts. They are all in Austin. They all know each other. They have lunch together once a week. They are all buddies. What they do is, they want somebody who will vote right on all issues affecting, say, malpractice, doctors, and insurance. So they get together, and they all decide whom they are going to support. They send out their "push" cards to doctors, nurses, hospital administrators, pharmacists, psychologists, psychiatrists, and therapists. Most of these people don't know and they don't care, but their professional associations say, "We should vote them."

The guy out in the middle of nowhere, who will not hear the candidate, is going to rely on what his state association tells him to do.

The lobbyists got mad at one of my opinions. They didn't know me. I didn't have any stroke with them. I had been a judge for twenty-five years, and I had never had anyone interfere with any of my decisions. I wouldn't have been a good team player. It was a wonderful experience to be on the supreme court for one year. It was the climax of my career.

How did you put together your campaign organization when you ran for railroad commissioner?

CAROLE KEETON RYLANDER, AUSTIN

The Texas Federation of Republican Women was a vital ingredient. I am not independently wealthy. I don't have my own plane. I am a working mama and grandmama. We had to go out and raise the dollars and build the grassroots base. There is no question that the TFRW is a great grassroots base. Republican Women were very helpful. Back when I couldn't afford to fly, I had to drive. There would be a TFRW woman there who would keep me overnight and get me to activities. Now, it is still the TFRW women who will meet me when I walk off the plane. I had friends that donated to the campaign and lent their airplanes. It is like campaigning in five or six different states. Texas has nineteen to twenty-two different media markets.

When I ran for comptroller in 1998, I was the only statewide officeholder who won and was out spent. We raised more dollars than had ever been raised for a comptroller's race, but I was out spent. My opponent could write his own check, million after million after million, and he did so. But we weren't out hustled. I had that grassroots base built running for the railroad commission. I am a real believer in TFRW, precincts chairmen, county chairmen, and other groups. When I was running for comptroller, the Texas Classroom Teachers Association members were very supportive, though the organization does not endorse. Grassroots is so important. I have got many, many friends all across this state. Obviously, you have got to raise big dollars to have a successful statewide race, but I defeated an incumbent on the railroad commission with less dollars. We raised them and used them wisely. And, as I said, I won this time when we were out spent but not out hustled. The grassroots effort pays off.

JANE NELSON, FLOWER MOUND

Before I ran for state senate, I was in Austin often because I was on the state board of education. I would come over and watch the legislature if I had some free time. My own senator was an incumbent Democrat, very liberal. He was carrying some workers compensation legislation that I, as a businessperson, knew was detrimental to business. I went to talk with him as a constituent. He didn't have time to talk to me. He never talked to me. I ran against him because I was so angry that he wouldn't even take the time to talk to me. Then when I decided to run, I started talking to people and found that more and more people had had that same experience with him and were willing to help me. Looking back, my gosh, I ran against a powerful incumbent with a boatload of money.

How did you beat him?

A lot of help from a lot of people. Of course, financially you don't get any PAC money if you run against an incumbent. My money came in $50 and $25 contributions. I had a huge number of volunteer workers that you couldn't buy. The district that I ran in was a 50 percent Democrat district. My base was Denton and Tarrant Counties where there were lots of Republicans. I was told by a lot of political consultants, "Don't waste your time out in those rural counties. They have never voted for a Republican, and they are not going to." I took it as a real challenge. They called me the "Dairy Queen candidate" because I would go to every Dairy Queen in every one of those towns. I would get up at three o'clock in the morning and drive four hours and be there when the dairy farmers came in from milking. Those were the most conservative people in the world. One man sticks out in my mind. I talked to him, and he looked at me after listening to my bit. He said, "Ma'am, I have never voted for a Republican in my life, and I have never voted for a woman in my life, but neither has ever come asking me for my vote. I'm going to vote for you." I won six of the eleven counties a Republican had never won. It is because I went to them and said, "This is what I believe." Yes, they were traditional Democrats but hard workers. The Republican philosophy is the philosophy that they arm themselves with.

Why did you decide you wanted to run for Congress in 1992?

DOLLY MADISON McKENNA, HOUSTON

I got into it because my husband and I started a small company. We were trying to get health insurance, which is almost impossible for a company that is under ten people. We were in a regulated industry and were having a lot of hassles with regulations.

My campaign was sort of unique in a way because I wasn't coming from a history of grassroots Republican activism in Texas. I was involved with arts organizations, the symphony, and the museums. Having worked with those organizations, I encountered a lot of people who were interested in politics and had some money and put money into my campaign. My first fundraiser was a women's fundraiser. Everyone said you couldn't raise money from women. It is more difficult, but I had a fundraiser and raised $35,000 from women. All of these people had been perfectly willing to write a check for $1,000 for the symphony. Somehow I convinced them to support this campaign. We were just really calling one-on-one. A lot of them were wives of husbands who had given a lot of money to Mike Andrews, who was my opponent. In fact, the fundraiser was at the house of someone who was one of his big contributors. It just threw him into a tizzy. He started calling people saying, "Get your wife in line." It got a fair amount of attention.

In 1996, I had not planned to run. At that point, I knew it was a Democrat district. Gene Fontenot, [*the Republican*] who ran in 1994 against [*Democrat*] Ken Bentsen, spent $4 million and didn't get any different percentage than I did [*when she lost*] in 1992. Then the supreme court came down with a decision to throw out a lot of the primaries, in effect having to do with segregated districts, racial balance, and so forth. They threw out the primary and held open elections on presidential Election Day. By this point, I had determined that it was clearly not a good thing for a moderate to run in any Republican primary in a pretty conservative district. You're not going to have a shot. But in open elections, the more people who vote, the more moderate the determination is going to be because the general population is fairly moderate. It worked. There were eight people running as Republicans, and I beat them all. I would not have run the first race any differently, but I would have run the runoff differently.

First of all, I was the recipient of the Republican Party wanting to pick up a Republican seat. So they sent down all of these campaign managers and strategists. Some of them were very talented, and some of them were not doing things the way they should be done. They put time and money into direct mail. It should have been to put on a get-out-the-vote effort. They should have spent four times as much money identifying the households in the precincts that I had done very well in to start with—for a very targeted get-out-the-vote. I didn't have the choice because I wasn't spending the money, the Party was. There were a couple of positions that I had not taken strongly. I think one was minimum wage. The national party people said, "If you're going to get the right-to-work people [*the anti-union vote*], you're going to have to take a stand on this issue." That was used very heavily against me in ads. I never would have done it of my own volition. The people that supported me probably would have taken my position, but not in such a strong way that it would mobilize them. Whereas if you are going to unions, which my opponent was doing, and using a lot of union money, that kind of issue is a mobilizer. So that is the one election I would have handled differently. Would I have won it? That was a pretty heavily Democratic year and even more Democratic district. I don't know. It is hard to say.

How many points did you lose by?

It was probably something like 45 to 55 percent, maybe even a little more. But when you're talking about a runoff, that is only 6,000 or 7,000 votes. Could I have found 6,000 or 7,000 people who voted for me before and get them out to vote? That is the question. The opposition had a much more sophisticated get-out-the-vote effort. They were doing daily get-out-the-vote fliers to only the identified voters. They weren't blanketing blocks, whereas our people were forced to go to targeted precincts where I had done well before and give them to everybody. You have 60 percent of the people that support me and 40 percent of the people that support him. That is not necessarily the best way to spend your money. I think that direct mail is often useless. Particularly blanketing it to lots of people in that kind of a circumstance. That is when you look to precinct chairmen [*to help identify and get out the vote*]. Effectively, the precinct organization and the party organization had been taken over by people who disagreed with me philosophically and were working against me.

Wouldn't you be better than a Democrat?

The fact that I would agree with them on 90 percent of the issues and not on 10 percent, I have been told right to my face time after time, doesn't matter. It is the 10 percent that we care about. We would rather have someone that we disagree with 100 percent and throw them out next time than have someone entrenched on those issues with which we disagree in our own Party. What I also found out, after the fact, was that they were running underground ads and radio against me based upon pro-choice issues. A lot of that was paid for by Ken Bentsen's campaign. I only found out because the campaign consultant who did it, in retrospect, had a falling out with the people he did it for and felt badly. He came and told me. He gave me copies of the checks from Bentsen's campaign.

PATRICIA LYKOS, HOUSTON

I received a call when I was in trial in court. They said, "There is a bench opening. Would you like your name to be considered?" The strong feminist that I am, I replied that I needed to talk to my husband and my mother. "May I call you back?" My mother and husband said, "It is really an honor to receive a call like that, so you should say yes. You are not going to get it, but that is the courteous thing to do." When I was in trial, my whole focus was my client and I forgot to return the call. I got interrupted in trial again. They said, "What is your answer?" At noon, the judge called a recess and asked me to approach the bench and said congratulations. I was appointed to County Criminal Court No. 10 to take effect January 1, 1980. It was exhilarating for the first few days, and then six people filed against me in the Democrat primary. They had never elected a Republican to a trial bench in Harris County. In fact, I was the first Republican elected to a county court at law. We didn't have any contested primaries because, who is going to contest a losing ticket?

The man who prevailed in the Democratic primary raised over $100,000. I raised $48,000. None of it came from lawyers. I always gave speeches for the Party, professional groups, academic groups, and all sorts of nonpartisan groups on significant issues of the day. So I was fairly well known in the community to Republicans, thoughtful conservative Democrats, and Independents. I tried fifty jury trials that year, all of the time that I was running for office. I would give 7:00 a.m. speeches, I would do luncheon speeches, and I made two or three appearances every night and did the same thing on weekends. I told them my philosophy and educated people on the three branches of government.

Did you have a campaign manager or any kind of campaign organization to help you?

Yes, I did. I had a Republican woman who was my unpaid campaign manager. Every single penny went to the campaign for radio commercials, yard signs, and brochures. Jim Culberson did my graphics work for me. Dr. Richard Murray from the University of Houston plotted out the precincts and told me which precincts were most likely to be Republican or Independent or swing precincts. That is where I concentrated my efforts as far as the paid media went, pushing cards on Election Day, and having clean-cut youngsters wearing my T-shirts, so if people didn't want a card they saw the name. We won. In fact, I went to bed thinking that I had lost. A friend from one of the newspapers called me up and said it looks really bad. We were used to the Democrat votes coming in last. But in 1980, there were precincts on the west side of town that didn't shut down until ten at night. That meant those people were in line before seven. Our votes came in last. I woke up a relatively substantial winner. There is no question that Ronald Reagan got that vote out. That is one of the keys to winning an election, turning that vote out.

BEVERLY KAUFMAN, HOUSTON

I was nominated for county clerk in May. [*Kaufman was appointed county clerk after the death of the officeholder but was required to seek the nomination of the Harris County executive committee because the deceased county clerk's name was already on the ballot*]. Then I started campaigning. I was on page twelve of a twelve-page ballot. I got 61 percent of the vote—more than the governor. I had a lot of training, through my political activities all those years, in nurturing the news media. The smartest thing that you can do as a public servant is to be a better spokesperson for the election process and let voters know what they need to know about elections and when early voting starts. So I put out a lot of press releases that helped the media. If they didn't call me, I called them and said, "Friday's the last day to vote early." They would do an interview. I was all over the press. I bet I got a half-million dollars worth of time. The day of the election I spent on the phone answering voter calls for information. I left to go to the Astro Hall to count the early vote. I ran into my old boss, Jon Lindsay, and Commissioner El Franco Lee, who is a Democrat. I said, "I've got to go count votes, and I need a hug. This has been the longest day of my life." I didn't know if anybody even knew that I was running. The judge said. "Are you kidding? They were talking about you on the radio." Commissioner Lee hugged me. So we counted the early votes, and I had 70 percent of the early vote. I just screamed. I couldn't believe it. I guess you get too close to the trees to see the forest after a while.

NANCY JUDY, DALLAS

When I ran for the school board, I had a lot of people who volunteered to help me. When I ran for commissioner, I had volunteers. When I ran for the congressional seat, I had people who wanted me to be in Congress—influential people here. Some of them had agendas, like oilmen, others did not. They were willing to raise money and have offices staffed for me. I had phone banks where volunteers would come. Dave Fox, who was the president of the firm Fox and Jacobs, was my finance chairman. A law student who had worked for Congressman Steelman gave himself to my campaign for one year. He would pick me up in the morning and take me to all the places. That was the greatest help of all.

Did you find it difficult to raise money as a woman?

It's just hard to raise money, period. I sent out letters. I got some PAC money. I returned some money that I didn't want. They were playing both sides against the middle. They gave to Jim Mattox [*her Democrat opponent*] also. I didn't want their money. I didn't go into debt. I am not a wealthy person. I had to do it through contributions. We would have to plan everything in terms of advertising, mailings, etc. based upon the budget. You could never get caught up in the moment and go into debt. So many people do. It is nervy of you to have fundraisers to pay off your debt if you have been defeated or, if you are elected, to come back asking for more money to pay off your debt.

I called a press conference right after the Democratic primary. I read all of my opponent's out-of-state labor contributions, and he interrupted my press conference and tried to takeover. Then he made disparaging remarks about me on Channel 13 KERA. They thought he was completely out of line, which he was. In high school assemblies when I spoke, he would make very disparaging remarks and appeal to the Baptists in the crowd. He was unbelievable.

The most difficult thing was to go to Washington on these congressional briefings with other congressional candidates from around a country. The Republican National Committee televised your speech. They would give you a subject, and then two seconds later you have to get up and speak and it would be televised. Then everyone in the room gave you feedback and criticized you in this room of thirty men. That was a challenge.

CAROLE WOODARD, HOUSTON & GALVESTON

I campaigned [*for county clerk*] with very little money. After everyone got me involved, I had very little support. I lost by about 1,000 votes. I ran against Patricia Ritchie, who worked as the assistant under the county clerk, who had been there for thirty years. She had been her assistant for all those years. I really thought that I was going to win. I campaigned with about $1,200. It was mainly with the work of my husband and my church that we were able to make our own signs. Steve Stockman ran for Congress, and he helped me. He included me in his mailers because I didn't have money to do my own. I carried all of north Galveston County. It was really the black people that did not vote for me. We were hoping that I could have gotten a small percentage of the swing votes from blacks, but I didn't get it because I was a Republican. That is what they told me in all of the churches I campaigned in. "We don't vote for Republicans." It didn't matter that I was the most qualified candidate, both in education and experience. What mattered was that I was a Republican, and they would not vote for a Republican whether they were qualified or not. The more vicious part of my campaign came from black Democrats. And I am black.

When I was running for county clerk, I went to a June 19th celebration. June 19th is a celebration that black people have in Texas because that's when the slaves were freed here. There are celebrations all over, and politicians use that time to make all of the picnics and the big gatherings where they talk to people about voting. All of the candidates go and try to reach blacks. A prominent black woman elected official stood up and said that the Democrats freed the slaves. I was appalled. I went there to speak, and they would not even let me speak. They let all of the black Democratic candidates speak, but they would not let me speak because I was a Republican. So I pushed my cards, and I spoke to people and said, "That is not true." Think about it—Abraham Lincoln was not a Democrat. Then when you brought it to their attention, it was like, that is right. He wasn't. But with her there saying what she did, they believed it. If you don't go back in your brain and pull up history, it is never even questioned. It is done so subtly. I was able to make it through the crowd. I stopped and talked to people and said, "With all due respect, she lied to you."

Candidates Helping Others

NORA RAY, FORT WORTH

When Betty Andujar ran for state senate, she was real supportive of other candidates. She helped them raise money and advised them, particularly the younger ones, about how to get the precincts organized, how to get out the vote, and where to look for support.

JULIA VAUGHAN, MIDLAND

Barbara Culver Clack ran and was elected as a Republican to the position of county judge, then was a district judge, and then was appointed to the Texas Supreme Court. She was a perfect example of how you overcome the gender barrier at the same time you are overcoming political party barriers. People like her, who were willing to put their reputations on the line, get their friends involved, and really turn it into a grassroots movement were very, very important. That was one of the things I learned from her. A lot of people were surprised when I ran for office in '94 that there were so many people nobody had ever heard of being a sponsor of a political event. They did it because I asked them. I'm sure it was the same way for her. That's the way she taught me. She said, "You have to be willing to ask people for help. Very rarely will they turn you down if they know you or if they really believe in what you stand for even if they don't know you."

How do you think your run for office in 1964 affected your ability in the future to work with candidates?

NITA GIBSON, LUBBOCK

I knew right where they were. Understanding things really helps you be successful. If you understand the role of the other individual or if you empathize with them a little bit by having been there and done that, you can talk their language.

SYLVIA NUGENT, DALLAS & AMARILLO

I learned two very important things running for state legislature. One is, you can't run your own campaign. Two, I like running campaigns better than I like being a candidate.

KATIE HECK, MIDLAND

I realized how hard it was to be a candidate when I ran myself. I ran for city council and had no objectivity at all. I couldn't even pick out a photograph of myself. My children just finally tore all the photographs out of my hands and said, "Mother, hire somebody." For all of the campaigns I had managed, I could not do it for myself.

Money

SHIRLEY GREEN, AUSTIN & SAN ANTONIO

As recently as maybe ten years ago, I think that nearly all women candidates and people that worked for women candidates acknowledged that the most difficult thing for them is to raise money. However, I found when I ran for state legislature back in '64, there were also some offsetting advantages that I don't think political operatives usually recognize because operatives usually think more of money and TV buys. For instance, when I ran, there were four state representative slots and we all ran countywide. I got many, many, many more speaking engagement requests, for instance, than the three guys who were running did. It was because I was a novelty. Organizations that were having a forum would have one Democrat and one Republican. Almost anytime someone meets a woman candidate, she is more memorable because she is different. So there are pluses and minuses to being a woman.

As a legislative candidate, how do you balance the need for money with the need for volunteers?

ANNA MOWERY, FORT WORTH

Raise your money early so that you're not having to in the later stages when you need to make contacts. Early money is very important. From the time you decide you might want to run, tie up good people and get some committees. What happened with my legislative race was Bob Leonard announced that he was going to step down right before Christmas. He had promised that he would call me since he knew I wanted the spot. He called me over the Christmas holidays on a Thursday or Friday night. I immediately hung up and started calling. I called the precinct chairmen, and I got 88 percent of the precinct chairmen committed to me. I called all the downtown people that give money or have influence. Being county chairman was invaluable.

GWYN SHEA, IRVING

The transition from being an administrative assistant to a candidate running for the office [*state representative*] is a real eye-opener. When I was the administrative assistant to Bob Davis, I knew where he stood and what he thought. It was real easy for me to be the spokesperson and say Bob Davis believes 1, 2, 3, and 4. It wasn't Gwyn Shea saying that. When I became the candidate, what did I think? What did I propose? What did I bring to that arena?

It was easy to raise money for my former boss. You were asking for somebody else and not asking for you. But when you have to ask for money yourself, that is still, after twenty-five years, the hardest, most unpleasant, most undesirable thing I do in politics. Having said that, it was really interesting in 1982 to go to the business community. You always know that if people will even give you a dollar then you have got their vote because they have confidence in you. I started out with the premise that if I couldn't raise enough money or have enough money pledged to run the race, then I did not deserve to have my name on the ballot. I was able to do that. That encouraged me, but the business community was real reserved. They really, really didn't want to do much, so they didn't do much. Of course in 1982, it wasn't as big of an expense as it is today. It was real interesting because then in 1984, I won by over 70 percent of the vote, and I have never had a problem raising money since. I would say that for Republican women, and it is probably the same for the Democratic women too, if you can instill confidence in the public that you are competent, that you are not an airhead, that you can do things, then they really get behind you. You have got to prove yourself first. That is basically what I did.

How were you able to raise enough money that first campaign?

I had an awful lot of help from my former boss, Bob Davis, who had been in the legislature for ten years. Anybody like that in your corner is going to give you a head start because people respect that person and their judgment of people. I had one or two in the community that were really, really supportive of me. But it was the Republican supporters, as opposed to a broad base of support. I want to give that credit to Bob Davis and to those people who were right there in my corner.

I Won!

What did you feel when you won a place on the school board?

SITTY WILKES, AUSTIN

It didn't register with me. I am not accustomed to losing. So it just didn't register with me, the impact of what happened. There was a guy on the school board named Roy Butler. He was a big LBJ man. He had to make up his mind to get along with me. Of course, I was younger then, and I hate to say I was more attractive. The reporters in the paper said, "The other candidates didn't have a chance when the comely Mrs. Wilkes walked in the room." I had to look up the word "comely" because I had always thought of myself as homely, and so that helped. I was something like thirty-eight, and that was an advantage. They were all shocked. They usually handed these positions down. They handpicked somebody to run.

MARY DENNY, DENTON

Winning! I can't believe they really do want me!

CHAPTER 14

Candidates' Wives

"They decided to send me out on the trail, too . . .
other wives weren't doing it then."   —LOU TOWER

*T*he role of candidates' wives changed through the years.
In most cases, wives were surrogates for their husbands, traveling
to remote areas of Texas to which the candidates' time schedule
would not permit a visit. They made speeches, generally avoiding
policy statements, and shook hands, making the electorate feel a part
of the campaign excitement. Although they won votes as they went,
in the early years it was often a lonely job, without many Party
faithful to support their husband's candidacy.

Some women were their husbands' campaign managers. They
did not let inexperience stop them and eagerly worked to do what
ever it took to mount a campaign. As the years passed, they used
statewide contacts developed through Party work and Republican
Women's Clubs to provide the backbone for their husbands' statewide campaigns. In some cases politically better known than their
husbands, wives made meaningful contributions, complementing
the campaign efforts of the candidate. Wives sometimes reached out
for support in nontraditional areas, taking risks their husbands
could not afford to take. This teamwork made a difference in many
campaigns, and it began to pay off with electoral success.

Wives Have Guts Too

MARTHA CROWLEY, DALLAS

My husband, Frank, was reelected as county commissioner in
'64 and then in '68. We decided to move up or out. They [*the Demo-*

cratic state legislature] just gerrymandered the Thirteenth Congressional District from Northwest Highway in Dallas north and central all the way to Childress. It was [*Democrat*] Graham Purcell's district. It took in Wichita Falls. We both went into it with full knowledge that it was going to be a tough race depending on whether the little tail of Dallas County could wag the dog. It darn near did. Dallas carried by a huge majority, but Wichita Falls carried for Graham Purcell. Of course, Frank was not known that well in that part of the state. The race itself was a great experience.

ROBBIE BORCHERS, NEW BRAUNFELS

My husband, Jack, ran for state representative in 1970 and again in 1972. Fortunately, we had so many terrific volunteers and friends who helped. Comal County was one that he was able to carry. Floresville in Wilson County was in the district at that time, the home of John Connally, the Democrat governor. It was just incredibly tough sledding. You just stayed in there. I spent many, many hours knocking on doors in Schertz and Seguin in Guadalupe County.

Was it hard to go and knock on doors when you expected an "iffy" reception?

You are all wrapped up in the campaign, and you know you have so many hours and so many days. You are just out there spinning as fast as you can go, trying to get things turned as far as you can in your direction, knowing that even if it doesn't work out you are planting some seeds for later on because he was a fine candidate. People were happy to have supported him—win, lose, or draw.

You convinced your husband to be a Republican?

BEBE ZUNIGA, LAREDO

Yes. I started telling him that our points of view were more in tune with the Republicans. We worked very hard for a job. We hated to give money from our paycheck to some people who did not even work. I think he saw the way that I truly believed. I started getting him involved in every meeting that we had. One day, he just woke up and said, "What if I ran for commissioner as a Republican?" I said, "Are you sure?" That time he got 47 percent of the vote, which was unheard of here.

Wives as Campaign Managers

SURRENDEN ANGLY, AUSTIN

They could not believe that a Republican was running [*for state legislature*]. We were in our twenties. I have often thought that we were so dumb. It never occurred to us that we would lose. There were very formidable candidates against us. We formed our organization from people that I had never met who came forward and helped us. Someone went through East Austin and said that all of the welfare benefits would go away if Maurice was elected. Of course, it had nothing to do with us because it was a national issue not state issue. We got hold of the letter and sent it all over what we considered our areas, verbatim. We turned catastrophes into neat things for us.

When Maurice won in the runoff in December of 1967, Lynda Bird was being married at the White House. I have it on very, very high authority that Lyndon Johnson was so mad that he flew home from the reception and arrived here about six in the morning. He had the county chairman, who was Mr. Snead, find out what in the world had happened. I remember the *Chicago Tribune's* headline the next day was "Republican Elected in Lyndon's Backyard." I find it very interesting that three months later Lyndon decided not to run for the presidency again. I also think it was interesting that in his bailiwick strength a Republican had been elected.

JAYNE HARRIS, SAN ANTONIO

The county organization, John Wood and others, were looking for lambs to run for state representative. They came and asked my husband, Bill, to run. At that time, you ran at-large. Being the freewheeling spirit that he was, he decided that he would run. He was a lamb.

A friend of mine, Nelda Hawkins, and I decided that we could run the campaign. We went at it full bore. In those days we didn't have computers. We worked with the advertising agency. We drove around town with signs. We drummed up endorsements. It's like anything else you organize. You go to your base—your friends—then from your friends to their friends. That's what we did. We probably had a whole lot of holes in our buckets and didn't even know it. Primarily, we worked our people who were going to vote with us anyway. That's just about it.

Did his loss discourage you?

No. In fact, that is when I met a lot of other people and got involved locally in our Bexar County organization. It was the genesis of involvement in the actual elections and judicial races, because I became co-manager for an associate supreme court justice, Will Garwood. Suddenly, it clicked in my mind that what had happened in South Texas [*election fraud*] and what was happening in Texas was going to have to be changed, not from the top. We were always saying, "We want to take over from the courthouse to the White House." We were always working nationally, but we weren't getting anywhere locally.

TONY LINDSAY, HOUSTON
When Jon was going to file for state representative in 1970, he said something about filing in the Democratic primary. I said, "Democrat?" He said, "Well, yes, you have to be a Democrat in this state to get anywhere. If you ever want to do anything more than just represent this little area, then you have to be part of a bigger picture. You have to be a Democrat." So I said okay. He said that we were conservative Democrats. I said that I really wanted to be a Republican but since there weren't any Republicans, I guessed it was logical to be a conservative Democrat. So that is the way he filed. Well, lo and behold, we had enough people who moved in from out of state that didn't know you had to be a conservative Democrat, and many were Republicans. My husband ended up losing that race by only a few votes. We had worked very hard. We had

done it on our own, financed it ourselves, and formed our entire political organization.

As 1974 was approaching, it was time for state reps to run again. Husband was planning to run again. Nancy Palm, who was then chairman of the [*Harris County*] Republican Party, approached him to run for county judge. Well, that was really a bolt out of the blue. It went along with what we had been saying to each other. As county judge, you have a responsible position and can really make a difference, but you don't have to leave home to do it. But that was a countywide position and just ordinary people like us couldn't finance it. We didn't have any organization, power, or backing. Who were we to think we could do a thing like that? From the very first, after Jon got the phone call, I just felt wonderful. I thought, this is it. Yes, do it!

In that election, we did the same thing that we did in 1970 only we had some people helping us this time. We got out and went door-to-door constantly. I would go day after day. Both of us got a lot of exercise that year. I really loved it. All the people were, with very few exceptions, nice even if they disagreed with you. However, for those two elections, the county judge election and the one before that, we still didn't have very much money. One of the few things that we could actually afford to go to were barbecues. We ate so much barbecue that I have never liked barbecue very well since. I was Jon's campaign chairman and volunteer chairman in both of those races and was on the phone from dawn to dark.

How did you work with the Harris County Republican Party in the county judge race?

Nancy Palm was very instrumental not only in getting Jon to run but in getting him Republican support and shepherding him through the whole election. When Jon said he would run, there was a meeting at someone's house—it may have been Charlie and Pat Alcorn's. There were probably a dozen people there. They were very active Republicans back when there were not all that many. This meeting was for us to be comfortable and know that they were going to support us at least a little bit. After that meeting, we were sure that we were going to do it. From there, we went to Republican Women's Clubs. There were not as many of those as there are now, but the Republican Party pretty much operated through the clubs and the precinct chairmen. The clubs held various events, which in those days did not draw huge crowds. They would do a little hoopla and encourage you, build you up and give you some confidence.

We tried to contact the precinct chairmen individually. A few of them we actually went and knocked on their doors. The rest of them we tried to call. We asked for their support. In those days, the precinct chairmen were expected to do their best to get all of the Republican candidates' material out in their precincts and hold parties or somehow get their candidates introduced to their neighbors. Many of them worked very hard for us.

We did scrape together a little bit of money, which I think Nancy Palm was largely responsible for getting. We got a little bit of TV right before the election. I remember the first ad I saw on TV, part of it was cut off. We only had money for just the few spots, and here this one didn't come out right. I called our media guy all upset because this ad had not run right. He knew that the station would run it over again. He kind of laughed at me a little bit for being *so* upset. Every tiny piece of media that we could get was so precious. Every bumper sticker and yard sign was so important.

There was a lot of tension between factions in the Harris County Republican Party in the 1960s. Was everyone working well together by the 1970s?

As far as I am concerned they were because they helped us. Everything that went before we didn't know about, and we had no reason to think that people weren't working together and just assumed they all were. So as far as we were concerned, they were.

Jon getting elected county judge in 1974 gave the Party a status, a way to build, and an access to the courthouse that they had never had before. We had Republicans there before but never in the kind of position that Jon had. I feel certain that was a big step in building the Party.

When your husband ran for railroad commissioner, you helped coordinate his campaign?

JUANDELLE LACY, MIDLAND

Polly Sowell, who was the vice chairman at that time, called out here and said, "Hey, Juandelle, would Jim run for railroad commissioner?" She said, "We're really trying to get a strong top of the ticket." That was when Bill Clements and Jim Baker ran [*for governor and attorney general*]. I was his campaign manager. I was his scheduler. I did all the washing and ironing. We ran a very low-budget campaign. I had done this before for other candidates, but I had not done a statewide campaign. It's a different ball game entirely. So we worked out a strategy. Out of 254 counties, we targeted 60 counties where there was the bulk of the population. We came close to winning the race. He broke the curve. Republicans in the state of Texas always used the railroad commission as their baseline. I drew from a wide range. I drew from the oil industry. I drew from the Republican Women. I drew from the Party itself. I drew from the Southern Baptists. Many times I would have a coffee in the morning, a luncheon at noon, a tea in the afternoon, a dinner or a picnic in the evening.

We were gone for ten days at a time, and then we came back to recoup for a few days. When I asked people to do something, they knew I expected it to be done. We had great response. We kind of went through an analogy with Jim Baker. He spent, I don't know, a million dollars on the race, and we spent about $90,000 and there weren't two points difference [*in the voting results*]. A lot of that depended on getting back to the basics. We picked up endorsements. Bill Clements won, and that could have helped. We had a friend in the Fort Worth-Dallas area that loaned us a motor home. We had it painted. Jim would drive, and I would try to get things all coordinated. When you are a candidate, you've got to walk out like you're fresh as a daisy with no problems at all.

MICKEY LAWRENCE, HOUSTON

In 1980, there was a position open as a justice of the peace for North Harris County. Tom ran. Five candidates ran. He won the Republican primary and prevailed in the general election. Through that experience, I got my feet wet in politics. That campaign was the most basic grassroots campaign that we have ever run. We didn't have that much money and were pretty much outsiders to the then existing Republican Party. So we started building our own base.

What kind of role did you play?

From getting volunteers, doing literature, and making sure that literature got printed to hosting suppers for numerous campaign workers, organizing block walks, helping Tom with his speeches, billboard design—you name it. You could effectively call me his campaign manager. We didn't really have anyone designated as such. People have made comments to us that it was such a well-organized campaign. We know our community, and we basically reached out and asked them to do things. They were always willing and supported us. We kind of knew what areas they liked to work in—whether they liked to get on the phone or whether they liked to endorse. It is a matter of building your data base and energizing your people to get out to vote.

Hitting the Campaign Trail

RUTH MANKIN, HOUSTON

In 1960, my husband, Hart, just completed law school, and he had a new job. He took it upon himself to run for the legislature. His employers would not let him take time off from work to run. I wonder why? I was his surrogate. I spoke at coffees and at luncheons and at rallies. How did I do this with two little children? My best friend was the Democratic precinct chairman. She was a conservative Democrat from Virginia. She was happy to help my husband because he ran as a forthright conservative. So she took care of the kids when I was on the stump. Hart used to say, "Look for Nixon at the top of the ballot, but you have to bend over and find me. I am Hart Mankin at the bottom of the ballot."

BARBARA FOREMAN, ODESSA & DALLAS

There weren't that many known Republicans. Ed ran basically an independent campaign. He had Republican help, but in a district that is predominantly Democrat you can't depend on the Republicans. We went to all of the Republican events, but we also had to court the Democrats. You would go into a little town, and you would go to see the newspaper editor and then check out the mayor. Then one person would say, you need to go and talk to so-and-so. So you'd go talk to so-and-so. Then you'd go to the cafe and have coffee at the right time. Everybody comes into town to do that. There are so many small towns out there. Ed had been in an oil field related business so he knew a lot of people in the oil field and where to find them. The first mailing, a friend and I put out.

What was it like being the candidate's wife in 1962?

It was pretty lonely. There was a lot of the district that didn't even have a Republican to run the primary. We had a two year old and a four year old. We would load them up and haul them around. We had an old Model T Ford. We would haul it on the trailer. When we got to the edge of town, we got out, unloaded the car, put the kids in, drove to town, and campaigned. I just went along and met people. I wasn't called on to speak. I went along and tried to keep the kids looking presentable and to put forth the picture of a nice family. Most of my traveling was done with Ed. A lot of sitting around and waiting while he was being interviewed by the editorial board.

What did they think when they found that you were Republicans?

We sort of soft-pedaled that. The Democrat out there was the one involved with [*convicted Texas promoter*] Billie Sol Estes and [*agricultural storage*] tanks that didn't exist. We had a sign on the back of the Model T that said "Cars go out of style but honesty in government never should." So that caught everybody's eye.

CHRIS HOOVER, CORPUS CHRISTI

My husband was encouraged to run for Congress in district fourteen in the 1960s. It was necessary that he have petitions signed by thousands of people in order to have his name appear on the ballot. We started a grassroots revolution to get his name on the ballot. We ran and lost, but we feel that we helped to build the Republican Party through that election. We tried establishing precinct chairmen in the 101 precincts in order that people might have a choice. If you don't have a polling place, then you actually don't have a choice. We felt that everybody needed a choice of whom he or she wanted to elect and from which party. We got voter lists and opened a small office with phones. Most of our first primary elections were held in garages. We did it mostly by phone and personal contacts, by saying we really needed to have a voting place and getting someone to serve. We got out the vote. We got people to man phone banks the day before the election and the day of the election to make sure that all of the Republicans got to vote. We had to secure volunteers and set up schedules.

The district included Duval County. We all went over to San Diego to a rally. We were all frightened because it was such a Democrat stronghold, but we had to go over there. Our stage was a flatbed truck. We were across the street from the county courthouse. We had to give a Republican message there. "There is a choice. You don't always have to vote Democrat." We didn't really ever have anyone angry with us except for some phone calls. We would get anonymous phone calls. They would say, "You really shouldn't be doing this." You just hang up and go on, as long as you are doing the best that you can.

"When I look at the old photos from 1961, I realize Lou and the kids did much to get me elected to the Senate. The girls then aged four, five, and six were so dear in their best Sunday dresses and pearls. Lou was the model helpmate to use a word that the

*newspaper feature writers were fond of back then. She could
have stepped off the cover of the Saturday Evening Post. We
exploited the photo opportunities in the best campaign tradition.
Mom and Dad Tower reading to the kids. Dad driving the
brood to school. It was good imagery."*

—A passage from *Consequences* by Senator John Tower

Describe that 1961 campaign.

LOU TOWER, WICHITA FALLS & DALLAS

Big surprise! I didn't know they [*state party officials*] were going to nominate him. We didn't have any money. They decided to
send me out on the trail, too. I don't know who really decided that,
but other wives weren't doing it then.

*Why was it such a surprise that they wanted the Senator to run
in 1961?*

John always thought that, sort of by osmosis, I knew everything that he did. I would read something or find out about something, and he would say, "Oh, you knew that." I would say, no. He
thought I knew about it because he did.

The state was divided into five sections. Whoever was in
charge of an area, a woman, would go out and drive the route they
thought I should take and time everything. I mean to the minute.
We did most of the trips by bus. They had banners on the bus and
a loud speaker that they used when they were allowed. John traveled all the time, but there was no way that he could get every
place. People wanted to meet me without him. In some cases, it
was sort of the biggest social affair that little town had had in
almost forever. Often, it was a totally Democratic town. Let's say
the mayor's wife had a coffee for me in her home. Then everybody
could come, and it didn't have to be political. It was the mayor's
wife giving a party for the people that lived in that town. It really
was great fun. I was fortunate. I really didn't have to make speeches.
I'd just get up and talk a little bit. Since John and I talked every
day, I would tell them where he had been the day before and that

day and where he was going tomorrow. It was just a closer connection for them to have a contact like that. They really were lovely to me. It was just great. People would do a broadcast from the radio station, or I'd get in the car with them and they'd sit in front of the house and interview me.

What kinds of questions did they ask you in the interviews?

I don't think it was like something anybody would get asked today. I don't remember that anything was of great importance. I didn't say what John believed because one little thing and I could throw the whole campaign off. It didn't usually get very deep. They found out that my life was very much like theirs—taking care of the kids, seeing that they are clothed, and going to the grocery store.

After the death of John Kennedy and the huge victory of Johnson in the presidential race of 1964, there must have been an enormous amount of pressure on you both to run successfully in 1966. Did you ever have second thoughts about that?

I don't think it would have mattered very much if we had. That group [*of Party officials*] had decided he was going to run. Of course, that group included him. But the Kennedy time was one of the worst I will ever know in my life. One of the worst. The press succeeded in making Dallas feel guilty. I remember one article that I was just furious about. It said, "at the time of Dallas." It wasn't Dallas! It was the time that some nut—he wasn't even a Dallas person—killed Kennedy. They just started out, "in the time of Dallas." People would act like Dallas was all right-wing nuts. Of course, we had some. I wouldn't say that the Democrats were free of them. John was in the air going someplace to make a speech when it happened. His office started getting calls from other nuts saying it was, in a way, John's fault. You know. His office called and said for me to meet the girls at school. Isn't that a wonderful thing to have to tell your kids? We spent a couple of nights with friends. It took people a long time here in Dallas to realize that Dallas really didn't have anything to do with that. It wasn't the right-wing nuts. It was a particular nut.

Describe the 1966 campaign.

Buses for Lou. Each town organized. Each hub had volunteers. Tower Belles. They had navy blue skirts and shirts with "Tower Belles" on them. It was a big hoopla.

So you actually rode a bus?

You don't think John would do that, do you? We would go, and somebody would take charge of the bus. This one gal said, as we pulled into a town and reviewed our assignments and agreed on a meeting time, "Okay, let's circumcise our watches." Of course, she meant synchronize our watches. Everybody knew exactly what was supposed to happen and at what time. The Tower Belles handed out campaign literature while I was at the coffee, party, or whatever they had lined up for me. John could do one visit to a big town with some television coverage what I could do in twenty or thirty little towns, but it was that touch. He wasn't going to be able to go there. They seemed real pleased that I went.

When you married the Senator, did you know that it was his aspiration to run for office? Did you know what you were getting into?

Somebody in Washington sent all of the congressional wives these questionnaires. I showed it to John one time. He was amazed that I had written that he had never discussed being a Senator. He knew he was going to be nominated, but I didn't know that. It was just one of those things that he thought I knew because he did. But there wasn't any arm-twisting. It wouldn't serve any purpose. I felt the same as so many people who worked so hard on this—that he would be a good senator. He was a very good one.

I didn't even know that much about politics. I had always voted. Members of my family were Republicans but not active about it. My dad was a businessman, and it probably would have been bad for his business for people to know that he was really a Republican. He also had a cousin who ran for governor against Ma Ferguson. Dad drove the car all over the state for his cousin. This cousin and John got to know each other real well. His name was Orville Bullington. They went together to the Chicago Republican convention.

John had one grandfather that really decided his fate. This grandfather—of course they were all Democrats then—talked Republican politics. When John was elected, his dad said, "Well, son, I'm real proud of you. I think most of the family voted for you." He wasn't kidding.

What did you do in 1972 as a Tower staff member?

VIRGINIA EGGERS, WICHITA FALLS & DALLAS

I was co-chairman with a girl from Victoria, Gloria Lee of Women for Tower. John by then was such a national figure that we didn't have to go in and introduce the candidate and do the same kind of work that we did in the early years. Our job wasn't emphasized as much in that particular campaign. We tried to provide the counties with whatever they needed. Most of the time they wanted the candidate. The Senator couldn't be everyplace. We went back to the bus trips. It just helped to bring the campaign to the counties. We emphasized the smaller counties. We would bring Lou into those counties and let people feel like they were a part of the campaign. They were really working, and we wanted them to have some of the fun. You could take Lou into all of the counties that John was not able to reach, and she would charm everybody.

How was Lou Tower as a campaigner?

She was just fabulous. She was just so congenial. She was so fun. She is the wittiest person in the whole world. She had some way of drawing something out of everybody she shook hands with, and they would have a little conversation. She would look them all straight in the eye. She never spoke to the issues because it wasn't necessary in those days. It was more "we want you to meet Lou Tower and see what a gracious lady she is." She wrote thank you notes every night. She enjoyed meeting all the people. She was so grateful that they came out on John's behalf. It really did spread the word.

DOTTIE DE LA GARZA, DALLAS

Of course, I wasn't working for Tower when I covered the 1966 race. I covered Ernestine Carr [*wife of Waggoner Carr, Tower's opponent*] and Lou Tower on the campaign trail for the *Dallas Morning News*. Lou was so superior to Ernestine Carr as a campaigner. I covered bus tours, and I flew on planes with Lou and Ernestine. Lou Tower was just unbelievable. Lou Tower had the people personality that John Tower never totally developed with strangers. He was wonderful with staff, but Lou Tower would get out on that stump and would win people over. Republicans did not have a country-club stereotype when she campaigned. She was herself. She had a total interest in whomever she was speaking to. She had a wild sense of humor that, of course, she had to temper when she campaigned. She has a humor that touches people wherever they are. She campaigned more in the smaller towns where he could not necessarily go. She won over editors of papers and she won over the ladies clubs and she did fine with men because she was so direct.

> *If she had not been out there campaigning, what difference would it have made?*

You hate to say that she was a critical factor, but not only did she loosen the Senator up but she made inroads into small rural places. Even though he said he was from Wichita Falls, and he was the son and grandson of circuit-riding Methodist ministers, I think she had the rural touch, even though she was a Bullington from Wichita Falls. She had the rural touch and the small-town warmth that he did not project. I think she helped cut into the traditional Yellow Dog Democrat, lock step, small-town image. She made the difference in small towns.

> *Since your husband ran for Congress, you have the experience of being both a candidate and a candidate's wife. What is important about the role of candidate's wife?*

ANNA MOWERY, FORT WORTH

I don't like it. I hate to say this, but we had a candidate's wife in Oklahoma and her slip showed all of the time. All of the time I was the candidate's wife, I thought about that. As a candidate, you're so busy that you don't feel like you have to worry about that slip showing. But as a candidate's wife, it's something you need to worry about—it's going to reflect on your husband—and you do feel like you're only going to be a negative and not a positive. When you are campaigning as a candidate, you're so intense about getting your message across.

PAULINE CUSACK, HOUSTON & WILLOW CITY

Callie Robertson and I put together a charm school for candidates' wives in the late '60s with one of the local, well-known modeling schools. It was several sessions over a period of several weeks. We tried to get them to wear pantyhose, which were brand new. They had to sit on podiums and the shorter skirts were prevalent then. These garter belts peeked through on rare occasions, and we didn't want that to happen. We taught them how to rise and sit gracefully in a chair on a podium when there was not a table and how to cross their legs so that they would sit in the "S" curve and all of these little goodies.

RUTH MANKIN, HOUSTON

When George Bush moved down from Midland and was considering a run for county chairman, we were told by Jimmy Bertron, the then incumbent party chairman, that he had a good friend he played tennis with at the Houston Club named Poppy Bush. We all kind of laughed. It was kind of preppy for us. Jimmy said, "He is going to be our next county chairman." There was a group on the executive committee that said, "Let's meet this fellow before we put this to a vote." So I volunteered to have a little picnic for him in our backyard out in the precinct in southwest Houston. He and Barbara came. Our cynicism was overcome, and Barbara said to all of us, "Well, you had better elect my husband because some day he is going to be the president of the United States." We didn't know if she was omniscient or a dreamer. Of course, like most things she said, it was indeed true.

Did you work on George Bush's run for the Senate in 1964?

I did some limited public relations work for Barbara Bush. The Republican National Committee sent down an "experienced" public relations person from Washington to accompany Mrs. Bush. I was escorting her to a coffee out in the Pasadena area, which at that time was very blue-collar. It was quite an unusual place for the wife of a Republican candidate to go campaign. We came to the house where the coffee was to be held and only saw two cars in the front. The "professional" from Washington said, "We can't let you go in there; it would be humiliating." I had made arrangements with the *Houston Chronicle* for photographers to be there because they thought it a very newsworthy story. I said, "Let's go around the block once." We went around the block once, and there was one more car. I looked at Barbara and I said, "Mrs. Bush, we really need to go in there. These people expect to see you." She agreed with me. We went in and there were eight or ten people. That wasn't what really mattered. What really mattered was it showed Mrs. Bush reaching out to a part of the population that we might not have considered talking to in earlier years. Secondly, I got my brownie points because there was a very big picture in the *Houston Chronicle* and an interview the next day, which reached hundreds of thousands of readers. Maybe there were only ten people at that coffee, but everybody learned who Barbara Bush was.

SHEILA WILKES BROWN, AUSTIN

Rita Clements supported Bill Clements 200 percent. She was right there campaigning with him, making speeches just like he was. I never remember seeing Janie Briscoe [*wife of Democratic governor Dolph Briscoe*] on the campaign trail. Rita Clements was either campaigning for him or she was campaigning with him and speaking at the podium with him. It wasn't just a "Hello, I'm Rita Clements." It was making statements.

What role did you play in recruiting your husband to run for governor in 1978?

RITA CLEMENTS, DALLAS

I didn't recruit him [*laughing*]. Bill Clements made up his own mind about it. Unlike a lot of people who think about running for office, he didn't fool around and conduct his own private little poll about whether he should run. The whole thing started right here in this room with Jack Schmidt, who was U. S. Senator from New Mexico. Bill had known him when he was in the Department of Defense. He had been an astronaut, and he was a geologist. He was here for a national seminar on energy. Bill was coordinator of the seminar. Since we knew Jack personally, we invited him to stay with us. After the seminar was over, we came back here and were visiting. Jack had caught a bad cold, and we told him we wouldn't keep him up, but he said, "There's something I want to talk to you about." He had recently studied or was familiar with enough Texas politics that he went through a litany of how close all of these Republican gubernatorial candidates had come to winning. He said, "It is a winnable race." And he turned to Bill and he said, "I've decided you are the one who can do it." Bill just shook his head and kind of laughed. He said, "Oh, Jack, they have tried to recruit me to run for the Senate, and people have mentioned running for governor, but I don't think so." Jack kept pushing him and discussing it and how it was winnable. Then he said, "Well, I had better get to bed."

Bill and I moved upstairs to our study, and we must have stayed up another hour and a half discussing it. The more we discussed it, the better the idea seemed. A couple of weeks later, we made a decision that he would do this. Really, the only person we talked to about it was Peter O'Donnell, who is a very good friend in addition to having the close alliance in politics. We really respected his opinion. Bill announced. It caused quite a stir because the Republican Women were having their convention. Ray Hutchison was the anointed candidate. Polly Sowell, who had been Republican state vice chairman when I had been Republican national committeewoman and was a real good friend, called me up and said, "Rita, what is going on? I have committed to Ray Hutchison.

Can't you talk Bill out of this? This is ridiculous," or something to that effect. I said, "No, Bill is going to do it, Polly, and I'm sorry but we are going to beat Ray. You will be with us in the fall." She said, "Oh, sure I will." She said it had caused a real uproar down there. I think Republicans were kind of used to candidates going around and feeling them out and seeing whether they might be acceptable instead of just announcing out of the blue that they were going to run.

It must have been an unusual experience to have a contested race, especially at that level. Was that a difficult situation to be the "outside" candidate?

Not really, because Bill brought a lot of people into the primary that might have otherwise voted in the Democratic primary. Word kind of leaked out when they were having that women's federation meeting, and Ron Calhoun of the *Dallas Times Herald* did an article speculating. So Bill decided to have a press conference and announce. The first question out of the box was from Ron, "Was it true that you voted for LBJ in 1964?" Where Ron had gotten that information, I don't know. Bill said he didn't really remember. Of course, he probably did tell some of his close friends he did, but he didn't remember. He just took a gulp and said, "Yes, that's true. I thought it would be good for Texas to have a Texan president." As it turned out, it was a one-day story. It wasn't exactly the way he wanted to start out with the announcement.

The time was ripe to really broaden the base for the Republican Party. Bill was able to raise the money. He used television very effectively and did win that primary pretty dramatically. He said, "I won't run out of cash in the fourth quarter"—or whatever football term he used—or run out of gas.

It was very helpful to have the political experience I had. A lot of the people in the Republican Party—the workers, the Republican club members—said, "Who is Bill Clements?" They really didn't know. A lot of them knew me better than they knew him. I sat in on all of the strategy sessions. During my door-to-door canvas in the Goldwater campaign, I had gotten to know

Nancy Braddus from Minnesota. So I immediately recommended that we get Nancy aboard, which we did. She helped with all of our telephone bank efforts in all of our campaigns. It was real helpful. I enjoyed campaigning with Bill, and I enjoyed campaigning on my own.

You had your own tour, didn't you?

We decided after he won the primary to spend the summer in the rural counties organizing. There were many counties that didn't have a Republican Party chairman. Our original plan was to rent two Winnebagos. I would go in one direction, and he would go in the other. The Winnebagos kept breaking down, and the young people that were helping drive didn't know what to do. I finally ended up with a station wagon, which suited me better, and with a couple of young people, which sometimes included my children. In one case, my two future sons-in-law went over to East Texas with me as volunteers. I guess my first foray up into East Texas was Greenville. We made several stops on the courthouse square and went into the coffee shop to talk to people. We would always visit the courthouses. We would hit some of the business places in town. We usually had interviews set up with the radio stations. There usually wasn't a television station but a radio station and the local newspaper. We had people working in advance planning. I probably ended up spending more time in West Texas and the Hill Country because I had grown up in the Hill Country and knew that area. It was a busy, busy summer, but it paid off. John Hill [*the Democratic candidate*] thought he had been elected governor when he beat Dolph Briscoe [*in the primary*] and acted accordingly through the summer. We spent almost three weeks in Austin doing intensive briefings on state government. Obviously, Bill did not have the knowledge of state government that most candidates who had run for governor had. We met with highway department people, and on down the long list of major boards and commissions, and were brought up to date on the issues.

Did you participate in those meetings?

I did. When I was on the campaign trail, I gave many political speeches about what he was doing. I tried to stick to evening events where both men and women were. As far as daytime events, I stuck to the downtown areas. I didn't do many coffees or anything like that. The real impact you made in those communities was when you got a radio interview and a newspaper interview and there was some kind of event, but we usually tried to hold it where it included both men and women. Campaigning is very tough, I will tell you. We made it very clear that Sundays were our day to be here at home and go to church and see the family. It was six days a week nonstop.

Wives Are an Asset

Have you seen candidates' wives make a big difference over the years?

BETTY RUMINER, SEABROOK

Oh, yes. They are in contact with people, and their overall activities just make a difference. You have got to have support from your spouse. I don't care if it's a man running for office or a woman. It just makes a lot of difference.

How have you helped your husband, State Representative Tom Craddick, stay in touch with the people in the district?

NADINE CRADDICK, MIDLAND

I have always been active in my community, volunteering. I served on a lot of boards and volunteered in schools when my children were at home. I was president of their PTAs and always involved. I now serve on a Midland-Odessa initiative for better transportation called MOTRAN—Midland Odessa Transportation Alliance. I was one of the founding members of that. It puts me in touch with totally different people than what he is in touch with. It gives me a pulse on what is going on within my community. I care about it. I am a Midlander. I want a better way of life out here for the people who live here. I didn't volunteer to enhance his career, so to speak. I did it because I wanted to do it.

You really didn't have a model since you were the first Republican first lady. What did you see as your priorities after the election?

RITA CLEMENTS, DALLAS

I decided I would limit my priorities. I have so many interests that it is hard to concentrate on a few. In fact, Bill counseled me on this. He said, "You need to think about a few things you are going to concentrate on." During the first term, education was certainly one of my priorities. Volunteerism was another, which was a natural for me. Then, restoring the Governor's Mansion, I got real involved in historic preservation. I helped on some historic preservation programs, like helping launch the first Main Street program we had in Texas, which is restoring small-town downtown areas. Then, during Bill's second term, the economy was down and we needed to really promote the economy in Texas. I took on tourism as my major project and added that to the other three. They still have pretty much the same ads on television that we developed—"Texas is like a whole other country." It really caught hold.

CHAPTER 15

Campaign Strategy and Management

"...if you have a good campaign plan that is well thought out and you stick with it, then you're going to be successful."

—MARY DENNY

*P*arty leaders developed political strategy in the 1950s and 1960s, discovering with each campaign what worked and what did not. In many cases, Republican Women's Clubs provided the starting place for candidates to recruit managers and volunteers. Both formal and informal kitchen cabinets formed to advise candidates in all aspects of campaign strategy, from volunteer recruitment to fundraising and media relations. These loyal supporters could be counted on for honest feedback as the campaign progressed. Campaigning in a state as large and diverse as Texas often required finding new ways to take candidates out of the comfort zone of Party regulars to meet and present their platform to all types of likely voters.

Some women started out as managers for local candidates while others became area managers for regional and statewide candidates. Women then began to manage campaigns at all levels as volunteers. They graduated to the ranks of paid campaign managers in part to command the authority they needed and deserved. For many candidates, paying for advice meant listening to it.

Convincing candidates to stick with a plan in the heat of the campaign, despite the second-guessing of friends and family, proved challenging at times. Even with effective planning and management, events beyond the control of the team sometimes detrimentally affected the ultimate success of their efforts. Through the years, Republican women perfected the art of *bouncing back after disappointment and happily celebrated their rare victories.*

In the early days, women did whatever they could to raise the visibility of their candidates. They learned to use new methods of contacting voters as they became available. With the large campaign budgets of today, it is difficult to imagine the transportation problems of yesterday. One of the biggest challenges was finding the money and people to get the candidates from place to place, especially in rural areas.

Whether paid or volunteer, managers learned to use their instincts wisely. With the rise of paid managers and staff, motivating and managing volunteers became a more important challenge. Volunteers viewed the campaign as a mission, devoting energy, time, expertise, and will power that paid staff, in some cases, did not have. If tension between volunteers and paid staff developed and went unrecognized by the candidate, campaign manager, or volunteer manager, the campaign suffered.

Strategy

Developing a Plan

SALLY McKENZIE, DALLAS

Campaigns are not that complicated. You identify your support. You're sure they're registered. You get them to the polls. I don't care how you do it. You can do it very simply or you can have a big fancy headquarters and lots of activity. That's ideal—baubles and balloons.

How do you approach developing a campaign strategy?

JANE ANNE STINNETT, LUBBOCK

You have to look at your district and know what will motivate the voters. Also, you have to look at the opposition and see what you think they are going to do. Then you have got to fashion a campaign that will put out the message that you want to put out but is realistic for your candidate. You can't have a candidate saying something that he doesn't deeply believe. I like to run positive campaigns.

POLLY SOWELL, McALLEN & AUSTIN

Living in the Valley [*in South Texas*], I knew that a vote was for sale. I tried to buy it myself. I know how hard it is. The laws may have changed, but what they used to do is pay somebody to take people to the polls. You give them however much, $50 or $100 for the day. That's all there is to it. However, it's very hard to find people who will do it for Republicans. We finally worked out a way of hiring people who worked for friends that we knew were trustworthy. We gave them a quota. We said, "If you can get fifty people to vote for our candidate in this precinct, we'll give you $100." It worked except that we could never do it in enough places for it to make much of a difference.

BETSY LAKE, HOUSTON

I have spent many, many hours talking to individuals who wanted to run. We had campaign manuals we would give them on how to run a campaign. You have to target. You have to look at your own finances and decide how much money you can raise. Mail-outs alone cost a tremendous amount of money, and you can't afford to send a lot of mail to all of the Republican households in Harris County. When I was county chairman, I rated precincts on the number of Republican voters, and I would tell a candidate, "Here are the top 100 precincts out of 1,200." We knew our swing precincts. In the primaries, you need to work with the Republican Women's Clubs because they volunteer. Most of the candidates who run in the county have to depend on volunteers.

SUSAN COMBS, AUSTIN

There is a difference in running for local office versus state-wide. If you run for local office you really do a more vertical, more intense race down through the community because you have time. You do a lot of door-to-door walking and neighborhood associa-tion meetings. It's smaller scale, but it is thicker and deeper through the community. When you're running statewide, especially in a huge state like Texas, you can't do effective door-to-door walking or neighborhood associations. Now, I try to go to every small town that I can and hit every newspaper editorial board. You work with groups that have a way of informing their members. You try to go to Republican Women's lunches so that they will get the energy up. You try to talk to some of the industry groups or chambers of commerce.

I have been on the road a lot for the last twenty-one months [*as the successful candidate for agriculture commissioner*]. What you can do is, you tell people "I'm going to be in Stanton," let's say. You tell somebody "I'm going to be there for an hour. Can you get me people?" They may get somebody from the school board, there may be a local mayor, there may be a neighborhood association, a farmer or rancher, and Republican Women. You work harder in getting representatives or people from various groups. Maybe you only go to Stanton once or twice as opposed to ten times. Days are longer generally because you're flying back from someplace or are driving back.

MARY ANNE COLLINS, DALLAS

Helen Harris's candidates won. She knew how to tell them to target—what areas they should target and how to target for what they were doing. She would even figure out a budget for them—an "A" budget and a "B" budget. If you have "B" budget, you can do this, but if you have "A" budget, you can do up to this. She knew by instinct what to do.

GLORIA CLAYTON, DALLAS

A kitchen cabinet is the backbone of the campaign. You would have someone in charge of canvassing, getting out your vote, fundraising, mailings, volunteers, and publicity. They are all volunteers. It is six or seven people who meet on a regular basis with the candidate and keep the campaign together and moving forward. How are the telephones going and what kind of results are you getting? Maybe we should send a mailing for that.

Let me give you an example. A candidate recently ran a television ad for his campaign. I was struck dumb when I saw it. It was so bad. If he had had a kitchen cabinet look at it and advise him, he wouldn't have run it. He pulled it after one day.

Sometimes the hardest part of the campaign is keeping the candidate out of it. They should be out making speeches, getting their rest, and shaking hands. Let all of the nitty-gritty be done by the volunteers. But they want to get in the act, too. If you can get the candidate out of the way, you can move forward. It is not just my thinking, it is a known fact.

BARBARA JORDAN, KINGWOOD

A kitchen cabinet is made up of the candidates' best friends who will stand by them until the very end no matter what. Then they have to look for a good campaign manager. Not necessarily somebody they really like but someone that they know can organize and stay on top of everybody and make sure that they are doing their jobs. The manager is focused on getting that person elected. The campaign manager has to be a mover and very aggressive but not offensive. Sometimes the candidate is not the same personality. They want to get elected, but they are timid in some ways about going about it. You have to have a manager that is going to move the candidate past the "I don't like to ask for money" or "I don't like to do this or that." If they are going to run, they have to do it.

CAROL REED, DALLAS

Oftentimes the frontal attack just does not work. That is the way women have had to do things. I don't care how you get from A to Z as long as it is ethical. I've seen a lot of people in this business, both on the volunteer side but mainly on the professional, that would rather lose than give up their position. It is an ego thing. If you look at the men I have had to deal with in the business over the years, everything is either a war or a football game. You just have to work not to giggle when they get their big map up and say, "We've got a frontline down here and this coming in." You'll say, "Well, maybe we ought to concern ourselves with what the average Joe out there is thinking about what we're saying."

What's their reaction when you say that?

Usually laughter, although some of them have not taken it that way, and they don't last very along. I spent years and years on the board of the American Association of Political Consultants. There are just twelve of us on the board—six Republicans and six Democrats. I think the reason they had me on the board was there were very few women back then who had their own companies outside of the Beltway [*Washington, D. C.*]. Roger Ailes was on there. Bob Squire on the other side. You talk about huge, giant egos. It would just amuse me the wars that they would have over internal stuff.

What is the most important thing to do during the last few weeks of the campaign?

ANNA MOWERY, FORT WORTH

It wouldn't be the last two weeks anymore. We have all switched because everything has to peak before early voting. The campaign is a lot like putting on a dramatic production. There's preparation, there's preparation, there's preparation and then there is the performance. Everything has to come together at the point that you want the highest visibility. You need to have completed the phone calls and disseminated your postcards. Everything in your arsenal needs to come together at that point. The main thing is to turn out the vote. It is not who your voter is, it's who your voter is that votes. You can have 40 percent of the vote committed to you and your opponent can have 60. If you turn out all of yours and he only turns out half of his, you win. It is mathematical.

Sticking to the Plan

NITA GIBSON, LUBBOCK

There are a lot of people in politics that just do what they want to do. That's not the way you are successful in politics. I agree wholeheartedly that you should be a part of the planning. But once a plan is in motion, I believe in going right down the line and keeping it and implementing it, not reinventing it along the way. There are a lot of people in politics that get to be like little Napoleons in their own county.

MARY DENNY, DENTON

When I was a county chairman, I used to give the candidates advice. Very few of them would take it. The last two weeks before election day, whether it is the primary or Election Day, candidates just go crazy. The tension is just unbearable. They have spent so much time and so much effort to get to where they are that they don't always think clearly. You really have to resist doing that because if you have a good campaign plan that is well thought out and you stick with it, then you're going to be successful. Throwing more money into buying more newspaper ads or trying to do something else is really futile. Candidates get short-tempered with themselves, their spouses, their volunteers. It is really, really tough. I swore to myself that I was not going to let that happen. Well, it's human nature. You can't help but go through all that. It was good to know that it was going to happen and to be ready for it. I still go through that now as a candidate. It is just the way it is.

Knowing Your Electorate

JUNE DEASON, SAN ANTONIO

You never know when to say, boy, do I think that old so-and-so is a dodo. You may be talking to his brother. When Tom Loeffler ran for Congress, Mary Lou Grier went out to every county seat. I've still got the book. It's a masterpiece. You flip to Menard and you see who the city council was, who they were related to, who they married. So when Tom went out, he knew not to do this or that. Not many campaigns have someone who is willing to get in that car and drive the Twenty-first Congressional District, which at that time was larger than the state of Pennsylvania. Hitting these counties cold was awful. If you get someone to walk in with you and say, "Hey, guys, I want to introduce you to Tom Loeffler here." That's a difference.

Planning Isn't Everything

FLO KAMPMANN CRICHTON, SAN ANTONIO

Politics changed a lot just by circumstances. The candidate can control some things, but sometimes there are circumstances that change everything.

GLENNA McCORD, DALLAS

Congressman Bruce Alger had been coming back to town and making speeches about what was going on in Vietnam. One speech after another, he was saying we are at war, an undeclared war. He said, "I see all of these newspaper clippings from all over the U. S., and they have notices that a private was killed in a jeep accident." He said, "You might hear about one or two of them, but I hear about all of them and they are being shot at." He said, "We are at war, and the people are not being told." For this he was labeled a warmonger. The other point was that Bruce had been elected and reelected on the premise that we can do it better in Dallas than they can in Washington. His votes were cast on what he called his yardstick. Do we really need it? Can we really afford it? It worked until all of a sudden a lot of the so-called influential people in town realized that they wanted a congressman that would bring some bacon home. We tried to get the point across to Bruce that he had to quit talking about Vietnam so much.

After the state convention in Austin, the campaign committee went into a room in the Driskill Hotel with Bruce and presented the results of a survey. Vietnam was at the bottom of the list as far as public interest was concerned. He said, "Look, I don't care what the survey shows. I'm the one who the morning after the election will go in and look in the bathroom mirror. I want to be sure I told the truth." That was Bruce. He was a man of principle, and he stuck by those principles through thick and thin.

Management

JUNE DEASON, SAN ANTONIO

I discovered that nobody paid any attention to you when you were a volunteer and said, "I think we ought to do this and I think we ought to do that." Even if you're supposed to be the campaign manager, you're a volunteer. So I started socking it to 'em for money. When somebody pays you, they do listen to what you say. They may not do it, but at least they listen.

JAYNE HARRIS, SAN ANTONIO

When you, as the campaign manager, interview the candidate, you have to ask the really hard questions. Hopefully, they will answer them totally honestly. You have to know if it is a stable marriage, not getting into the personal things like they do right now. Can your wife take the adoration that goes with this sort of thing? Is there anything that someone can start a rumor about so that you are prepared? In other words, it's no one's business but, at the same time, if you are going to have that kind of relationship with the candidate you have to know what is going on. There are some people who run for the salary. You never want to work for those.

MARTHA WEISEND, DALLAS

You help candidates by settling them in and by being realistic with them. You say, if you think you are going to work five hours a day—forget it. This is a ten- to fourteen-hour day. You need your shoes polished and all of that. It is the simple things that get your candidate elected. It's not rocket scientist stuff. It's grungy, hard work. I try and keep them from going to the same meetings month after month. I say, reach out and make new friends. Every day I expect them to make a minimum of fifteen calls and not leave a number on an answering machine but one-on-one calls to ask for votes and money. You give them guidelines that this is what you do on Monday and this is what you do on Tuesday. I don't work candidates on Sundays. It is family time.

Our candidates don't want to embarrass their grassroots supporters, their families, or themselves. They need someone with whom they can bare their souls. I try to have a relationship with them so that they can say, "Look, I'm afraid." I try to smooth the way. It's necessary because we campaign for a year to a year and a half and there's no one who would not become afraid or down about all of this. They meet all kinds of people from all walks of life.

They need to know their issues by doing background and research. If they're going to talk about a shortage of water, why, when, how do you fix it? Once they know their issues, they are comfortable with the substance of their speech. Then the more people they know, the more comfortable they are going to be because friendly faces help. When you have a campaign theme, whether it is more jobs or better education, you stick with that and give them the basic ingredients that make them secure. It takes thought about the message, and then you back up the message with facts. I insist on integrity. If you don't know the answer, say "I'm sorry, I don't know the answer, but I will have it the next time I see you" or call the campaign, but please don't act like you know when you don't. It comes back to sting you.

In the early 1960s, when you went from envelope stuffing to running campaigns, what did you do right and what mistakes did you make?

SHIRLEY GREEN, AUSTIN & SAN ANTONIO
What we did right was work very hard and learn the craft. We never had any money. Everyone learned to do a little bit of everything. The first thing you do is start trying to build support with a steering committee. If the campaign was going to be big enough to justify headquarters, try and find someone who would donate the headquarters. You had to build a schedule. Think of good speaking opportunities. Learn to write a press release. We were all just kind of teaching each other, actually. Certainly, there were some people around who had been involved long before I had. At this time, in the early '60s, Marion Findley was the county

chairman in Austin. He and his wife had been active for many years. You learn from watching the smart people who made it work.

Experiences as Campaign Managers

POLLY SOWELL, MCALLEN & AUSTIN

I wanted to work on the 1960 Nixon campaign. So I called Robert N. Clark, and he was an old, old man. He remembered marching in a parade for William Howard Taft [*Republican president elected in 1908*]. When I called him he said, "Okay. You're in charge." I didn't know what to do. There was no Party structure. There was nobody to help. There were no big campaign gurus that said, this is what you're going to do. You had to do it all yourself, which is more fun than you can possibly imagine. When you run the Nixon campaign in your local area, you raise the money, write the ads, and put them on TV or in the newspaper, whatever it is that you want to do. The downside of being a total amateur and having nobody to help is you make big goofs.

ANNA MOWERY, FORT WORTH

Campaign management was mostly people skills—making people enjoy what they are doing and feel part of the process. What motivates people to really enjoy it is the feeling that they are part of something bigger than they are and that they are going to make a difference. You have to make it fun to come and work for twelve hours.

POOLIE PRATT, VICTORIA

I was George Bush's area chairman when he ran against Ralph Yarborough for Senate. I was his chairman in nine counties. I would go around to all of my counties and try to get women's clubs in every county and did in most of them.

There were so few of us. For instance, when John Tower would come to town he would come into Victoria. The candidates didn't have money back in the early days. We would give him $20 to get him to Goliad. I would have Dorothy Ramsey meet him at Goliad and whoever Dorothy would send him to in Beeville, she would give him another $20. That is how he got around the state. Nickel and diming it. It was important to have a women's club in each town so that there would be some sort of reception for him and he could meet some people. The women's clubs ran all of the headquarters.

NITA GIBSON, LUBBOCK

I became John Tower's Lubbock campaign manager. You've got to realize that back in the old days of the Republican effort in Texas, I was the only one to do it. It wasn't necessarily talent. The person that really made me determined was Charles Guy, the publisher of the *Avalanche Journal*. John Tower wanted to come to town. So they called me and they said, "Can you get some stuff going?" I took him to the *Avalanche Journal,* and Mr. Guy leaned back in the chair and put his feet up on his desk—he could hardly see us for his feet. He said, "Tell me, Mr. Tower, do you think you'll come in fourth or fifth?" I determined right then that this man will be elected Senator. It was certainly not what you would think would come from an unbiased newspaper.

People came from headquarters to tell us what to do. For the phone bank, we rented a building, put in the telephones, and got our message, telephone numbers, and people's names to call. I couldn't find enough volunteers to call. I hired girls from the business college to telephone. We began having a little money come in because people would drop by the headquarters and they would make a little contribution. We started having some fundraisers with Tower out here. We invited Barry Goldwater for a breakfast. Lou Tower came in with John. I picked them up at the airport. They asked how many we thought would be there. I said, "Well, maybe 400." There were over 1,000. Who in the world in Lubbock, Texas would have thought that at six o'clock in the morning at ten dollars a plate we could have 1,000 people for a Republican "John who?" We asked Ronald Reagan, and he came and spent an entire day.

GWEN PHARO, DALLAS

In 1962, Mary Anne Collins and Dorothy Cameron got a guy

named Bill Hayes for lieutenant governor through the primary process. They said, "You get to do the general [*election*]." I said, "I've never done a campaign." They said, "That doesn't matter. We'll help you." I was too dumb to turn them down. I got this brilliant idea to attract some media attention and get some free media—fortune cookies! I called around the yellow pages in San Francisco and found a fortune cookie factory. One day a truck drives up in front of my house. For a day and a half, they unloaded the truck. I called all of my friends' kids, and I said, "On Thursday we are going downtown, and it's going to be Fortune Cookie Day in Dallas." I went to a costume place and bought coolie hats, white cotton gloves, and shopping bags. I got some parasols, too, not knowing they were Japanese, but who cared?

I thought, "I have got to get some coverage on this." So I went down to the TV stations with some of my girls and their hats and their white gloves. Eddie Barker, the news director at Channel 4, said, "Oh, Jesus, what has she done now?" They read the fortune, and they thought it was wonderful. The fortune said, "Good luck those voting Bill Hayes Lt. Governor."

There were probably twenty of us. Millions of people crossed Main and Akard at high noon every day, and we were stationed on all corners. As people came by, we would ask them, "Would you like a fortune cookie?" Then out of the Baker Hotel walks John Connally, who was running for governor, and Clifton Cassidy, who was an old friend of mine. Cassidy said, "What are you idiots doing?" We said, "Oh good fortune. Have a fortune cookie." Connally opened his and said, "Listen to this, C. W." He read it, and Cassidy said, "Mine says the same thing." Everybody laughed. They said, "All right, girls, see you later." He was running against Jack Cox for governor that year, but he thought that was very funny. We got on the national wire.

Now I am panicked because I don't know what to do with all of the fortune cookies. We didn't make a dent. But then I started getting phone calls when everybody in the state saw the coverage. They said, "Would you send us some?" And I said, yes, I would send them for $100 a box or something. I paid all of the money back that I had borrowed for the campaign. We carried Dallas County by quite a nice margin.

SHIRLEY GREEN, AUSTIN & SAN ANTONIO

Every year that I was in San Antonio I would be somebody's co-chairman for a race. In '68 and in '70, I was co-chairman for Paul Eggers' race for governor. It was always a man and a woman that were co-chairmen. In 1978, I barely knew Jim Baker, but I had been so impressed with the job that he had done for [*President Gerald*] Ford in 1976 [*as campaign chairman*]. I saw him at the Republican Women state convention. I said, "You know, rumor is you are thinking about running for attorney general, and I'd love to help you in San Antonio if you need any help." A while later I got a phone call. He had been checking me out and wanted to know if I would be his San Antonio chairman. I said, "I would love to. Who is going to be the co-chair?" His response was, "Well, I hadn't planned to have a co-chairman. You can have one if you want it." The way to endear somebody forever, and it's one of Jim Baker's great strengths, is that anybody he authorizes to do a job he gives not only the responsibility but the authority to do it. My attitude was now, finally, I can do it the way I want to. I don't have to wait for my co-chairman to get around to calling back or authorizing me to spend money. It was one of my favorite campaigns ever.

RUTH COX MIZELLE, CORPUS CHRISTI

I was addressing envelopes and spending thirty minutes at the telephone bank. I went to a reception one day, and a neighbor of mine walked up to me and said, "I want you to meet this gentleman, Mr. Bush, from Houston." She turned to Mr. Bush and said, "This is the lady that I suggest for your campaign chairman." Well, I will tell you the truth, I really didn't know what a campaign chairman was. My family talked about it at dinner, and I told them sometime later that's the last good dinner they had cooked for them. I started in 1963 for the 1964 campaign. He was running for the Senate against incumbent Ralph Yarborough.

The first thing I did was go to the person that I had addressed envelopes for because there were three men in the race. They thought that enough people were in the race, and we did not need another strong candidate. They didn't want to give me the list of addresses I had been working on. That served a good purpose because I started from scratch. I started asking everyone. We rented a fire truck one time and brought Bush home from the airport. The kids would say, "Mom, vote for George Bush so I can ride the fire truck." We had a Neiman Marcus style show. We gave the models hats with "Bush for Senate" on them to wear with each costume. Their pictures were in the paper. Some of the men called me and said, "I am a registered Democrat. Quit having my wife's picture in the paper with a Bush sign on." We just organized the campaign the way we would organize something for the school or the community.

We had to have a runoff with Jack Cox, who had made a valiant race for governor in 1962. I remember learning a very valuable lesson from the Bush family. The advance man came to town and said, "How is everything going?" I said, "Everything is going just great. I'm having a reception after work. I sent out an oriental invitation. It says, 'Take a second lookee' and it has George Bush's picture. I'm going to serve fortune cookies, and I have written the fortune." I proudly told him that the message said, "Vote for a Republican tried and true instead of a loser of '62" Well, this man just turned red in the face and said, "Ruth, I will eat every cookie if you won't serve them." So I canceled the order. I learned that you never go for the jugular. George Bush taught me no matter how much I want to win, it just pays to be decent.

Another thing I remember about Barbara was when someone walked into a reception we were holding for them, and I said, "Barbara, these people have contributed a lot of money." She said, "Ruth, don't tell me about who gives money." I really found out that they were public servants. They were people you could always be proud of whether you win or lose. We lost that campaign.

I went to Houston to watch the returns. I was sitting next to Barbara. I didn't understand things too well. I said, "Well, that's okay. He's losing now, but he's really going to win." Barbara turned around and looked me square in the eye and said, "Ruth, in your eyes he will always be a winner, but I want to tell you, honey, he's losing now and he is losing big."

IDALOU SMITH, WACO

I was disappointed when George Bush wasn't elected that first time because we had worked so hard. Jean Lupton and I put that together with our own money. We just did whatever needed to be done. We didn't do a drop in the bucket, but we thought we were. We were both young and idealistic.

What did you do to organize the campaign committee that got Ron Paul elected in 1976?

MARY JANE SMITH, HOUSTON

In '74 we had a special election. The universe was smaller and easier to target. Our universe was three counties totaling 200,000 voters. I knew that only 15 percent was going to vote, which was 3,000 people.

If we can get 1,501 votes, we win. I know where the 35 percent that are Republican primary voters are and where the 35 percent that are Democratic primary voters are, so there are 30 percent in the middle. That totals 900 people. I need to get 451 of those people. So we have gone from 200,000 to 451.

How do you find those 451?

I know they lean Republican. It is very easy to target precincts. I prioritize the very best Republican precincts with the 35 percent primary voters. I need to turn them out, but I don't need to put the candidate there. Then I get to the other "leaning" precincts. That's where I send the candidate to walk. I had a clipboard for him. He knew who to talk with. He checked them off the list. If no one was home, he would leave a signed piece of literature saying "sorry I missed you" and go on to the next house. I tried to get the precinct chairman or someone who knew the neighborhood to walk with him. When someone comes to the door, they say "Hello, I'm working for Ron Paul" and introduce him as he walks up to the door. As the conversation winds down, the volunteer goes on to the next door. After a while, we would only do one side of the street because the word travels.

In the next election, someone called me and said, "Let's do a telephone bank." The place had a boiler-room effect. About this time, John Connally switched parties. We said, "We want Ron Paul elected. Would you help us?" We got John Connally to record a message. It was something like, "Hello, neighbors, this is former Texas Governor John Connally. As you know, I just switched parties and I am a Republican now. I am happy to endorse my good friend, Dr. Ron Paul. He is running for Congress in district twenty-two. I hope you will vote for him. Thank you so much." We had a recorder, and the worker had to dial the phone. We had light bulbs. It was real primitive. You had five different little recorders. You would sit there, and as soon as you heard a voice saying hello you punched the button. You had to get a rhythm flowing. The newspapers came out because it was so gimmicky. He won. We called into each primary voter household and into the 30 percent in the middle, too.

KATIE HECK, MIDLAND

I was always on Tom Craddick's campaign committee. The first time he ran for state representative in 1968 was difficult because he was so young and the opponent was a well-known local guy. The second time was the hardest because he had been there long enough to make an enemy or two. So it is the most fragile time to run.

The first race he had some issues, fairly general kinds of things. He knew so much about what could be done, so we were never worried about that. What he needed was name recognition. He had lived in Midland for a long time, but he was untried. We pushed him as a person and the choice that voters would have. We did everything that we could do to put his name in front of the people. We designed campaign materials so that if people threw it on the ground they could still read his name. We picked up on the colors that John Tower had used because they were highly visible—navy blue with a fluorescent yellow. Everything that he did had his name on it. It was reinforced on TV and on radio. But mostly it was the visual reinforcement. We had yards signs. We had four-by-eight plywood signs. The second time around, pretty much the same. By the third time he had a record and could run on the record.

What position did you hold in the first campaign?

Payton Anderson, George Conly, and I were the three that were Tom's committee. One of them was a money raiser, the other one signed checks, and I did the campaign material design and took care of all the advertising, placing the ads, that kind of thing. They never questioned any of my expenditures. I called Payton and said, I want to place radio advertising in the amount of such-and-such and we've only got such-and-such in the bank, can you get more? So he'd call up George, and they would go hit up whomever they hit up. We all trusted each other, and we didn't interfere in each other's area of expertise. My area got a little bit bigger, and gradually those guys kind of faded out.

MARTHA WEISEND, DALLAS

We had Clements people in all 254 counties. It was a first, if I remember correctly. We knew that we needed 1.8 million votes to win. That's why we had such a passion about it. We knew that we needed a businessman for governor because our five major building blocks were on their knees—savings and loans, banking, high-tech, farming, and the oil business. We did not want Clements to lose. We had been very sad about his first loss [*Governor Clements, who was elected in 1978, was defeated for a second term in 1982 and ran and won again in 1986*]. We did not want a repeat performance in 1986. So we had an absolute drive about us. We were to do our work and to do it expeditiously. We had wonderful, wonderful volunteers.

How did you communicate the urgency of the campaign through such a huge organization?

We were very structured. For instance, there were certain people I called on certain days so that I knew what was going on in their districts. South Texas is different than East Texas, and East Texas is different than Houston and Dallas and the bigger cities. We needed to know what the message was, what had changed. I needed to be in touch with the volunteers because they were our producers. I wrote job descriptions so that there would be absolutely no doubt of what they were supposed to do and what their time line was. We relished being structured, but it took a lot of night oil to get the organization set with that much structure in a state as big as Texas. I was available, night and day. We didn't know what time it was until we found 1.8 million people who said they would go to the polls and vote for Bill Clements. We found them the last of September. But we kept working to be sure our numbers were good. We had get-out-the-vote and phone banks that worked beautifully. We identified our voters and then, prior to the election, we asked them to go to the polls. We did as many as three calls to a person until the person said, "Yes, I have voted."

JANELLE McARTHUR, SAN ANTONIO

In John Tower's last campaign, I was his state deputy chairman and did a lot of traveling with him, setting up events. We went to all of the marginal counties where an appearance would pull just enough votes to put him over. Those were wonderful experiences in that you learn. John Tower was the master.

There were about eight or ten of us that met every Sunday afternoon the last two months of the campaign. He had refused to shake hands with Bob Krueger, his opponent, in Houston and there was a photo taken. That Sunday the polls went down, way down. Each one of us gave our "should you" or "should you not" apologize opinions because that was the big deal. The majority said you need to apologize. He said, no, I'm not going to apologize, and he was right. He made a big issue about his daughters and his wife and that a gentleman does not extend his hand when another man makes statements against your wife and family.

As a politically interested, young, up-and-coming person, did you find that longtime campaign manager Nola Gee had some

*qualities that you could use in your own political development
and career?*

SHEILA WILKES BROWN, AUSTIN

She was able to sense the exact kind of reaction that was needed.

I don't remember Nola ever being the person that was upfront at the podium. She worked behind the scene, and she knew exactly what needed to be done. I admired that because it was more my nature, too. I saw it, as my career progressed, as being my role. I certainly learned from her how effective it was to be that way—not to toot your own horn or to let your ego get in the way. At that point, we were all there to do the best we could in order to see that Senator Tower remained in office. She was very tuned in to details and follow-up. Her communication skills were excellent. She always knew in terms of the chain of command who to call first so that toes didn't get stepped on and feelings hurt. Whatever her personal thoughts may or may not have been about various issues, you wouldn't have known them. She truly was in there to represent the Senator and to do the best for him.

RUTH MANKIN, HOUSTON

We elected Bill Elliott to city council. At the beginning of the second term, he decided he wanted to be a county commissioner. He lost that election, but he stayed on the city council. He ran again in '67. I managed his campaign. It was a rip snorting, tough race because the last thing that the Harris County court wanted was a Republican commissioner. It was challenging for me because I had never run a countywide campaign before. I had only worked my husband's legislative campaign. There was a lot of skullduggery. Signs were cut down at night.

Something almost tragic happened to my family. My oldest daughter, Margaret, was sitting at the piano in our home out in Memorial. She got up and walked in the next room. At that moment, we heard a bullet come through the window and pass over where she would've been sitting and lodge in the wall. We called the police, and they came out to investigate. We talked about the idea of it being a random shooting, but we personally believed that it was done to scare us off. That made me angry because no one scares me off. I am an old Montana girl. We requested some help from the county police, and they guarded our house for the remaining ten days until the election. Bill Elliott won. That was a great, great triumph for all of us. That race was the beginning. We had to take little steps before we could take big steps.

Why did you entrust your campaign for Congress in 1978 to a woman campaign manager?

TOM LOEFFLER, SAN ANTONIO

I never have had a gender preference or prejudice with respect to my first congressional campaign. Mary Lou Grier had shown the leadership and the skills for managing the campaign. That coupled with the fact that she, Janelle McArthur, and Jim Lunz really knew the congressional district. She worked in other campaigns outside the greater San Antonio area. Mary Lou had an inherent understanding of West Texas, the Hill Country, and San Antonio. She was also a real friend for Tom Loeffler. I could totally rely upon her. Her loyalty and dedication were absolutely steeped in doing whatever was necessary and correct in the direction of the campaign and following up to make sure it was done.

Urban vs. Rural Campaign Management

FRAN ATKINSON, LUFKIN & SAN ANTONIO

As a regional campaign coordinator, first, you find a campaign chairman in each county. This has nothing to do with the Party; this is for the candidates. They give you some leads on names, and you check them out and tell the candidates what you think. In some counties it's, who can we get? Then you go on to get a finance chairman and you set up the organization. The finance chairman will raise money, the chairman will solicit assistance in the election and in doing the mundane day-to-day things. If the candidate comes to town, it's the candidate's chairman who puts on the function.

What was it like to run campaigns up in the Panhandle?

GAIL WATERFIELD, CANADIAN

If you believed in the candidates, it was very easy, which is probably a universal statement for the state. If you had a campaign, let's say for example, that had thirteen counties—piece of cake compared with Houston or Dallas. By the time I actually did it seriously, there was a chairman in every county, there was a Rotary club, a chamber of commerce, a newspaper, and sometimes a radio station. You set up a day in that town and reached everybody. You walked Main Street and got yourself in with the key people. Now, whether they agreed with you or not was not too important because they were going to be fair with you until you stuck your foot in your mouth. The press and radio might make remarks. The Rotary, the chamber of commerce, the Lions club—all of those organizations want speakers. They want to be informed. So you actually had an easier set-up than in the big cities where they could have the president of Phillips Petroleum come and speak to them. After we got county chairmen, they were always willing to head up the campaign.

LILA McCALL, AUSTIN

My mother, Margaret Luckie, was the county chair in Wharton County, which has a significant minority and Democrat population. When Kay Hutchison ran, Wharton County carried for her. Mother was a very dynamic person with very strong opinions and a great politician. Many of those Democrats crossed party lines to vote for Kay.

Staff—Paid and Volunteer

DOTTIE DE LA GARZA, DALLAS

I left the federal staff to work in the Tower campaign and worked out of the Dallas County office with Carol Reed. I was pregnant with my fourth child. I think a lot of women who built the Republican Party in Texas were doing it in between babies. Carol Reed was so energetic and so funny. She attracted volunteers to the campaign with her personality. In 1978, on election night, I was at the Tradewinds Hotel. We couldn't get the results fast enough. It was so close, that was one reason. The Senator sent Shan Pickard and me to Dallas to the Associated Press Bureau. I don't know why it was so bad. I guess because we didn't have all the communications that we do now.

The turning point of the campaign was the grassroots organization. You have to credit Republican Women's Clubs. Having the support of Republican women and having really good women staffers kind of subliminally helped play down some of the rumors about the Senator. You had women like me, a straight-arrow Catholic mother of four, attesting that the man was a good man and statesman. Carolyn Bacon, his administrative assistant, and Molly Pryor, who ran the Houston office, and others were credentials for the fact that there was a lot more to John Tower than what the rumor mill might have engendered about his womanizing. Reaching into the Hispanic electorate made a big difference in 1978. We had Lionel Sosa and those guys doing Hispanic media. That was one of the constituency groups that he worked with the best.

In addition, Cyndi Krier going to the San Antonio office and running the campaign in his opponent Bob Krueger's backyard probably turned the corner there. The Senator gave a lot of credit to the fact that he put one of his sharpest staffers in Krueger's backyard. He put that woman there for a specific purpose because that also deflected a lot of rumor mill stuff. She was very masterful at dealing with Senator Tower's second wife, Lilla, and also reaching the Hispanic vote there.

JUNE DEASON, SAN ANTONIO

I start out telling candidates I don't even want to talk to you about strategy or numbers because we both know why you're running—your opponent has done thus, thus, and thus. Your qualifications are givens. You start out with that—otherwise what are you doing in this race? You don't do anything except shake hands and raise money. No, switch that, raise money and shake hands. Money, money, money. It has to be the first thing. I'd get that basset hound elected over there if you give me enough money. Well, he's photogenic and probably as smart as some of those we've got in office already.

How would you get your basset hound elected?

Well, first of all, you have his honest countenance. Isn't that right, Clyde? The sincere look and the fact that he loves children. Because he's got short legs, he's really closer to the people. He's right down to the ground on all the issues. He was bred to be honest.

CAROL REED, DALLAS

I had a unique situation because I was on staff but I didn't need the job. Consequently, anytime anyone did something that I thought was inappropriate, dumb, or not the correct strategy for the Senator, I would state my case. The worst thing that could happen to me was to get fired and I'd go back to playing tennis. It was nice being able to start in this business without needing the money. The campaign was pretty much controlled out of Austin. Ken Towery and that whole gang. I'll never forget going down to Austin for the first time with my new briefcase, all dressed up, and getting on a plane. That was a big deal for me then. Well, you know, you walk in and after the meeting you think, these guys don't know what they are talking about or they do but it is still a bunch of smoke and mirrors. Everything that I have done, I've thought, "Now I'm going to meet the ones that really know." Then it finally dawned on me that I know as much as all these people do.

I would go to Austin to the meetings, and they would set strategy and we would agree. If Tower was in North Texas then it was my responsibility. Dottie De La Garza would handle the press portion of it. I would handle the political side of it. That meant if they decided that they would schedule him for a meeting out at a defense plant, I would make sure it was set up and advanced properly. Of course, there would be these times where they would dream up something down in Austin, and they'd call up here. They'd say, "Now, Carol, we decided to have a rally in downtown Dallas on Friday afternoon next week." I'd say, "You did?" They'd say, "Well, yeah, and the Senator can go around and pass out materials." I'd say, "I don't think I have a picture of the Senator doing that." They'd say, "What do you mean? We have decided we want to have these rallies all over the state." I'd say, "First of all, he's horrible in a crowd. Why would you do that to him? He's fabulous when we can drop him into an auditorium and have him give his incredible speech." He was a great orator and horrible on the handshake deal. John was a statesman. That's how he viewed himself, from his suits to his gold cigarette case and his very expensive taste in brandy or anything else. It did not transfer to the little guy on the street. But, yet, if they saw him on TV that night or they read what he said in the paper, they would think, well, this is a Senator. We would have these constant wars.

Finally, I'd say, "I will get right on it." I've always not been afraid. I'd call Tower on the phone, call Washington or wherever and just say, "Have the Senator call me when he's got a minute." He'd call back and say, "What do you need, Carol?" I'd say, "I'm so excited that you are going to be here next Friday for this big old rally in downtown Dallas. I want to let you know it's kind of hot right now, so you probably want to cut down on what you are wearing. I have set stuff up, and we will go door-to-door and meet some of the shop owners." "Who's idea was that?!" I'd say, "Well, I don't know. I just got this call from Austin, and we're going to have a great day. We can get a little sack lunch and go down on the Trinity River." Well, the call would come from Austin in about an hour saying, "We've had a change of mind." I'm not sure that they ever knew what the deal was.

LINDA UNDERWOOD, HOUSTON

I got a job in Youth for Nixon. From there, I went to work for John Erlichman in the Committee to Elect Nixon. In '68, I went to Miami Beach to open the convention headquarters for Nixon. When we were finished with the convention, John Erlichman said, "What would you like to do?" I said, "I want to travel with him on the campaign trail." He said, "That will not be possible, but I can probably get you on the Chuck Percy plane." This was before the vice presidential nominee had been selected, and we all thought that it would be Charles Percy from Illinois. As it turned out, Spiro Agnew was the nominee, and I remember John Erlichman looked at me and said, "Spiro Agnew?" He didn't even know. We were all shocked. The day before we were leaving to go on the first leg of the campaign trip, John Erlichman said, "Okay, I will take you with us on this leg and you can help out and see how things go, and we will take it from there." I went and I stayed. I got along with everybody.

We went all over the United States. It was the most exhilarating and the most exhausting time. Since I had been in the Young Republican National Federation, I knew people from all over the U. S. So every time we landed somewhere I had a whole group of people that would be there. John Erlichman was like the advance director. I was assistant to John Erlichman, working on all of the logistics for the next stop. Although we did have advance men, there would be a lot of changes, and we called ahead and made plans. Rosemary Woods and everybody else wrote speeches. We would type. We didn't have faxes and all of those wonderful things.

Ever since then, campaigns have tried to copy that one because it was so well managed. It worked like clockwork. We put out a schedule every day and a list of everybody that would be on the plane. There were two planes. One was the main plane with Nixon, and I traveled on that one. Then there was a press plane. We did six or seven cities a day.

LOUISE FOSTER, AUSTIN

I worked at Tower's 1978 campaign headquarters here, which was his statewide headquarters. Of course, I knew absolutely zilch. I was doing grunt work. I didn't know why I was putting all of those stamps on a mailing. It all had its purpose. Having worked in many, many campaigns now, if you put a dollars and cents value on it, it is surprising how many volunteer hours our ladies do give. There would be no way that our candidates could afford to pay for these services.

There is a lot of difference between a busy Republican headquarters and a Democratic headquarters. Years and years ago when Ronald Reagan was running, the television stations here came and took pictures and then they took pictures of the Democrats. Ours was very busy. Nobody was paid. Yet we would go down and spend an eight-hour day. Sometimes I brought work home and spent another four or five hours and took it back the next day.

Is there tension between volunteers and paid staff?

ANNA MOWERY, FORT WORTH

Yes. It is usually when the paid staff is aggressive and does not work as hard as the volunteers. It doesn't always cause a problem. Sometimes it works out very well. It just depends upon the people involved on both sides. You need volunteers that are not resentful and paid staff that knows how to handle the problem. Quite often you do get paid staff that are young and less experienced, shall we say. They really don't realize the necessity of being appreciative. I will say, too, that some of us who have been around a long time think we know everything, which is not necessarily true.

BECKY DIXON, WACO

I was able, with my background in working with volunteers, to bring in all of the support groups that the political consultants needed. We had the money guys, who brought in the money, pay for the big guns to bring in the ideas. Then they came to me to put those ideas to work by calling on my contacts out in the district.

In a rural area, you cannot go on TV around the clock because people are not going to see it. You need a good grassroots county organization in each county. You start with Republican clubs. That will be your core group for contacts. Then work with them to get a county chairman in that area. The network and the word-of-mouth gets out saying, "Look, this is a great candidate." Then they start putting together little groups. The grassroots element is still there regardless of the other money that you pour into a campaign.

Media

BARBARA NOWLIN, HOUSTON & FRIENDSWOOD

Des Barry was running for Congress. One time he was invited to go to Channel 13 in Houston to appear on a question-and-answer show. Callers could ask questions that were going to be more or less scrutinized by his campaign manager. He invited me to come down. We would look at the questions together. This was before the day of videotapes, or I would have a funny videotape. I had on a dress and high heels—that was back in the days when everyone was all dressed up, in the '60s. The campaign manager was very tall, so I was standing on my tiptoes to see a question and all of a sudden I lost my balance and started falling backwards. I hit the backdrop. It didn't fall over, but it went "boing, boing, boing." Des Barry and the people sitting at the table with them were looking like, what happened? I have never been so embarrassed. I said to the people at home, "Did you hear a loud noise?" and they said yes. I said, "That was me."

During the 1960 presidential campaign, Lyndon Johnson made an appearance with Lady Bird in Dallas. Before he arrived, a Kennedy-Johnson ad ran, which included the names of prominent Dallasites. Many who read the ad, to their surprise, found themselves listed as Kennedy-Johnson supporters. The visit also coincided with a scheduled "Tag Day" for Congressman Bruce Alger. The events of the day provided fodder for the conflict-driven press and resulted in unflattering publicity, which benefited the Kennedy-Johnson ticket.

Efforts continued to communicate effectively with the media through better preparation and knowledge of the issues. Sometimes, though, women found the portrayal of Republican candidates so inaccurate that they formed new campaign organizations to educate the voters.

MARTHA CROWLEY, DALLAS

Tag Days had become a traditional thing in campaign years for Bruce Alger. The Tag Day Girls were known for their red vests and beanie-type hats. The girls were almost without exception cute young girls, very gracious, nice, and fun. After we had our coffee and put on our little hats with "Vote for Bruce Alger" tags, we hit the streets. We had assigned corners, bank buildings, lobbies, or whatever. After people got to their offices, we all went back to the Adolphus Hotel on the mezzanine and had another cup of coffee before the lunch hour. We got our bags refilled so that we could tag everybody. Then we went back and hit our corners again when the lunch crowd came out.

What happened the night before the infamous Tag Day when LBJ and Lady Bird were present?

In the newspaper the night before there was an endorsement ad for Kennedy and Johnson in one of the papers. My husband's mother's name was in that ad. The list of names was like a telephone book. People couldn't believe their names would appear in this ad. A lot of those people were mad enough about it that they apparently came downtown to greet Lyndon Johnson.

JOY BELL, DALLAS

I remember being inside the Adolphus behind one of the brass rails. I think John Tower came through first. After Tower came in and went up the stairs, that is when Johnson came in. We were in there cheering for Tower, but I don't remember anything against Lyndon. I'm sure it was pretty quiet. It wasn't that big of a deal. It was made to be a big deal. Everyone was so far away from him. It was just LBJ and Lady Bird and maybe another person or two plus the news cameras. She stopped, and I don't remember exactly what she said. I think she said, "You know you are on the wrong side," or something to that effect.

Accounts say the women in the crowd physically assaulted Lady Bird. Was that true?

No. If she was, I wasn't there because there wasn't anyone inside that center lane. I guess that's why I was so amazed how they could turn it. I don't think there was anything bad about it at all! I just couldn't believe that the press could do that. They call it spin now. There are a lot of people who believe everything that they read and go through life that way. It hurt, what they said about us. I just kept quiet and let it go.

FLO KAMPMANN CRICHTON, SAN ANTONIO

I had been active in George Bush's campaign for Senate in 1964. I remember going with him and Fred Chambers to Dallas to meet with Felix McKnight, who was publisher of the *Herald,* to introduce George to him. He had been a friend of my family. The *Dallas Morning News* people had been friends, and so they were very helpful to George.

MARY LOU WIGGINS, DALLAS

The Buddy MacAtee newspaper ad when he ran successfully for the state legislature was kind of a big deal. I don't think people had done something quite on that scale before, with hundreds of names in a full-page ad. That was pretty impressive. That, of course, cost money. A lot of it didn't cost money. You'd go to the newspaper in Rockwall, for example, and try to get free press. You had to pay for ads of course.

GLENNA MCCORD, DALLAS

Republicans probably had more strategy exhibited in state legislative races because of Ann Good and Dale Yarborough. They took the legislative candidates as a group and drilled them on issues. You can do strategy to the "nth" degree but if you can't get your message across to a newspaper, forget it. We had this fellow who worked for the *Dallas Morning News* as a reporter. He left the paper and came to work for the Republican Party to do research. We had volunteers who ate up this stuff—Bonnie Hurst and Vic Robertson in particular. They did clipping and filing, and it got to the point that in about two years time when any issue or political problem came up, he could pull it right up out of the files. Ann and Dale used his knowledge and expertise because he knew the political writers, what they looked for, when you would get something across, and when you wouldn't. He tried his best to convince people that the paper was going to have the last word—you would never have the last word. Be careful what you say. There are a few people who should have listened to him more closely.

JUDY CANON, HOUSTON

It was after the 1980 election, actually about midterm. The media started this mantra about Reagan doesn't do enough for women. The National Organization for Women [*NOW*] attacked him in the media about what he hadn't done for women. You looked closer at them and realized that those women were not nonpartisan women. They were Democrats who were going under the nonpartisan banner trying to attack Reagan for their own purposes. I was working at the Republican headquarters in Harris County. I had listened one day too many to the morning news.

It just came over me that somebody ought to do something about this and somebody ought to do it the same way they are doing it. Ann Lee was the Republican Party secretary for Harris County. I talked to her and a couple of other buddies of mine who were all in the Magic Circle Republican Women's Club that Barbara Bush helped found years ago. Why can't we do something in some way to counter this and form a nonpartisan organization too? Our agenda will be similar to theirs, but we are going to show the positive side. We believe the glass is half full and not half empty. No president has done it all. We have to be practical about it. That was our whole theme.

Republican campaigns will have women for whoever the candidate is within the Republican umbrella. This was outside of the umbrella. It was not paid for by or a part of Republican politics. It was supported by individual contributions, and it was nonpartisan. We started out with four or five women. Penny Butler had our first organizational meeting. It was Penny, Ann Lee, Marie Clark, Senya Lemus, and Stephanie Milburn.

First, we had to make everyone aware of what we were doing. The National Federation of Republican Women was about to have their meeting in Louisville. We thought that was the best way to go nationwide with it. We devised a brochure "Women for Reagan." We got a logo—"American Women Supporting the President" with a woman's profile in the middle of it. There was a blue and white bumper sticker that said "Women for Reagan." Our brochure spelled out all of the things that he had done and was doing for women. We designed a button that said "Women for Reagan."

We got on the plane and went to Louisville. We got a table and started selling our buttons, brochures, and bumper stickers for two dollars. Our organizational meeting was on the agenda. I got up and talked about what we were doing. Women could take our idea back to their precincts, their hometowns, and set up Women for Reagan there. All they had to do was send us names and a dollar, and we would send them a button, brochure, and bumper sticker. Darn if these people didn't start ordering our materials. People ordered from all over the country. Everyone felt some relief—okay, we are doing something. NOW and the media mantra are not just going unanswered. We were just amazed at the number of people that came along who were Democrats that wouldn't have done anything because they were not going to follow along the Republican line, but because it was a nonpartisan group they participated. I would say around 25 to 30 percent were Democrats. We worked not to be connected with the Republican Party. We were in about 30 states. When he won, that was it. People would say, "Aren't you going to do something else?" We said, "No, that is all we wanted to do."

So many times people sit around and complain about the media. What made you decide you could make a difference?

I guess I was young enough to be idealistic. I felt like there were enough people out there like me who didn't find the facts were there to support the way Reagan was being presented. The hypocrisy! I couldn't stand any more, and I wanted to do something. I don't think that I have ever felt that strongly about anything before or since.

CHAPTER 16

Campaign Nuts and Bolts

"Campaigning is really hard work, not only for the candidates,
but it is hard work for the workers."   —KAY DANKS

*W*ith the strategy formed and the managers in place, the
time came to execute the campaign plan. Most plans
incorporated two basic parts: identify the voters and get them to
the polls on Election Day. There were two types of voters, those
who enthusiastically sought the opportunity to become informed
and even worked on campaigns and those who went to the polls
on Election Day. Ideally, strategies maximized the motivation
of the first group to reach the second.

Each campaign established a headquarters as its nerve
center. The headquarters also served as a meeting place and
raised the candidates' visibility in the community. Developing
enthusiasm and sustaining it through Election Day was critical.
Campaigns brought the candidates to the voters whenever
possible by holding rallies, hosting coffees and teas, and taking
bus tours. When it was not possible for candidates to reach each
voter personally, surrogates went out to campaign—most often
their wives. Loyal followers also sent postcards to friends and
associates, called on local media outlets, put up signs, and
creatively helped generate enthusiasm.

Campaign headquarters, phone banks, and get-out-the-
vote efforts have all become more sophisticated through the years.
In the early days, calling a page from the phone book was a
common method of both identifying voters and pulling crowds
together for political rallies. Women turned the vote out on

Election Day by relentlessly calling identified voters until they said their ballots had been cast and by giving voters rides if necessary.

In the beginning, most campaign workers knew they did not have a prayer for victory. They hoped to hold on to the few seats they held and make strides toward a higher percentage of votes than the last election. Women often developed their own definition of the word "win" so that they could keep motivated and look forward to the next election. Regardless of their objectives, women all worked toward fair and honest elections in which Republican candidates received the benefit of the votes from their followers and could expect a proper vote count after the polls closed.

Campaign Headquarters

CLAUDETTE LANDESS, AMARILLO

People were interested in coming by Nixon headquarters and picking up the literature in 1960, which is the reason you wanted a very prominent location. Knowledgeable people were behind that desk and talked to people as they came in.

JANELLE MCARTHUR, SAN ANTONIO

Every Tuesday I went downtown to the little Bush headquarters by the Milam Building. Around the corner from us was the Goldwater campaign headquarters. We were kind of in competition with one another. Lillian Schnabel taught me how to stuff, seal, and stamp envelopes. I don't know how many hundreds of women since that time I have taught. They are always amazed that there is a way to stuff hundreds of letters.

ANNA CLAIRE RICE, HOUSTON

When David West was running for a district judgeship, we didn't really have a headquarters for him. Often I would use my house. We sat around the table and did mail-outs.

FRANCIE FATHEREE CODY, PAMPA

Headquarters helped get things going in Pampa. When we had the opening, the radio stations came and the newspaper came. We let people know that we were alive. We staffed it for two months, and we lost the election.

RUTH McGUCKIN, HOUSTON & WASHINGTON COUNTY

Usually, the candidates wanted to run their own headquarters. They got their own volunteers. That was better because the county headquarters couldn't do all of that. Most people don't know what the county does. When I was vice chairman, it was my job to run the headquarters. My biggest job was to prepare the financial statement for the cost of the elections. Everything was listed, including clerks, judges, and polling places. It was several hundred thousand dollars. Headquarters contracted for about 400 polling places. We had to write to the schools, talk to them on the phone, go and look at the facilities. We had to talk to the people who were in charge of the voting machines and tell them how many voting machines we would need and at what address, what time, on what day.

The hardest thing besides the financial statement was figuring out which names to put on the ballot. It would be the same for every precinct as far as president and vice president and state offices, but then it would start changing from state representatives on down. We would go to the printer, sit down, and go over all of the ballots with them. We did mailings occasionally for the Republican ticket, but we weren't supposed to take sides in the primary.

JACQUE ALLEN, WICHITA FALLS

My first campaign was for George Bush. Paul Eggers was running for governor. We had one little room that was campaign headquarters. When Eggers was coming to town, his chairman, Mary Jane Maxfield, would call and say, "Come on down and help me pull all that Bush stuff off the wall." So we would take the Bush stuff down, and we would put all of Eggers' up, just like it was his headquarters. He would come in. Well, then Mildred Staley would come in and say, "You're not doing anything for George." So we would take everything down and put up George's stuff. There were so few of us that we all worked for every candidate. Most of the candidates thought, "Gee whiz, they are really for me."

FRANKIE LEE HARLOW, DEL RIO

People liked the fact that they could come down there and express their opinions, get some free literature and a cup of coffee. It was a small town, and it was easy to get people in. I won't say that all of them that came in and got bumper stickers and coffee voted for us right at the moment, but we kind of put a bug in their head about why are you voting for those Democrats?

CINDY BROCKWELL, BOERNE

Betty Nuss had been here in Kendall County Republican Women forever just doing the grunt work. She wasn't interested in doing more. She was interested in stuffing envelopes. Just the basics that are important.

Why is it important to have people like Betty Nuss around?

The basics never changed no matter the size of the campaign. With the size of the campaign, the candidates have more money, but your local candidates don't have the budget to pay a mail house to send out their direct mail pieces. Volunteers do it. So people like Betty Nuss were dependable. It saves the candidate money so they can spend their money on things that you can't do with volunteers, like newspaper ads.

SHIRLEY GREEN, AUSTIN & SAN ANTONIO

In those early days, volunteers did almost all of the work. I was never paid until I went to work for George Bush for president in 1979, and then we were paid pittance wages because Jim Baker can stretch a penny further than anyone.

I developed and always used a little device of day chairman

for the campaign. Very few people could work every day of the week, but a lot of people would give a day. So someone would be the Monday headquarters chairman, someone else the Tuesday headquarters chairman, and so on. It was a matter of learning to apportion your resources. One hour you'd be cleaning out the potty in the headquarters, and the next one you would be trying to learn to drive in a motorcade, and the next one you would be trying to get ten dollars out of somebody. We just had to do it all. There were people that worked campaigns who really weren't that active in the clubs. But the Republican Women's Clubs did the bulk of the work in the early '60s at least.

NADINE FRANCIS, ODESSA

I had strict instructions on how to run a headquarters. I always had something for the people to do. There was a saying, "if you don't have something for the volunteers to do, make up something and throw it away." That was not my philosophy. By this time, I was holding a full-time job. I would take my kids to school then go to the headquarters and get things lined up. I always had a headquarters chairman, Willie Shortes. She was a former office manager for a title company. We would lay out the work, and then when people came in we had it there for them to do. It was run like a business office. We eventually had to have a set of rules for how people dressed when they came to the office. No curlers for example.

DEE COATS, HOUSTON

Sometimes you worried about people infiltrating. We did have one of those during the 1988 primary. She came in saying she wanted to volunteer. She wasn't anyone that I knew. She was a reporter who was not on our side. I don't remember how we figured it out, but we did. She was trying to sabotage our campaign. We had her typing up volunteer cards. She was changing one number in each telephone number so that we couldn't get a hold of them. We discovered it when we were merging a list. We realized that on all of the cards she had changed one number.

Let's Meet the Candidate

Personal Contact

ANN HARRINGTON, PLANO

In 1961, [*Speaker of the House*] Sam Rayburn died. Our cousin Conner Harrington ran for his seat in a special election. We went to McKinney, Texas to campaign around the old courthouse. There were benches that the older men sat around on. We called them the Spit and Whittle Club. They would sit and talk, and Conner was giving out brochures. This man looked at him and said, "Boy,"— Conner was probably thirty-eight at the time—"are you a Republican?" Conner said yes, and the man threw the brochure down on the ground and spit on it. When we went to Wylie campaigning for Goldwater we had tomatoes thrown at us, but we were glad they weren't bricks or rocks.

BEBE ZUNIGA, LAREDO

We have *pachangas* here in Laredo, which are very, very popular. Someone in a neighborhood decides they want to get together. So someone says "I'll bring the meat," and somebody says "I'll bring the beer," and somebody says "I'll bring the mariachis." There are no strangers there. The minute you meet them you automatically become their friend. This is where the Republican Party has had problems in the past getting to talk to people and telling them what we are all about. The people were afraid to invite Republicans because we have the reputation of being snobbish with so much money (I wish). My house has been a railroad station. We have had parties for many statewide candidates. Coming to the house, they know it is not an elaborate house and the minute you walk in the door you are one of us. It has really helped. We have a very popular restaurant here named Cotulla, and every morning, especially on Saturdays and Sundays, you literally have to wait in line—and sometimes the line is a block long—but every single person goes to Cotulla for breakfast. We have taken George Bush and Kay Bailey Hutchison there to go around the tables and shake hands with everybody.

JESS ANN THOMASON, MIDLAND

One thing that works in campaigning is the candidate him or herself goes to the main post office in the morning and the afternoon, takes material, and shakes hands. You will not believe how well that works. Is that country or what?

Rallies

FRANCIE FATHEREE CODY, PAMPA

We had this big rally and a barbecue at the rodeo ground. All of the people running as statewide candidates were coming. Jack Cox [*who was running for governor*] didn't want to be with any of them, which made it a real problem for those of us that were holding it. Finally, we said, "You have to do this. This is the way it is billed." So he did do it. He didn't want to be seen with them because those other people had no chance of winning

GLORIA CLAYTON, DALLAS

George Bush was running for the Senate in 1970. Anne Nicholson, who was the president of the Dallas County women's assembly, called me frantically mid-afternoon and said, "Gloria, I have just had a call. George Bush's plane is coming into Love Field. We have got to have a rally." I said, "When?" And she said, "Tonight." We called women's clubs and put phone committees into action. We went to the dime store and got red, white, and blue crepe paper. We went out to Love Field and decorated—very little but enough that it looked a little festive. I got a call that said the staff has not had a bite to eat and they don't have much time. Could you pick up some Colonel Sanders chicken and bring it out to Love Field? My station wagon smelled like Colonel Sanders chicken for a week. I had boxes and boxes of Colonel Sanders chicken in my car. The rally actually came off pretty well. He spoke for a few minutes and got back on the plane, and the staff grabbed all of the chicken and went running out to the plane. We were just so eager to do what we could.

KAY DANKS, GALVESTON & AUSTIN

Campaigning is really hard work, not only for the candidates, but it is hard work for the workers. We worked in '80 and '84, we worked probably fifteen hours a day in headquarters doing whatever needed to be done. Linden Heck [*Howell*] ran the '84 campaign. Linden called me into her office one day and said the president and vice president are going to be here next Thursday. The advance team will be here tomorrow. We will need to pick them up at the airport and have five sites in mind. She said, "You'll need a bus." So I called the Kerrville Bus Company, and they said it was almost closing time for them. I said, "We have to have this. I know we're supposed to have a check for you up front, but if you will send the driver with the bus in the morning, I will walk straight out to the bus and hand him the check." We picked up the advance team. It was July, and it was hot. They came in their three-piece suits. So the first place we stopped was the baseball field and it was so hot. We got there, and they started taking their ties and jackets off. We ended up using Auditorium Shores.

They said, "We have to have 10,000 people." I said, "Ten thousand people? There are not 10,000 Republicans in Austin. I don't know how we are going to get 10,000 people." So we gave away tickets, and we acted like it was a big deal. We had hundreds of people who made signs. I called a woman and said, "I need some help, the president and vice president are coming." She said, "Why did you call me? I've never been on the same side as you." I said, "Well, we have to have everybody." She did her job beautifully. We had to get people from San Antonio to come and set up the stage. It was frantic because when the advance team comes the Secret Service comes and so do the communications people. They all set up in a suite in the Hyatt Regency. They go inspect the tops of the buildings downtown. Most people are not aware of how much it takes to move these people from one place to another. You have to have cars. You have to have a bus. You have to provide food and drinks for the press on the bus. We had to have a press platform built. I thought, "Why are we doing this? They are not ever nice to us." They came, and it was really exciting. We were really hot.

Postcards and Letters

MARTHA CROWLEY, DALLAS

Frank and his supporter would have their picture taken together. A "Vote for Crowley" sign was somewhere on the wall. It would be put on a postcard. "Hope you will support Frank Crowley" was printed on the back, and there was a space left for the supporter to write and sign his name. We encouraged these people to send postcards to places they traded, like the gas station, the cleaners. We did it for Bruce Alger. They would do the addressing, then we would make them bring the cards back and mail them to be sure that they would get out.

DEBORAH BELL, ABILENE

You need to make an effort and not assume that people know. Very intelligent businesspeople don't read up on issues. They depend on word-of-mouth. My goal is to reach the people I know or I meet. I send out postcards giving them my opinions about who they should support. It means a lot to them because nobody else is doing it. We had a city treasurer who came to me. I said, "The best thing that you can do, Lisa, is to do a postcard telling your qualifications. City treasurer is kind of low on the totem pole. Get people to commit to mail so many and stamp them for you. If I send it to people and say "this is who you ought to support" and they like me, that might help sway it.

PENNY ANGELO, MIDLAND

When my husband, Ernie, ran for mayor, I set up a telephone list and gave volunteers areas to call. We sent letters every night. Ernie would wake up in the morning and say "Now, we need to send a letter." By night, they would have them printed, and the next day he'd say, "We need to send another letter." We must have done that ten days in a row. We were running against a popular incumbent mayor pro tem.

We had to do it all by hand. First, we didn't have the money to do it any other way. Second, frankly the technology had not caught up with the way that we wanted to do it.

Bus Tours

MILLIE TEAS, DALLAS

We were Pioneers for Reagan. We went in Pat Jacobson's motor home. Jane Bergland, Betty Ambrose, Sharla Moore, Pat Jacobson, and I were going to travel all over these little counties and reach out to people that were away from the campaign. Right before we left on a trip, the *Dallas Morning News* said that East Texas is a landslide for Carter and that Reagan probably wouldn't be looking for any assistance in that area. Well, we went down through Central Texas and all over East Texas.

We had the bus decorated, and we were all in red, white, and blue with hats with streamers and buttons all over them. We went up and down the street asking everyone to vote for Ronald Reagan. We stopped once, and there was a crew of telephone workmen. A picture should have been in *Time* magazine of Pat hanging out of the motor home handing this guy a Reagan flyer. We had a ball doing it, and we made an impact.

CATHERINE SMYTH COLGAN, DALLAS

In 1974, I was appointed by state chairman Jack Warren to chair the Candidates Caravan. It was the first time that we had candidates for all of the seven statewide offices. We had a motor home motorcade and went to sixty-nine towns in thirty days. One day, we got off to a fifteen-minute late start, and we were fifteen minutes late everywhere we went. But the other days, we were right on time. There were two fascinating things about that trip. Number one, most of the candidates traveled with us the whole time. Polly Sowell, the state vice chairman, traveled part of the time; Barbara Lewis, president of TFRW, was off and on; and I missed a few days. But most of us traveled the full month. One of the young staff people at Republican headquarters who had just finished at the University of Texas helped arrange our logistics. He was Jeb Bush.

In a number of towns, particularly in West Texas, many people had never laid eyes on a Republican. We would pull up in front of the newspaper office and walk in unannounced. This, I am told, paved the way because the next time we had statewide offices four years later a trail had been blazed. They knew there was such a thing as a Republican.

The other interesting thing that happened is that we were all together on the tour the night Nixon resigned. That was absolutely riveting. We were dumb struck, but the man who was the lieutenant governor candidate stood up and proposed a toast to President Ford. We carried on from there. We were supposed to fly the next day to El Paso. We called ahead, as we did every time, to make sure that they were ready for us, and they said, "Are you really going to come?" We said, "Absolutely!" But we knew that literally sealed the fate of all seven of our candidates. They were determined to proceed. Promises made, promises kept. People had made arrangements, spent money, and planned parties. We completed the tour with style.

Coffees and Teas

NADINE FRANCIS, ODESSA

When Jack Cox ran for governor, it was back in the days of the coffees. Coffees, coffees, coffees. They were in people's homes. Of course, it was mostly women. I would often try to set up a luncheon for men if I could, but for the most part, it was coffees. I was at the airport lots of times at eight o'clock in the morning. We would have a couple of coffees, even three, before lunch and then have lunch. The instructions out of Austin were to keep him as busy as you can. Then we would go call on individuals and businesses. When you don't know how difficult a job is, you just kind of go do it. I was very naive. If Peter O'Donnell sent something out that said "do this," I would have gone to the end of the earth practically to get it done.

LOU BROWN, MIDLAND

Barbara Culver Clack basically ran her campaign for county judge. That was before the times of campaign chairman and campaign treasurers and filing all these papers. Katie Heck was helping her and her husband. She would call somebody and say, "Would you invite the people that live on your street?" They would basically have cookies, punch, and coffee. The candidate would be there to greet everybody. The candidate at that point did not walk in the door and everybody was there to greet her. Barbara was there greeting everybody at the front door. Maybe she even brought the cookies. She would tell them why she wanted to run for county judge. She was very articulate and convincing, and she was very warm. A lot of people would go away shaking their heads saying, there's no way they are going to elect a woman to political office in West Texas. She's got good ideas about running a county, and I like what she says about ad valorem taxes. I might vote for her, but I don't think there's any way we're going to do this. Sure enough, that was the first win that gave the Republicans that first breath of life.

ROBBIE BORCHERS, NEW BRAUNFELS

The Tom Loeffler campaign took about a year of my life. We were absolutely determined that this was our chance to get a Republican congressman. So here in Comal County I started in '77 inviting people to events for him here at home. It would be breakfast or cocktails or something just for people to come in and meet him. When he came to town, I would take him place to place for days. He stayed sometimes two or three days. We would just hit everybody that we could think of to visit. He was a delightful candidate. I never will forget that after the parties he was always there to help with the cleanup and always insisted that he'd take the garbage out.

BECKY CORNELL, SAN ANGELO

Congressmen Collins from Dallas ran against Lloyd Bentsen for the Senate. I was his chairman for ten or twelve counties in the area. One time, Mrs. Collins came and there was a tea party for her in Murchison out west of town. I dreamed the night before that I was late and had to pick her up at the airport in my bathrobe. I said, "Oh, don't worry. We will take the shortcut by the Boys Ranch, and we will be in Murchison in plenty of time." I was up at the crack of dawn the next day so I would be sure not to pick up Mrs. Collins in my bathrobe.

Car Caravans

MARY ANNE COLLINS, DALLAS

We would ride around in these caravans for "Bruce Alger for Congress." I had my first baby then and put her in the car seat. We'd have big signs on the car and ride all around neighborhoods and shopping centers.

MARTHA CROWLEY, DALLAS

Rita Clements was Rita Bass then. She was very, very active in the early days. We used to do car caravans. She and I were pregnant at the same time and could barely squeeze behind the steering wheel. We used to get antique cars, and if that didn't work we got convertibles. We went to shopping centers and drove slowly around with the candidates. I don't think that we could blare too much music. It was a no-no. Get little kids and hats. Red, white, and blue everything. Something to draw attention to the candidates.

MARION COLEMAN, PASADENA

I got a motorcade together when Nixon was coming into Herman Park. I went before the city council and asked if we could get motorcycle police officers. They laughed at me. They said, "Oh, we will give you a car. How many cars do you think you'll have,

Mrs. Coleman?" I said probably about 75 to 100, and they all laughed. We had 257 cars. The Houston Police Department met us on the Gulf Freeway and led us into Herman Park. I had a little boy who brought a bicycle, and he decorated it because he thought he could go with us. I just stuck him in my car. We really made a mark in Houston and Pasadena.

Creating a Presence

JOCI STRAUS, SAN ANTONIO

In 1960, they asked would I head up the Nixon Girls? I got every high school and college signed up, and I got a group from each one. We met every Saturday at a parking lot at one of the malls. We got permission from the mall keepers to be at the parking lot, and we would stop as a car would pull up and ask if we could put a Nixon bumper sticker on the car. We always had to ask. We had training sessions on how to ask and how to take a "no" nicely. We were at every function that was possible with our uniforms on.

One of the most fun things was when John Wayne came to open the new Alamo movie. My husband and my father-in-law were out of town. They had tickets to the opening of the movie. What an opportunity to have my Nixon Girls there outside the theater giving out bumper stickers and buttons. First, I called the chamber of commerce who was sponsoring the opening, and I said, "Would you mind if I came to the reception at the St. Anthony. I have a ticket. And would you mind if I wore my Nixon Girl outfit?" I asked Theo Weiss, the president then. He said, "No, I wouldn't mind. Of course not! You go right ahead." So I did. I picked up my mother-in-law. It was pouring rain, and I had on my raincoat. I walked into the party, and everyone in there was dressed to the teeth in their furs and jewels. I took off my raincoat and everyone said, "OH!" It was the first time you could tell your real friends from the people who were embarrassed for you. It was really interesting.

I was approached by this young man. He said, "Miss, would mind taking off your hat?" I said, "It's part of my outfit. It's okay.

John Wayne is a Republican. Who are you?" He told me he was his press agent. "Oh, fabulous. Let's go over and meet him." So I locked arms with him, and he took me over to meet John Wayne, which was the most wonderful moment. Then all my girls were standing outside of the theater. There were six on each side as people came in. We had a presence. Somebody had to know we were out there, and we had to have a chance.

SITTY WILKES, AUSTIN

I was on a Bush Belle committee. Rita Clements was involved with that in 1970. She had us go down on Congress Avenue and do "Buttonhole for Bush Days." You would feel like a prostitute if you did it now. I went down there and stood on Congress Avenue. We put a campaign button in the men's buttonholes. You could never do that today. I still have my Bush scarf that she had us wear.

Anything to Generate Enthusiasm

MARGARET BAIRD, HOUSTON

I had a little toy Pomeranian dog back then. We made a campaign outfit for him, with the candidates' names on either side of the outfit, and on top we had a small piece of wood, which had a little hole for a flag. When he ran, the flag would wave. He also had a little hat, which had campaign buttons all over it. However, he wasn't as willing to wear that. The first election in which my dog campaigned was the Nixon-Agnew race against George McGovern in 1972. We always hoped that the candidates' names would not be too long. Every election, we would update the campaign outfit.

When my youngest child was born in 1973, I used my baby and her baby carriage to campaign. The carriage was covered with bumper stickers. Later, she helped me campaign using her wagon covered with bumper stickers, and she would cover herself with them. As my little Holly grew older, she would entertain at the polls. She and friends would dance and sing political songs, some of them original. My feeling was you had to generate enthusiasm. Animals and babies will always attract attention, and attention is the name of the game.

What is your sign strategy?

First of all, you need to get a lot of signs up. Signs are extremely important psychologically. I try to find visible corners on busy streets first of all. You make sure you have every other block covered. Some people would allow me to put any sign up. They'd say, "If you are supporting them, then I trust you." Signs, particularly all over the important big streets, have a positive impact on voters. I can remember elections where all of a sudden, overnight, dozens of signs disappeared. It was so depressing. Psychologically, it is really important to have signs to generate a good voter turnout and enthusiasm.

BILLIJO PORTER, EL PASO

In 1980, when George Bush ran for president against Ronald Reagan, I was going to support George Bush. Of course Patty Bruce did, too. We were the chairmen for the Sixteenth Congressional District. I said, "Let's get it going because there's no organization in some of these little counties, like Hudspeth." There weren't any Republican county chairmen. I said, We're going to go out in our Levis and be one of the group." We went everywhere west of Odessa including Pecos, Valentine, and Fort Hancock. We spent three or four days getting Bush chairmen. We took the material and told them what we wanted to do, and we met with them and drank beer with them. Whatever we had to do, we got these people. I remember the Bush people were so proud of us because we even had a chairman in Loving County with only 300 people.

I understand that later on when the Reagan chairman in El Paso found out what we had done they were mad because we had organized. We had gotten all of the people. In some of these counties, there were only two Republicans. I talked to them and said, "Now, George Bush is a Texan and we have got to support our fellow Texans." I had done some organizing when John Connally had run for president. I already had some contacts there. Here was a chance to really sneak them into the Party. That was my main motivation. Here was my chance to say, "You are going to have to make a commitment. You are going to have to vote in the Republican primary if you are going to vote for your guy." We had these people committed. Some fell by the wayside early on, but I had their names. By god, I supported Connally. You are going to support my guy now.

Phone Banks

REBA BOYD SMITH, ODESSA & ABILENE

In Taylor County, we got out the vote. We did what Nancy Braddus said. If you follow instructions, you get the job done. There were four steps. You identified the voter. We zeroed in on the undecided voter. We sent them information. We called the undecided voters back to say, "We hope you received the information. Could you join us now and support Bill Clements?" Then we got out the vote. We called every one of those people.

BARBARA NOWLIN, HOUSTON & FRIENDSWOOD

Running those phone banks back in the early days when volunteers were hard to come by was challenging. It is an absolutely grueling experience to be there every day. You get the location, set it up, staff it, and then are there all the time. That experience, that teamwork, that camaraderie is probably the best. You learn their names and that was not hard with someone there day in and day out, but we had 600 volunteers. Looking back on that experience, working together really drew us together. There was a bond. It was a wonderful experience. Very rewarding, very gratifying.

JANIE BROCK, SAN ANGELO

In spring of '84, we were getting ready to set up the phone banks. A friend of mine accepted the chairmanship of the phone banks and asked me to be a captain. They were having training in Midland, so she took me to Midland for the training. By the time we came back, I was the assistant chairman of the phone banks. She got sick two or three months into the campaign, and I became chairman. I was brand-new to Republican election procedures. Gladi Wright was my right hand. I put in about sixteen hours a day at the headquarters, and Gladi was usually down there to help. Before the election was over, I had been completely indoctrinated in the procedures.

BARBARA PATTON, HOUSTON

Phone banks are one of the best ways to reach out and connect with the voters and show some excitement about a real opportunity to elect someone to office. The other thing they are, is an opportunity to get volunteers involved in working for the candidate. A lot of times you found a volunteer that came in and wanted to help with one aspect of the campaign and do the telephones, and you found out they had all of these other marvelous skills—perhaps being a surrogate speaker or writing press releases or being a field rep for the campaign or eventually going to work for that particular candidate. Working on the phone and other volunteer positions in a campaign can be a wonderful training ground for a career or for being called upon to do another job.

PENNY BUTLER, HOUSTON

If we don't have a personal touch at phone banks, we are going to lose our vital nerve. It is simply amazing what kind of stories and information you can gather if you get on the phone and talk to some of these people. I think that is part of what is really missing these days. Some people feel so foreign about campaigns and about leadership because candidates are not getting good feedback. They're looking at polls that "high-powered people" are doing, and we are not really talking to people on the ground. That is a real mistake. We need things that volunteers can do and that will bring out some of the younger people.

PATTILOU DAWKINS, AMARILLO

Martha Weisend was Bill Clements' overall campaign chairman in 1986. She was a general if there ever was one. She would call and bark "Pattilou Dawkins!" I would say, "Yes, ma'am?" "Now tell me, what were your numbers today? How many calls did you make? How many were Clements'?" We had to report into her every morning by 9:00 a.m. So of course it was very important that the people who worked at night got all the numbers correct. Invariably, they didn't. I'd get over there by 7:00 a.m. and make sure that the numbers were all correct because she scared the pooh out of me. I lived in fear that Martha Weisend was going to call, and my numbers wouldn't be accurate. I tried not to fabricate, but there were sometimes that I would lie on those numbers to make sure I didn't incur the wrath of Martha Weisend because you didn't want to do that. She was a general, and it worked. We had the number-one phone bank. We got out 98 percent of all of our identified voters.

How in the world did you do that?

I had drivers. Everybody had a Suburban. We would go to rest homes. We would go everywhere. Our phone bank kept working. We called people until they said that they had voted. We would maybe call people two or three times the day of the election. We would ask had they voted and they would say, "Quit calling me. I'm going as soon as I put the wash in the dryer." We would say what time do you think that might be? "Well, in another fifteen minutes, I guess." We would call them back in fifteen minutes and we would say, "Have you voted?" We had people working from their homes. We probably had 100 phones working that day calling people to make sure that they had voted.

Voter Identification

MARY ELLEN MILLER, AUSTIN

All of the campaigns that I have been involved with I have always felt that voter identification was extremely important. Without it, a manager can not use money or the candidate's time to the highest degree of productivity. You need a guideline for where to put your volunteers, where to schedule your candidate, and where you spend your bucks. So the first thing that I do in every race is all of the arithmetic for the campaign. I get all of the statistical information on past voting patterns and know what is a reasonable expectation of votes, the ones that you can forget about and the middle ground—the savable. I set the vote goals before we ever start. I want to know where we are every single day, what we need, and where we are going to get it.

What was your role in John Tower's 1978 race?

They wanted me to be in charge of voter I.D. Phone bank results plummeted after Tower refused to shake hands with [*Democratic opponent Bob*] Krueger. I'm surprised the photo didn't win the Pulitzer. Polly Sowell and I cornered John in a limousine in Dallas and said you are in big-time trouble. He said, "I know it." I said to him, "I have an idea, but we will never get the money from finance to do it." I will never forget what he said. He looked at me and he said, "Do what you have to do, Darling." So Polly and I went to southwest Harris County because that is where most of the new people were. We sent out some teams door-to-door asking if the election were held today who would they vote for. We found seven or eight out of ten were Republican. That is one of the times that we didn't turn out the vote by identified vote. We called everyone and turned them out by the percentages. That was a turning point in John Tower's election. There is no question about it. Later I did a total, just like I would do before an election. County after county after county, Krueger beat Tower. If they had had a turn-out, Krueger would have beaten John Tower.

Do you think that it would have been as successful if it had not been for the volunteers who were willing to get on the phones and make those calls?

No. John Tower was so well loved by party members, and you see how that shines through in conversations with other people.

Volunteers were fundamentally important because it was like a holy crusade to them to reelect Tower. He and Lou were both so well loved, and anyone would do anything for them. That was the ingredient. You couldn't put a dollar value on it. There is no way you can put a dollar value on that.

If you don't have a phone bank you are inviting defeat every time. We wouldn't have known what we had to do if we hadn't had a phone bank. Maybe it doesn't matter if you have a real popular person who is going to win by 70 percent of the vote and has been reelected three times. When you are serious about it, it's more than just winning. It's getting the best investment of their time, spending your money where it will do the most good.

Get-Out-the-Vote

GWEN PHARO, DALLAS

No job was too dirty for any of us. We were on a crusade. We would sit at the headquarters on Lemmon Avenue, and they would give us a phone book. They would say "you call this page," and we would sit there like idiots and call every number on the page in an afternoon. We would pretty well get the phone book covered before Election Day. We would just say, "Is this Mr. Jones? Mr. Jones, this is Gwen Pharo at Republican headquarters. We'd like for you to vote for our candidate, Mr. X." They would say yes or no, and we put a little mark by their name. That's how we developed lists for phone calls.

KRIS ANNE VOGELPOHL, GALVESTON

The first phone banks that really stand out in my mind we did in our house. We brought in eight extra lines. We had phones in all of the different parts of the house. We had women who were taking their children to school, dropping them off at nine o'clock, and coming back here to phone. Then they would go and pick up their children at noon. Then a group of women who didn't pick up children until three or four o'clock in the afternoon came at noon and called until three o'clock. Then we had a group of widows who came in about three and worked until six on the phones because they did not have to prepare an evening meal. I would prepare an evening meal so that before these widows left we would sit down and have a hot meal. Then we would have a hot meal ready for young couples coming home from work who would come by here and call until nine. We had a real system going, and we kept all phones full at all times.

Some women could not walk into a Republican headquarters as they can now. The people who helped us with our early phone banks were the parents of our children's friends. The groups that came in the evening were our friends' mothers. It was through friendships. Recruiting is the hardest thing we had to do.

GLENNA McCORD, DALLAS

[*County Chair*] Harry Bass took our strongest precincts and figured out where all of the known Republicans lived distance-wise from the polling place. He put these phone lists together and brought them up to headquarters on Election Day. Bobbie Biggart and I were at headquarters. He came in around six o'clock. He said, "Are you two the only ones here?" He said, "We are going to call all the people on these lists. These are our strongest precincts." He said, "I have figured out how long it takes them to get from their house to the polling place. We are going to call until five minutes to seven." The three of us sat there with the phone lists. He had listed all the people that lived the farthest away first, so we would call them first. When you talk about getting out the vote, that was getting it out until the very last minute.

MARGARET BAIRD, HOUSTON

In my neighborhood, people started voting without having to be reminded because they became interested and felt like their vote counted. I would tell them how many elections have been won or lost by less than one vote per precinct. It all adds up to victory if you make sure that you get those votes out.

THEO WICKERSHAM, SAN ANTONIO

I found that one way to help get more people interested in your Party was a ride to the polls. As we are riding along to the polls you are hoping that they are not going to vote for a Democrat. There was one old couple in Cibolo. They said, "We just appreciate you so much for coming way out here in the country and picking us up." I said, "Well, you are adamant about getting to the polls. I could tell that when you called." They said yes. Come to find out, they were Democrats. I said, "I want to show you my ballot before you get out of the car. I want to tell you about each one of these people—which ones I know and why I want to vote for them." They were so interested. From then on, they'd always call me to take them to the polls. I am sure by word-of-mouth they have a lot of their people turned.

CAROLE RAGLAND, LEAGUE CITY

Turning out the vote is very difficult now. I have enough Republican voters in this county to make a difference in any race—4,000 or so. I sent a letter out before the last election, and in Galveston County none of our candidates won. In our precinct, we only had 1,500 votes. Only our precinct commissioner in our gerrymandered precinct won. The letter said, "Gov. John Sharp. Think there's no way? Think again. How would you like to wake up the day after the election and have John Sharp elected Lt. Governor? John Cornyn is trailing in the polls because Jim Mattox has name ID. This can happen if you don't vote. Did you know that there are three candidates that live right here in our precinct? Please go vote."

Ballot Security

PAT McCALL, HOUSTON & UVALDE COUNTY

Ballot security is making sure that those people who come in to vote have the right to vote. We had poll watchers. Men. As you know, this is ranching and farming country. We had a lot of big farmers and ranchers who went down to poll watch. It was a small county so it wasn't difficult. Everybody knew everybody else. If they came in and they weren't legal, they would look at one of the poll watchers who knew them and turn around and leave.

How did you figure out that you needed a good ballot security program?

Because of what I had gone through in Houston and Harris County. People had always said we would never carry one side of town, and I said, "Well, if we get ballot security, we might have a chance." We put it together and it worked.

BARBARA PATTON, HOUSTON

Back in 1965 through '67, Mildred Fike would always be in charge of ballot security for any election. She was a very meticulous person. She was very talented mathematically and very distrustful of people [*laughing*]. She was perfect for the job. She analyzed the election returns—the demographics. It helped to plan for the future for another campaign.

MARY ANNE COLLINS, DALLAS

We had a very good ballot security program. Helen Harris was a prime mover. She was one of the brains of this Party—our little old lady in tennis shoes. She knew political strategy and was a meticulous person. Candidates like Ike Harris would go to her for advice in their campaigns. She also would figure out the number of delegates per precinct, and she was just meticulous. She ran one of our first ballot security programs. She had regional poll watchers in Dallas County before we were able to get election judges.

GLENNA McCORD, DALLAS

We became aware that we were going to have to do something about poll watchers at an early stage. Democrats weren't accustomed to having anyone look over their shoulders. The evidence of vote fraud was all around us every election day. We had to devise some way to try and counteract that. You could have affidavits galore and people willing to go into a courtroom to swear what they saw, but if you didn't have a judge in place to hear the case you could forget it. We're talking about the days when there wasn't a Republican judge in Dallas County. Maybe there were one or two in the whole state. So we couldn't get the cases heard, but something had to be done. If it hadn't been for the women who gave their time to volunteer, we would not have been able to do what we did.

Volunteers took the obituary list, and as soon as the voter registration list came in from the county for the election of 1968, they went through those voter registration lists and made notations as to who was dead. In so doing, they also found a lot of duplications. So we put all our data together on three-by-five index cards, and then we put them in alphabetical order according to precinct. When I was vice chairman, I had a call from a lady in Dallas who was a liberal Democrat. She was trying to find polling places for the Democratic primary in precincts where there weren't very many active Democrats. We were having a hard time finding a place to vote in areas of Dallas that were her precincts. She said, "Do you think that we can work together on this?" I said, "Sure. I need help too."

She called me at home one night, and said State Senator Mike McKool was having hearings around the state trying to get some good information together to knock out some of this voter fraud that was going on. The conservative Democrats were doing the same thing to the liberal Democrats that they were doing to us— stealing elections. They would steal their election in the primary and steal ours in the general election.

In September 1970, as co-chairman of the Dallas County Republican Ballot Security Committee for 1970, I appeared before McKool's State Senate Committee for Election Law Reform. I presented an exhibit of the poll books from a number of precincts with the combined total number of duplicate registrations from those precincts, which totaled 791. I also pointed out that in 59 precincts of commissioners district one there were 681 voters listed in the wrong precinct. I also informed the court that volunteers at Republican headquarters had checked the obituary lists in the daily newspaper. The deceased voters were listed by precinct on slips that, upon request, would be available for the purpose of purging the list. Judge Sterrett and the commissioners agreed that it would be impossible to purge the list of convicted felons unless every person in the state were fingerprinted. I turned to him at that point and said, "Judge, we just sent men to the moon and back. If computers can do that, then I think they can purge these lists." He almost swallowed his cigar.

We requested that some guidelines be drawn for precinct election officials to determine qualifications of the voter who has lost his certificate and whose name is not in the poll book in his home precinct. We had one report after another of people who had registration certificates but got to the polling place and their names were not in the book. My sister was one of them. In October, we were given permission to talk to the tax assessor-collector and to his assistant in voter registration. We discussed using the computer to delete the duplicate social security numbers. We purged the list of 7,048 duplicates. This is the possibility of 7,048 people voting twice. Then, physically scanning the list, we deleted an additional 7,438 for a total of 14,486 names. We printed Dallas County's first master list of registered voters in alphabetical order so that if an election judge had questions about a voter's qualifications he could learn if a voter had been listed in the wrong precinct. In addition, we shared the list of deceased voters. With the addition of the 1987 deceased voters, a total of 16,473 names were removed from the poll books.

BERYL MILBURN, AUSTIN

I think the Clements election for governor was fair because we watched the ballot boxes. I remember meeting at the Clements headquarters, and the vote was so close. They said, "You've got to go back, and you've got to contact all of your county chairmen to be sure they know where the ballot boxes are and stay with them." So we did. All through the night, people went and found the ballot boxes and stayed with them. We guarded that ballot box, and that's what made it a fair election, and Clements won.

ESTELLE TEAGUE, HURST

In the early '60s I started doing early voting for the county clerk. I was known as the token Republican. We had chief deputies that we used to chase down the stairs to get the ballots. The deputies would say, "I've always sent loose ballots out. Now, why can't I take one to these old friends of mine?" We sat on the cans all night long in the basement of the courthouse to keep people from getting into them. We've gotten it cleaned up, but it took us a good while.

We had a precinct judge who got mad at one of our poll watchers and slapped her and told her to get out. The poll watcher sat there and said, "I'm entitled to be here and I am staying." We had nursing homes that voted 75 percent of their patients when I was in charge. The handwriting didn't compare so I threw them out. When they took it to court, the opponent won the election by fifty-five votes. That is the only time in the history of Tarrant County that the ballot box was ever opened to match up votes. The judge ordered that all of the mail-in ballots be matched up to the stubs. That's when he declared that they were illegal, just as I said they were.

FRANCIE FATHEREE CODY, PAMPA

I guess it was 1962. The state party wanted us to get poll watchers. The poll watchers were to be there to make sure that the elections were being run correctly. We had a cantankerous little guy who was the presiding judge. They counted the ballots all by hand. There was a big precinct and it was late. He decided he was going to quit counting that night, take the ballots home, and start the next day. The poll watcher called me. I said, "No, no, he can't do that!" I said, "Tell him to meet us at the courthouse." I called Clayton, the county chairman, and said, "We have got to go to the courthouse." There was the sheriff, the deputy sheriff, Clayton, the judge, the poll watchers, and me. I said to the judge, "I understand that you're tired, but you can not take the ballot box home with you. How about locking it up in the sheriff's office?" He said, "No, I am in charge of these until they are counted, and I am taking them home." I convinced him that I didn't write the Texas election law, but I was just trying to go by the law. I got the sheriff to chime in with me. The sheriff said, "She would like to lock them up here. Will you do that?" This poll watcher had already missed one day of work so he had to miss two days of work.

RUTH McGUCKIN, HOUSTON & WASHINGTON COUNTY

I believe it was 1968, soon after Nancy Palm became the county chairman. We got in the election returns from several precincts in the west part of Harris County, which we knew were Republican precincts. But the vote came in overwhelmingly Democrat. So we knew something was wrong. Nancy Palm got a court order to go to the storage facilities and inspect the voting machines. She went with a marshal and a screwdriver and opened up the machines. They had rigged from the straight Republican lever a wire over to the Democrats. If you pulled the Republican lever, it would vote straight Democrat. She went throughout the warehouse unscrewing the machines and changing them. The county judge was furious. He was not elected after that.

ESTHER BUCKLEY, LAREDO

All of the hoodwinks of voting, we had them. There was the folded ballot, where a guy would come and ask for a ballot and have a folded ballot in his pocket. The folded ballot was voted. He would drop the folded ballot in the ballot box and take the new one and put it in his pocket for the next voter. The trick with the string. Strings were cut the length of the ballot. They would line them up to the side of the ballot and tie knots on the squares where they were to vote. All of these things that they would do because the people were illiterate in many cases. In a lot of cases, we knew they would come up from Mexico. In one of the 1972 elections, there was a truck that had forty people in it. This truck would drive up to a polling place. They would get out of the truck and get their voting cards, go in to vote, come back, and the driver would pick up the voting cards. We could never prove corruption.

One of the things that helped a lot is when we could pay poll watchers. It made them [*the Democrats*] nervous. We have documented something like 500 cases of things that they did. Like a voter would come in and they would say, "What is your name?" "Juan Gonzales." "Oh, which Juan Gonzales are you? The one that lives at 1302 or the one that lives at 101? Oh, 101." Of course it wasn't him. There'll be a Juan Gonzalez or Juan Rodriguez in every single polling place. They never ever asked for I.D.

ANNE SHEPARD, VICTORIA & HARLINGEN

In 1984, I was running ballot security in the state. We called all of the Republican County chairmen to make sure that all of their precinct chairmen were on target and knew exactly what they were supposed to do during the election. One part was the legal side. You have your attorneys lined up with what to do in the event of irregularities. Then we had the organization side of it. The poll watchers had to be organized and trained.

In my opinion, most people didn't want to break the law. They just didn't know the law. In some cases, they had been election judges for years. They just didn't know the law, and we just had to help them out. Then there was intimidation. If you have a voting booth in someone's garage or a volunteer fire station and you go in and say "I want to vote Republican," and the Democrat county chairman is sitting there looking at you, and they say, "You want to do what? Vote in the Republican primary? You have to walk through five of us here and then go to the back of the room." It would be intimidating. There were pictures taken. That was tough. Both parties have frankly done a better job of letting their election judges know what the laws are.

MARION COLEMAN, PASADENA

In the 1960 Nixon race we had poll watchers because there were no Republican judges. I had canvassed every member of my precinct. Every single door I went to, whether they were registered or not, and asked for support, even a dollar, or gave literature. On Election Day, all of a sudden, this bus load drove up. All black people. They went to the voting booths and were instructed, "See that lever? Just pull that." I went up and said to the election judge, "I have to challenge this because these people do not live in this precinct." "How do you know that, young lady?" Then I opened up my portfolio and said, "I canvassed every one of these houses, and there is not one black person living in Pasadena, never mind my precinct." He said, "Well, honey, I don't want to disappoint you; we just love you to death. We wish you were a Democrat." He said, "We have this election already won. Right here in Texas and in Illinois." No sooner had they left than another bus load drove up, and they all voted a straight Democratic ticket. That was shocking to me. Of course, I took all of this down, but it didn't mean anything. I know that it sounds unbelievable, but I witnessed it.

FRAN ATKINSON, LUFKIN & SAN ANTONIO

Our women's club studied the Texas election code ad nauseum. We wanted to get poll watchers because we could not get clerks appointed by the commissioners court, which were all Democrats. So the only way we could get our people into the polls was to appoint poll watchers. I learned it so thoroughly that I could train poll watchers, and I did, frequently in other counties. Angelina County was written up in 1960 for voter fraud. There were boxes that came in doubled in votes. There were all sorts of shenanigans. There were indictments. *Look* magazine, which was popular at the time, was one of the magazines that mentioned Angelina County along with Cook County in Illinois as high points of voter fraud. The only way you can cure that is to have both parties represented at an election.

The poll watchers were there to observe and report any wrongdoing or ask the judge to correct it on the spot. You had to know many points in the law. For instance, a judge is not allowed to pick up a ballot and hand it to a voter. The voter picks up his own ballot. They used to just stand there handing them out like a deck of cards. I'm not saying that there was anything wrong, but the potential was there to hand out pre-marked ballots for people to cast. In those days, you were not allowed to carry a list of who you were going to vote for into the polls. Husband and wife could not vote in the same booth. I had one old fellow tell me one time, "Well, why not? We sleep together." And I said, "Mister, I didn't write the law, the Democrats did." "Oh, it's bound to be a good law then," he said. We had one precinct where there was a lot of suspicious nonsense going on. So we put five poll watchers on duty, the absolute limit of what we could put in, and the judge never came back. It was not our intent to run her out. It was our intent to make it clear to her that we expected an aboveboard election.

LIBBA BARNES, SAN ANTONIO

I went to poll watching school. Arthur Seeligson and Fred Wright and I went to this precinct way on the West Side. It was when Lyndon Johnson ran against Barry Goldwater. Arthur Seeligson had sent out all of these registered letters to everyone in the precinct. They came back no such address, no such person, a variety of reasons. So when these people would come to vote we knew that they were not legal voters, and we would challenge them right there. The election judge herself was saying in Spanish when they went in, "Pull the left lever." She called Democratic head-quarters, and their lawyer told us that if we caused any more trouble he was going to throw us in jail. When we left at eight o'clock that night, a cheer went up.

GAIL WATERFIELD, CANADIAN

We were beginning to get a little more professional and a little more organized in Hemphill County. Francie Cody called up one day and said, "You have got to be a poll watcher." I hate to admit this—I said, "What is a poll watcher?" She told me, and I said, "Well, Francie, that's like telling people you don't trust what they're doing." She said, "It is not. You need to get down there and get yourself registered and your papers turned in to be a poll watcher." I said, "Okay, Francie, I'll go do that." The morning I had to go down, I was actually trembling. I thought these are all my friends. I am here as a poll watcher, pretending to watch for something to be done wrong. I spent the whole day and learned a bunch. I found out that day the only way you are going to learn the ropes is to climb them. From that year on, I had poll watchers at every single election. It was no big deal.

Transition between Primary and General Elections

How do you bring the campaign volunteers together behind the primary winner so you can win the election in November?

FLORENCE NEUMEYER, HOUSTON

The first thing is winning over the opponents to endorse the winner. If they come out and endorse, then usually their volunteers and supporters will take the lead from that. Now, sometimes they don't endorse and let everybody choose for themselves. Sometimes the winner lets it been known that it is time to close ranks and continues to try and win those people because you don't always know who they are.

You just have to put your best foot forward. You find out who the key players are. The candidate goes to them and says, "You know, I would like your support. Tell me what can I do. Tell me why you chose my opponent over me. What can I do to convince you I am really the person that you can support now?" Chipping away at it. Of course, at your first speech, the very night of the election, you reach out to everybody that supported the other candidates and say, "Now I want your support."

What Makes Campaigns Fail?

FLORENCE NEUMEYER, HOUSTON

A lot of things can make a campaign fail. Lack of enough funds to get your message out. Candidates do have to have the right balance of money, commitment, and knowledge of the electorate. They can fail due to mismanagement of volunteers, bad campaign management, or lack of a candidate that is really dedicated.

A lot of times candidates would be great and could be elected, but they are a bit lazy or get shy about mixing with people.

Bad strategy might be a better way to put it. It doesn't have to mean that it is the campaign manager. It can be the candidate's advisory committee. The whole committee can take the wrong stance. For example, they run a campaign like they are running for something in Washington and they are really running for the school board. They never really get down on the local level where the people are. Candidates can side on the wrong issues. Their message is not quite right. They don't choose the right management of volunteers, supporters, and information that they pick up from the grassroots. You would be surprised how many people who run for office really are reluctant to mix with the average Joe in a precinct. Sometimes people are telling candidates a certain thing is wrong or they are concerned about an issue, and candidates don't pay attention. If you go to several civic club meetings and you hear the same thing, then maybe you just need to do something with that information in those precincts. You really have to be in tune to what you are hearing.

Some candidates choose the wrong campaign to get in. That is one of the biggest things. They are set up for a fall from the beginning. We had people that would file against Congressman Bill Archer. You can build up name I.D. for something in the future knowing that you can't win. But in this case, you can make people mad just because you file against someone that they love and respect so much. Are you going to win friends and influence people or make people mad so that they are never going to forgive you? Sometimes you have a lot of good people running in the same race. Then it gets down to who can run a well-funded campaign, choose the right issues, and be articulate in conveying to the public what their concerns are and what they are going to do about them. So it can be choosing the wrong race at the wrong time.

In the general election, any number of things can happen. Those failures come from higher up. For example, when [*Republican gubernatorial candidate*] Clayton Williams made the remark that he made [*a joke about rape*], I was doing a state rep race and we picked it up on the phone bank. My guy was an incumbent, and he had won in a special election. It was a slightly Democratic district, which was always difficult to overcome. Our guy was very popular. We were going great guns. When that statement was made, we began to hear from the women on the phone bank, "I am voting for the woman"—meaning Ann Richards—"and I am voting straight." We knew in our district that if they turned out and stuck to that attitude our guy was done. It wasn't anything to do with him because he had a good record and was well liked and supported by a number of Democrats. If we had had a million dollars, we couldn't have done anything.

Staying Motivated in the Face of Defeat

FLO KAMPMANN CRICHTON, SAN ANTONIO

Victories, I have discovered, were not achieved or accomplished. They were built step by tiny step. Just don't leave a stone unturned. Take every opportunity you can.

VERA CARHART, RICHARDSON & HOUSTON

I went to Del Rio one time when Tom Loeffler was running [*for Congress*]. It was a night meeting and involved a lot of men. They were upset because Tom had not been there. I said, "Well, I know he is coming, but don't expect candidates to spend all of their time here, and don't be upset when I tell you why. They have to go where the votes are. You just told me how many votes you have here. Set goals and start working to develop the potential you have." I quoted some election where a Republican lost by half of a percent, which equated to so many votes. I said, "If Del Rio, El Paso, and some other towns could have all contributed about twenty more votes, we would have won those elections. So if you turn out a thousand more votes than what you normally have, you are making a big contribution toward electing Tom Loeffler and Bill Clements." Several of the men came to me after the meeting and said, "Thank you. You said something that makes sense. I have never thought about it that way."

ANNE BERGMAN, WEATHERFORD

Shirley Green said one time, "We all worked so hard back in the years when we didn't expect to win but we wanted to turn out our vote." If we got 47 percent of the vote, we thought we won because we turned out our vote. We'd sit around after the elections in this little county and just go over those votes and all of the voter I.D. calls. We'd say, "Well, we turned out our vote. That's all we can do."

ANN WALLACE, FORT WORTH & AUSTIN

We lost so many times. You would just think, "I'm not going to do this anymore." But then here would come a good candidate, and you'd think, "I'm going to give it one more good try." We lost so many more than we won. All and all you made a lot of good friends that you still have. It's kind of like the old dalmatian dog at the firehouse—when the bell rings you get up, shake yourself off, and get ready to go again.

CHAPTER 17

Money

"Money could not have been all-important, thank goodness, or the
Republicans never would have won."   —ANNE ARMSTRONG

*P*olitics used to be a low-budget endeavor, but as campaigns
became more sophisticated and the role of the media grew so
did the need for money. Early on, volunteers conducted low-key
fundraising efforts to pay their candidates' expenses and buy a
few ads. An effort was also made to collect as little as five dollars
from as many people as possible in the hope that this would raise
the stakes for those individuals and motivate them to go vote on
Election Day.

As expenses grew, so did the magnitude of the fundraising
effort. Women planned events, asked for money, and followed
up, in many cases developing an admirable list of contacts. They
learned to ask for a lot of money from those with a lot of money.
Throwing a fundraiser became an art—in planning a party,
getting the word out, generating enthusiasm, and collecting the
money. The state party created the Key Republican program to
support its operations. State Republican Executive Committee
members and others were expected to raise $1,000 each year.
Some women also became prominent national fundraisers.

Women worked hard to learn to ask for money. Some thought
they did not have the personality or the contacts to be successful.
Developing a system that worked for them personally and following
through with it became the key to success. Overcoming the fear of
rejection was sometimes the least of their fundraising problems.
Most members of the business community did not find it politically
expedient to give to Republicans, and it was not unusual for donors

to remain anonymous for fear of retaliation from the Democratic machine. Once people were persuaded by philosophical appeals and convinced of the potential impact of their contributions, wallets started opening and money came into the Republican Party and Republican campaigns.

Role of Money in Politics

The Early Years

FLO KAMPMANN CRICHTON, SAN ANTONIO

Fundraising was confined to a few occasions. When you talk about dollars then and dollars now, it's just unbelievable. We had a loyal bunch of small givers. People didn't mind sending five or ten dollars. We worked with very little money. When John Tower was first running [*for Senate*], we ran that campaign on a shoestring. Probably the whole statewide effort cost $200,000.

KATHRYN McDANIEL, BORGER

Campaigns didn't cost as much as they do now because so much of the campaign was done on a volunteer basis. For example, instead of having to run newspaper ads or television ads people would just go door-to-door and ask everybody on their street to vote for that candidate. Many times that was more effective but took time not money.

ANNE ARMSTRONG, ARMSTRONG

Money could not have been all-important, thank goodness, or the Republicans never would have won. It's hard to remember now that the Democratic Party was weak except for labor. Labor was never as strong in Texas as, say, in Michigan or Pennsylvania although labor money flowed in here at times when there were important races. The Democrats had a pretty good noose around most of the money in those days because at that point it was largely a conservative party. The main campaign cry of the conservative

MONEY

377

wing of the Democratic Party was, if you vote for those Republicans they are never going to win and you're going to put in the Ralph Yarboroughs and the labor lovers. Very rarely were we able to keep up financially with the Democratic candidate. Money was not all-important but as Phil Gramm said in the 1996 presidential election, "Money is the mother's milk of politics." We made up for the money we didn't have in enthusiasm and drive. We really had a feeling of mission. Women were much more apt to be at home. They were the civic backbone of the small towns and the big cities. They turned a lot of that effort to the Republicans and to the Republican Party.

LIZ GHRIST, HOUSTON

Media is very, very expensive. It has become a major business. When we first started, everyone volunteered. Someone was a research person—that was a volunteer. Someone was an administrative assistant that handled all of the correspondence and the calendar—that was a volunteer. Now, we pay people to do all that. In order to have any hope, you hire "the best people." The best people are identified by their previous successes. You have to set up the office, the staff, the equipment, the technology. Raising money becomes paramount. A candidate for Senate now has to raise $10,000 a day in order to plan for his reelection. Not only do they have to raise money but they have to spend it effectively.

How can you be an effective fundraiser but not leave anyone expecting favors?

What I fall back on in every bit of fundraising that I do is the personal philosophy of the candidate or the party that I am raising the money for. There are so many people who give money in this community with no strings attached. They just want the person that they support to be elected and do a good job. I know that is not true universally. There are those who every time they pick up the phone and call they want a response. Every time they want a meeting or special favor they expect to be handled. They are money givers, too. The person that is the recipient of the money has to learn how to handle that, to not offend, and to not violate his personal convictions.

JUDY JONES MATTHEWS, ABILENE

The way things are now money is 75 percent of it. Sweat equity is important, but money buys the publicity. That's what counts. That's what they all tell me anyway. I never thought of money as being as necessary to politics in the early days. It has grown exponentially in the last few years. Too much really.

RITA PALM, FORT WORTH

In those days, fundraising was not done by third parties. It was usually the candidate himself or a friend of the candidate or a friend of yours. Not many people had that kind of money or thought it was politically expedient to give money. You had contractors that wanted state contracts, and there were a few big boys. But most fundraising was much more personal. When Bush ran for the Senate in 1964, you would go to a party and people would just hand you a check. You would just make kind of a slight comment like, "George is really doing a good job. I hope you can find some change for him." It was really low-key.

JANE JUETT, AMARILLO

It is important to get funds whether it's big dollars or little dollars. If somebody donates even five dollars to the candidate, they are probably going to vote for him. They want to protect their investment. So I think that fundraising is good.

GLENNA McCORD, DALLAS

We never had enough money! When John Tower ran the first time, it was the funniest operation, as I look back. The women made all of the yard signs. Stuart Tears was precinct chairman. He and his wife, Fran, both worked so hard in the Party. There is nothing those two wouldn't do to help. Fran was a public school art teacher. Stu built two silk screen frames for us. We put these silk screens in the garage out back of the headquarters. The women would go out there during the day and make the signs. The men would come at night and nail them on the stakes and get them distributed.

Can't Do It without Money

LOU TOWER, WICHITA FALLS & DALLAS

You can't do without money. So you have to get people to believe in you enough to put some money into the campaign. Campaigns just got wild as far as what they cost.

ILLA CLEMENT, KINGSVILLE

When you are giving money to the Party to help them get a person elected, it's not really for self-dealing. You want that person elected because the country needs them whether it's the president or a state office. We are lucky that we are a free country and can have a choice in an election.

You need an organization that helps people get elected. It takes money, like anything else. If you are building anything, whether a company, a store, or a school, it takes money. People may think it's terrible that money makes a difference in an election, but that's life. Sex makes a difference in marriage. You are not going to change some things.

LINDA UNDERWOOD, HOUSTON

We used to say, it takes three things to win an election. Number 1 is money. Number 2 is money. Number 3 is money. It was true then, and it is true today. Money bought exposure—travel, television, and billboards. Now it is an electronic age but then it was billboards, yard signs, and walking a precinct. People wanted to meet the candidate or speak with somebody. This is what women did more than anything. They were advocates who were going out and talking to people and telling them about the candidates. The importance of human contact should never be diminished. You can't just do it by television.

MARTHA WEISEND, DALLAS

You don't get there from here unless you get on TV. Anything that has to do with print and electronic media is expensive. There is some earned media [*free*], but in relationship to every bit of earned media you get you have to pay big bucks. It takes money for travel, bumper stickers, yard signs, postage, and staff. If you're running statewide in Texas, you need an airplane because it is such a vast state. It gets expensive to run in Texas. It takes both money and volunteers. Televisions do not vote. They certainly will carry the message, but once they have, your message is dead unless somebody picks up on it. So when I see a campaign without people there on a daily basis who believe in the candidate, I'm very afraid. Candidates need people. It's where the enthusiasm is, and it's where the vote is.

DEBORAH BELL, ABILENE

Fundraising is important for a city. Abilene was known years ago as not giving money. Yes, they would vote Republican. I am not saying that candidates look only at that because at the same time you have got issues, but you need to show that you are working to contribute your part.

Who Is Effective and Why

Were there many women involved in fundraising in the early years?

PETER O'DONNELL, DALLAS

Not very many. There were a few and Flo Kampmann Crichton was one and she was awfully good at it. By and large, they weren't. You don't get a big, long line of people standing at your door asking to raise money. We had to recruit people to do it. You could ask them, and they would say, "Oh, I will work, but I'm not any good at raising money." It was hard to recruit them to do it. You can't make them. It is all volunteer. We had our needs, so we had to just keep moving and find someone who was able and wanted to do it. There were a few. In San Antonio in addition to Flo, Irene Cox Wischer was effective, but they were few and far between. There are more than there used to be. Nancy Brinker is a terrific fundraiser today.

Why was Flo a good fundraiser?

In the first place, she could make a substantial contribution herself and that is important. She was charming and persuasive.

GWEN PHARO, DALLAS

I was privileged to sit in on the Saturday morning Marching and Chowder Society. I was included in that as was Rita Clements and I believe Dale Wigley and Bobbie Biggart. There you were given a sounding board. I saw that the people who either contributed money or could raise money had a louder voice than people who didn't involve themselves in fundraising. I decided I could become a good fundraiser. I did.

ELLIE SELIG, SEGUIN

You have to work very hard to get that inside track. Don't misunderstand me, I don't think everything that was accomplished cost money to get there. I think it helps. Money is a way of getting into the inside of politics. If you can do that, you can talk to somebody that knew somebody. You got a little higher up. You could get an invitation to a party. It sounds hokey.

Just Do It

FLO KAMPMANN CRICHTON, SAN ANTONIO

Fundraising is something that I learned. When you first get involved in politics at age twenty-one, you are so starry-eyed and think everything is going to work. Then I discovered the most important and first lesson of politics is that just being right doesn't necessarily mean you're going to win.

You have to figure out the way you do it best. Whether it is writing letters or going to see people, the main thing is to do it. Most fundraising committees are a lot of talk. They could talk about how they were going to do something or how something should be done, but the point is they never did it. So you had to get behind them and say, we have got a deadline on this. We have got to raise so much money because every campaign has a budget.

JUANDELLE LACY, MIDLAND

All women have to do is ask, and if they say no you can't fall off the ground floor. Women can raise money as easily as men. If you really and truly want big contributions you go to the person eye to eye. If possible, the candidate should go. A lot of candidates are reluctant. It is not easy to raise funds. It is probably one of the most difficult things to do. Women are prone to say, "I just can't ask for money." It's no worse than asking for something else. That's a cop-out as far as I am concerned.

Know Your Target

LIBBA BARNES, SAN ANTONIO

I think I have the reputation that, if I have not given, I'm not going to ask you to give. I knew on a very personal basis a lot of these people. It got there toward the end they'd see me coming and say, "Now what do you want money for? That's all you want." After a while, you get tired of doing that because people think, "Do you really like me for me or is it because you know I'm going to give you some money?" I really limited myself to whom I would go ask for money, and they would know that I had checked the candidates out.

Strangely enough, not a lot of people like to do it. Working with Joci Straus made me realize that there was a real need because we did not have any strong men back then. We did not have people like Red McCombs, Lowery Mays, and Gene Ames. Raising the money was left to us to do.

LIZ GHRIST, HOUSTON

You have to know your case. You have to get in to see the right person to present your case. Sometimes you have to convince people that they feel the way you know they feel, but most often they are ready and you just have to ask. When you bring closure, you get out of there. It is business. It is a consistent, organized campaign you put yourself on to get the job done. There is nothing grandiose about it. It is just hard work.

BARBARA BANKER, SAN ANTONIO

It takes time and it takes persistence. It's just like a dog with a bone. You can not give up. Once I identify a little softening that you might consider a contribution, then I'll call you tomorrow. I will stand in that door to keep you from going out if I have not had the opportunity to tell you what I came to tell you. I am assertive in that respect. It takes a determination that is almost akin to rudeness, but you can't open people's minds for them. You have to get them to a point where they're receptive to listen. That's when you've got to know what you're talking about. You can't just sluff it off saying, "Oh, he's a great candidate and he's a friend of mine." You have to spend time to know what their platform is or where they stand on issues. Friends and business associates say that when Barbara Banker calls for money it is not "if" but "when and how much?"

The first thing I try to do is to figure out a pocketbook issue that they support because you're only going to get a person's attention for a very finite amount of time. You want to talk to them about an issue that they are going to get excited about.

HALLY CLEMENTS, VICTORIA

I have more nerve than the law allows. I enjoy calling people up and persuading them to give to a good candidate. I do not enjoy working with any professional fundraisers. I much prefer volunteers. Victoria is small and you also get the "you scratch my back and I scratch your back" sort of thing. Truly, it is a round-robin sort of a situation. I think that it is important if you want to be a fundraiser that you go to these public functions and be seen and get to know people by their first names.

To be a good fundraiser, you need a bunch of easy bullshit. Make a person feel comfortable even if he is not going to give anything. Make it a pleasant experience. Let's forget this business about idealism. People think of the pocketbook first. The men do. Education is always a safe bet. Mainly, try and stay away from anything controversial. You don't want to get in any type of argument with people.

Match Them

KATIE SEEWALD, AMARILLO

In 1962, Dr. Tom Duke and I were co-chairmen of the Jack Cox [*gubernatorial*] campaign. Tom was a very busy doctor so I did a good deal of the work. I raised a lot of money just by going in and staring people in the face and saying, "Look, I've given a thousand dollars. You're giving a thousand dollars." I knew that was the way that Johnny O'Brien did it. He was our chief fundraiser for the Party. One day the president of the bank called and said, "I hate to tell you, but the Cox account is overdrawn." I said, "It is not." He had me mixed up with one of the Democratic candidates. So I said, "Well, I just feel so bad that I think you're going to have to give me a big contribution for the campaign to make up for this." So he did. I used every angle.

SHIRLEY GREEN, AUSTIN & SAN ANTONIO

In my experience, most of the women who were successful in raising money were of a social or economic class themselves that they could lean on their friends who had money and raise money as much through personal friendship and loyalty as through any real commitment to the Republicans. Certainly in the early days that was true. We had some very good women fundraisers, not many but there were some.

BECKY CORNELL, SAN ANGELO

Some friends were very generous when I had to ask them for money. Sometimes the businessmen who have helped one another were able to raise more money than a volunteer. That is very effective, certainly more so than the volunteer saying, "We would love it if you would give us $10,000." I told one person how much I had given, and they gave that, too. I thought, "Wow, this is great."

Don't Be Afraid

PENNY BUTLER, HOUSTON

A good fundraiser is not afraid to ask. You have to ask and then follow up quickly and say thank you. A person just wants to be acknowledged. Enthusiasm and a lot of persistence help. Unless you ask, you will never know. The worst they can say is no. That happens a lot.

SYLVIA NUGENT, DALLAS & AMARILLO

People are afraid of fundraising. Everybody thinks that fundraising is some magic. Fundraising is just work. It is very simple. You identify your universe. You contact them by letter and then you contact them in person. You make sure that the best person asks them. Then you collect the money. Then you have the party.

Believe in It

SALLY McKENZIE, DALLAS

I've been on the national finance committee and the state finance committee for just about everybody. I always said, "I'm not a good political fundraiser, but I can raise money for George Bush until the world looks level." You can do it if you believe in somebody.

GWEN PHARO, DALLAS

I learned to go ask for money for candidates by getting it in my head that this money was not for my personal gain. It was for a greater cause. I really believed in what we were trying to do, which was to give the people of Texas a choice politically and to get rid of the back-room deals and to force the Democrats to have to work to maintain their party. If something isn't for your personal gain, it makes it a whole lot easier to beg. They would say, "Give her what she wants so she will get out of here."

JUDY JONES MATTHEWS, ABILENE

Good fundraisers like people. They have a light touch. I am convinced that people aren't good fundraisers unless they are doing it for something they really believe in. I do not think people who raise money professionally are nearly as effective.

JOCI STRAUS, SAN ANTONIO

Joe and I had Desmond Barry, the candidate for lieutenant governor in 1962, to dinner. We both thought, "Wow, this guy is worth working for." I put together a luncheon on the telephone and talked to every single person that came. We had 150 people. He gave such a good talk that people were just mind-boggled. I got my finance chairman from that luncheon. We got free headquarters downtown. We raised so much money that we had more money than we could use. We went door-to-door. Got $100 here, $100 there. If I came home without $1,000 a day, I had a bad day.

I walked down the street and attacked a building. I called ahead, and I knew who was in each building. I said, "Can I come by and see you?" It was pretty scary the first time. My palms were really perspiring, and I was really nervous because I had never asked somebody for money before. But if you believe in something, you can do anything. I believed in this person. So it wasn't so painful after the first day or two. It became kind of fun.

Fundraising Methods

Candidates Raising Money Themselves

JANELLE McARTHUR, SAN ANTONIO

One of the things Joci Straus and I would do when Senator Tower came to San Antonio was meet at her house and dial for dollars. I'd get the phone number and Joci would say, "All right, Senator, this is a man that you met thirty-five years ago. He was the best man at your wedding." You know, that kind of thing because the Senator was not good at names. When he walked into a crowd, he always felt like someone wanted something. They did. This is how we would get him to make phone calls.

BARBARA BANKER, SAN ANTONIO

Candidates sometimes show weakness when they make calls because sometimes people perceive that they are getting panicky that the money is not coming in. So they are sitting down and dialing the phone themselves. I've had calls from people and wondered, "Why are you calling me? Are you out of money?"

You have been an effective fundraiser. What advice would you give to candidates, both men and women, on how to develop a good fundraising effort?

KAY BAILEY HUTCHISON, HOUSTON & DALLAS

I did different things according to where I was positioned in a particular race. When I ran for the legislature, my fundraising was very grassroots oriented with small fundraisers. Women were very instrumental in helping me with little donations. I also gave the impression that I was going to win. I was able to show the numbers of people in the district that were Republican. I had six opponents in the Republican primary, so I had to get through that first. But I looked like a winner. I think that is very important in fundraising. I was supported by businesspeople. As I went up the ladder and ran for Senate, I was at a disadvantage in fundraising because I was running against an incumbent Democrat and two incumbent Republican congressmen. All of the big money went to them. I was unknown in Washington, and none of the PACs [*Political Action Committees*] or business groups supported me. So I was very grassroots oriented in my Senate campaign. I was able to raise about a million dollars in the first race with people I had worked with who knew me and thought that I had a good chance to win and that I would be the right candidate for the Republican

Party. I put together a good solid team of men and women in that race. Once you are an incumbent, people think you're going to win so it makes it easier.

Dialing for Dollars

LINDA UNDERWOOD, HOUSTON

It seems like every time I called and said, "This is Linda Underwood in [*National Committeeman*] Albert Fay's office," I was calling for money. I was so naive at the time. I would call anyone. I will never forget in Des Barry's campaign [*for lieutenant governor*] they had such a hard time raising money. They would put a list in front of me, and I would just go down the list and call people in Houston. I raised a lot of money because I didn't know it couldn't be done. People were just amazed that I had no fear. Albert Fay would say, "You call. You get more money than I do."

ISABEL GRAY, PASADENA

One time my husband, Fred, was out of town when he was precinct chairman. He was supposed to raise so much money. I got on the phone, and I raised more money than he did. He would call two or three of his old pals. They would give him the money, and he would turn it in. Well, I called everyone that voted and asked them for money. I just asked them for whatever they could afford $1 or $15. Some sent $50. It was not big money, but I raised it.

So We Need to Throw a Fundraiser

POLLY SOWELL, MCALLEN & AUSTIN

I realized that we had to raise some money. I had a friend from McAllen, Kay Wharton, who had actually worked in Washington and was a Republican. She said to call Peter O'Donnell in Dallas—it was before he was state chairman—and she gave me his number. He said, "Yes, I'll be glad to come down and help." He told me exactly what to do. I needed to get somebody's house, invite people to come, and serve dinner. He would come down and talk to them about money. So I did everything just like he told me. I asked Marian and Forest Finch, who had a nice pretty new house, if we could use their house. I called people. The women stayed in the kitchen. We cooked. Even me. I was the one who organized the whole damn thing, invited the men, got them all there, did the whole thing, but I stayed in the kitchen with the women while Peter talked to the men about giving money. Nobody thought a thing about it.

When did women get out of the kitchen?

Shortly thereafter. It was all gradual, an evolutionary thing.

JAYNE HARRIS, SAN ANTONIO

Some fundraisers fail because they put too much into them. At a lot of the fundraisers that I have done, the hosts furnished the food. Our costs were wine, invitations, and postage. When you do not have that situation, you try and go to the simplicity of it. If you get into dinners and things like that, you get into a lot of money. If you do it with finger food from five to seven o'clock and catch people going home, you can have something very nice. The presentation is everything in my book.

I have seen fundraisers that are total busts. It is poor planning and in some instances it is the candidate. It takes in-depth planning right down to who's going to work your table. You have the name tags ready. You make it as efficient and as lively as you can. I am not talking about giddy stuff. If you have someone who knows the guests when they come in, greet them by name. Being real is very important. People know when you are not real. They pick up on it in a minute.

MARY BODGER, CORPUS CHRISTI

We held the Pachyderm Polka. A union leader called me and said he was upset because we hired a nonunion band. I said that was too bad because that was the price and the kind of band we wanted. He said, "We just may come out there and picket you." I said, "Please do. It would help us." But he didn't do it. That dance was a huge success.

PAULINE CUSACK, HOUSTON & WILLOW CITY

In 1970, Bill Archer asked me if I would be special events chairman, which was for fundraising. At that time, he was a state rep. That was a wonderful job. One of our events was a box supper out in the Sharpstown area and Senator Goldwater came in. We charged twenty-five dollars per person. The place was full. There were other events along the way. In 1972, it was kind of a repeat of the same thing. We didn't have as much fundraising then because it wasn't as needed. He was taking something like 80 percent of the vote in those days. Bill was elected [*to Congress*] in 1970. It was not until 1994 that he became chairman of the House Ways and Means Committee. Had I thought "I am doing this because someday he is going to be chairman of ways and means" I would have worked even harder than I did. I just wanted to get him into office because I trusted him.

Key Republicans

MARY JESTER, DALLAS

When Peter O'Donnell was state chairman, he made all of the people on the state committee sign notes for $1,000. Sure enough they did. They all raised their $1,000 to pay off their notes and become Key Republicans. We would use any way to get the money.

POLLY SOWELL, McALLEN & AUSTIN

When I got elected to the SREC, our state chairman was Peter O'Donnell. He made us all sign a pledge that we would raise $1,000. I thought I would die! A thousand dollars was a lot of money. I thought, "What in the world am I going to do?" I worried about it for six months. I'd wake up in the middle of the night in a cold sweat. What if my husband finds out that I have signed this pledge? What if I can't raise the money? I was just beside myself. I finally decided that I would just have to go try. There was only one person I knew who had $1,000 and might even remotely consider giving it to the Republican Party. I circled the block around his office about ten times trying to get up the courage to go in and ask him. Finally I did. Quivering I said, "I'm here to ask if you would give the Republican Party $1,000." He said, "Sure. How do I make the check out?" I almost fell out of my chair!

LIBBA BARNES, SAN ANTONIO

When Joci Straus and I were working together, we would go downtown and call on ten or fifteen different people. Joci would say, "We're coming with our hands out. We want a little contribution for the Republican Party of Texas." She was raising her Key. Finally, she turned to me and said, "Now we've raised my Key, we'll start on yours." I came home and I thought, that's hard work for $1,000. So I picked up the phone, and Tim Hixson was the first person I called. I said, "Tim, I'd like for you to give me $1,000 for the Republican Party of Texas." He said, "When do you want the check?" I got my Key before Joci got hers because I went down and got that check right then and sent it in.

Then, of course, you get so paranoid about your list. You really don't want anybody else calling on your people. Well, that didn't last for very long. Ace Mallory was another one of my donors. All of a sudden, I saw that Diane Rath had a Key on her lapel. I thought, "How in the world did she get that?" Well, when I called Ace, Diane had gotten there before I did. I said, "Where is your loyalty?" He said, "Well, it's all going to the same place." It is but it isn't.

THEO WICKERSHAM, SAN ANTONIO

Rejection doesn't bother me. All they can do is say no. One of my old mentors years ago back in the late '60s or early '70s taught me one of the things that works best. If you tell somebody how you are going to use the money, they will help you. For example, "we're going to use $300 for a mail-out" or "2000 signs cost so many thousands of dollars." You always ask for a little bit more than it takes. When I was on the SREC, George Strake would say you must raise so much money per year. He used to tell this story at our meetings. "You know we have got to raise this money. Why not do what Theo does? She sends me these tacky $15 and $25 checks every month." I was getting them from widows on fixed incomes. I'd tell them that I was on the SREC and we raise so much money per year. I sent a copy of my quarterly report to the people who had contributed for that quarter. I circled things that their money helped buy. By getting people involved, they're going to trust you and believe in you and your candidates.

BETTY STERQUELL, AMARILLO

I had trouble because when I volunteered, they would hand me the $25 and $50 contributors. You have to call a lot of contacts to raise $1,000. I would rather they give me the $100 cards because it is just as easy to ask somebody for $100 as it is for $10. I had to overcome that. In that phase of my life, I couldn't contribute $1,000 for a Key. I earned mine.

Letter Writing

FLO KAMPMANN CRICHTON, SAN ANTONIO

For me, letter writing is the most effective. The people that you want to reach, their time is fairly valuable. You have got to have respect for other people's time. So rather than make a phone call or ask if you can come by and visit, they've got something on paper and they can look at it and read it and decide what they want to do. Of course, you can have a follow-up phone call. But I believe in giving people time to think about it. That's not everybody's way of doing it.

Make fundraising letters short and personal, and write a little extra P. S. at the bottom. It takes a lot of work, but it is worth it. You simply just spell it out. Generally, when you have a committee, you divide up the names and people take people they know best. It's done a thousand different ways.

Candidate Fundraisers

PATTILOU DAWKINS, AMARILLO

Emmy O'Brien organized "Babysitters for Ike." We would babysit for people. The money they paid us, we gave to the Eisenhower headquarters. Well, they wanted to support Eisenhower and gave us a lot of money—certainly more than we were worth. We spoiled the kids. We would take them to the country club and feed them under their parents' names on the country club tab. Yet they still had us back.

SURRENDEN ANGLY, AUSTIN

When my husband ran for the legislature, we raised money mostly by direct mail. From the very get-go, he had a lot of parties at private homes. Toward the very end of the campaign, he bought thirty minutes of television. He had a call in question-and-answer show. That night was our biggest campaign contributors' party. He would leave the station and come to the big donors' party.

MARTHA CROWLEY, DALLAS

We did "Crowley Follies." It was mostly publicity. I don't know whether we raised any money or not. It was a lot of fun. Frank and his niece Peggy were really good at song parodies. They would use familiar show tunes, like "Big Spenders" and "The Country Needs a Man Like Me." We would get a hall with a stage. Kitty Harrington was the director of so many of them. A couple of them turned out to be really pretty good shows. In fact, the press club came down there. It's a shame that I had to get so old before I realized I was such a good chorus girl.

PAT JACOBSON, FORT WORTH

I ended up doing a Wayne Newton concert to raise money for Ronald Reagan. That is the hardest thing I have ever done. We sold tickets at various amounts, like $10 tickets for up in the balcony and $25 and $50 tickets and then up to $500. The difficult part of it was Ronald Reagan was there, the national press was there, but we were not sure the people would show up. I looked out at the crowd in the Rogers Coliseum and said a prayer of thanks. It was standing room only. It's a terribly frightening thing. I later called [*Reagan advisor*] Mike Deaver, and I said, "Don't you ever ask me to do a concert again."

Personal Effort

MARJORIE ARSHT, HOUSTON

You're not involved unless you're interested, and you're not interested unless you're involved. Writing a check is a way to get someone involved.

They credit me with being the originator of the neighbor-to-neighbor drive because in the '50s, [*party activists*] Albert Fay and Dudley Sharp and Ted Law had funded the Party. I kept saying, "Get people to give you a dollar." Of course, it would spread out the Party and bring people in. If they are going to give you a dollar, they are going to vote. When George Bush became county chairman, he said that he wanted everyone in the Party.

CAROL REED, DALLAS

I raised money for Senator John Tower. Tower and Fred Agnich [*state representative and national committeeman*] used to just take great joy in sending me places that no one else would go. I didn't know it. Here I am twenty-nine or thirty and kind of cute back then. They would just howl, I know. They would send me over to get money out of Joe Staley. He was drinking a lot. Well, so was everybody. I would call Joe and say, "It is that time of the year to make your contribution to the Senator." He'd say, "Great, meet me for lunch at the Cipango," which was across the street from where the Mansion is now. It was "the" private club in Dallas— "the place." So I'd show up at lunch and at four o'clock in the afternoon I would crawl out of the place with a check. Women's groups would just have a heart attack. But this was all part of the dance. I thought there was no way I could make it through another lunch with those guys.

Tower and Agnich would say, "You go see Herb Schiff." They used to love this—you don't have to do this to me but once. I'm pretty bright. But then it got to the point where I kind of enjoyed it. Herb Schiff, he was oil and gas; he is now dead. The first time they ever sent me to Herb's office they said, "Now, Herb gives big checks." They said, "Don't leave there until you have your $1,000 check" or whatever was the most ludicrous thing they could come up with. Herb used to tell the story about the first time I marched into his office and he said, "So glad to see you. Here's the check." He slides it face down across the desk to me. I thought, well, this is much easier than I expected. Then, doing what a man would never do, I looked at the check. It was like $50. I thought, well, he is teasing me. I thought, what the heck I have nothing to lose. So I said, "Mr. Schiff, I can't possibly take this back." He said, "What's the matter? That's what I normally give." I said, "No, that's not what you normally give." I realized that I had been had. "Tell you what," I said, "I'm just going to tear this little check up, and I'm going to give it back to you because if I were to take this check back, word would get around Dallas that you're having financial difficulties. It will just be our secret that you can't afford to give but $50. So why don't you just keep that check?" Well, he looked at me. I'll never forget it. I wasn't sure whether he was going to go ballistic, but he just burst out laughing. He said, "How much did they tell you I was going to give?" I said $1,000. He took his pen out and wrote me a check.

When I got back to the two clowns that had sent me on that little mission, they were just dumbfounded. They always sent me to the ones that were their good friends. They always gave me terrible information.

The bottom line is, I wasn't ever afraid of asking for money. I could get away with stuff that no man could. There was nothing wrong with it. There is an ego thing that goes on, and so I always assumed that they would love for me to call on them and ask them for money. I don't always get what I want, but I get closer to getting what I want.

RITA PALM, FORT WORTH

When Phil Gramm came into the Party, he was still a Johnny-come-lately. In 1983 and '84, he was running for reelection and needed some cash. I asked some of my real estate guys, "You have been making deal after deal after deal. How about giving Phil Gramm some money?" For years, I had taken Shaklee vitamins. I met the Shaklee government liaison at the convention in 1984. I said, "You know, Shaklee needs to give to the states that contribute to their well being." She agreed with me. They had a Political Action Committee. She gave Phil Gramm $5,000. It was just because I asked. Then, I was so successful with my one real estate guy, I asked the next one. I raised probably $60,000 or $70,000 in one afternoon, just asking. I couldn't believe it. It was so easy. We did that some for Bush. They can say no, but you have to be willing to ask.

SYLVIA NUGENT, DALLAS & AMARILLO

It's like a game. You just take one person and you follow to the next person. You call one person and say you want to have a fundraiser. You go to your Republicans first and then ask, "Who in your town would be good for that?" Who are the presidents of the banks? Who has the most money in your town? Who is the most respected? Who would want to do this? Then you guide that person to maximize your dollars.

ANN WALLACE, FORT WORTH & AUSTIN

In 1960, I decided we needed an airplane with "Tower for U.S. Senate" on it to fly over the TCU [*Texas Christian University*] football stadium. It was going to be $250. I called ten people and asked them for $25 apiece. It was something that they could see. So you nickeled and dimed it. You didn't dare ask anybody for $250. In those days, if anybody gave you $1,000 you would think they were trying to buy you.

JUDY JONES MATTHEWS, ABILENE

The most effective way to raise money is to ask people who have a lot of money for a lot of money.

National Level Fundraising

FLO KAMPMANN CRICHTON, SAN ANTONIO

When you operate on the national level, so to speak, you do not get involved so much in individual fundraising as in the setting up of benefit lunches and dinners for a cause. The Republican Boosters was a congressional committee that made direct gifts and donations to a candidate. They held booster lunches all around the country. We worked on those. We worked on the Senate-House dinner they have in the spring.

I was going to be appointed to the national finance committee in 1965 or '66. There were one or two women on it. I asked John Tower and told him I was thinking about resigning as national committeewoman because I wanted to be with my children a little more and the finance committee wouldn't be as demanding. I ended up on the executive committee of the finance committee, which was fine with me. The congressional committee and the congressional boosters, particularly, raised money for Party candidates and for the incumbents. The national committee raised money and would divide it up. We had to select cities for fundraising dinners or luncheons, and we had to get a chairman for it. That was my job.

I had to get a chairman for the boosters in Houston. I got George Bush to get Jim Baker [*Bush's eventual secretary of state*] to head it up. I think that was the first time he had done something politically. He may have been involved somewhat on the local level, but I don't think that he was involved nationally. He did a superb job.

The trouble was, when Nixon was running again for president and I was on the finance committee, he arbitrarily moved it into the Committee to Reelect the President—CREEP. All of a sudden, I found out I was no longer on the national finance committee. It was nonexistent. It worried me a little bit. Of course in an election year, the function of the national finance committee is to elect the President.

Later, I worked as a founder of the Republican Eagles. We met with President Ford. There were about fifteen of us. It was really Jerry Millbank's idea. He got us invited to the White House. We listened to President Ford's ideas and organized it. We tried to recruit people into the Eagles. Amazingly enough, there are quite a few people. We started out at a $10,000 contribution, now it's $15,000 a year. I would rather give to individual candidates than do that. I still think that's a good program for those corporations and PACs that can do it.

Fundraisers as Recruiting Opportunities

THEO WICKERSHAM, SAN ANTONIO

We would tell Democrats in the '70s what wonderful candidates we had, and we would also question them about who the opponent was. Joe Sage was a Republican who ran against Al Brown [*for state representative*]. When a friend of mine said I'm voting for Brown, I'd ask, "Do you know him well?" "Well, I know that he's a good Democrat." I would say, "I'm giving a fundraiser for Joe Sage at my house. I'm having a backyard party with lots of cold margaritas and barbecue, and it's all free. I'm sending out 2,000 invitations, and you are going to be one of them. Not only did they come, but two years later when Alan Schoolcraft ran against Al Brown those people all came and helped me.

BILLIJO PORTER, EL PASO

The first thing I ever did was go with my husband to a fundraising dinner with Spiro Agnew in 1971. We went to that, and then I became involved. I was a real fan of John Tower and so was my husband. In 1972, when he ran, I volunteered. I guess they were really glad to see a volunteer because everybody else was working for Nixon.

MARY TEEPLE, AUSTIN

The women I watched doing fundraisers were really good at recruiting people to help. It was opening up the arena and involving as many people as you could to help you make the telephone calls, write the letters, visit the people that you know want to give the money. Women are good at enlisting people and convincing others that causes are important. They make it a lot of fun to work. Women have no fear of going to their peers or even people that are outstanding in the community and asking.

Once, we had a goal of raising $20,000 for Senator Gramm. It did not occur to me that perhaps I could get that from twenty people. So instead, we formed a team and worked very hard at getting two hundred people to give $100. Nancy Braddus was always talking about how important numbers were in politics. The whole Hyatt Regency was full of people wanting to give Gramm $100. He raised his goal, but it took a lot of time and we enlisted an army of people to do that. It is very necessary to ask people who can contribute large amounts to get involved, and it's also fun to involve people who give $50. It just takes longer and you work harder.

Who Gives and Why

JUDY JONES MATTHEWS, ABILENE
    I think it is so important to be involved in fundraising for candidates that people want to be elected—to get money behind them for publicity, the mailings, and particularly television.

> *Why would somebody want to give money to a political*
> *fundraiser if they could invest the same money or give it to a tax*
> *deductible charity?*

Don't you feel really strongly about politics in this country? Don't you feel really strongly that we need to get rid of the people in the White House now? Well, I think that's it. I think you find people that feel really strongly about a particular candidate or a particular party and think it is important that we get things done. Of course, there are people who give a lot of money and expect something in return, and I am sure that they get it.

> *Do you think that politicians have a big problem with that?*

It seems to me it should not be a problem. I don't believe a politician should let himself be blackmailed. That may not be the right word. I think men like Ronald Reagan or Dwight Eisenhower wouldn't do it.

ILLA CLEMENT, KINGSVILLE

I was willing to donate money to the Party to get things done that I believed in and that I felt the Party was right about. Or for the person. But I think if you are donating money, well, there may be certain people who have things they want in return. Maybe somebody wants a road built, and somebody in local politics will do it for them. But mostly I was just thinking of the leadership of the country. Of course, getting the people elected that are really good—that is the most important thing.

DONA BRUNS, NEW BRAUNFELS

When Craig Enoch and Tom Phillips were running for the Texas Supreme Court, they came to town several times. One thing about New Braunfels, we can get them to vote but they are not very generous about giving money. For the first time, we were getting people to give more money to those offices because they were really concerned and wanted very much for those people to be elected. They felt that we had such good candidates that we needed to support them.

Associated Republicans of Texas

FRAN ATKINSON, LUFKIN & SAN ANTONIO

Associated Republicans of Texas [ART] is a funding organization. When the Party changed hands back in the Reagan years, the people who came in were not fundraisers. So we set up this organization to raise funds and dispense them according to our formula. Our formula is this—first we target races. We don't put a Don Quixote to tilt at windmills in a totally hopeless district. We target races, say, for the state house or senate or some judicial races.

We don't give money to candidates who won't work and who won't raise their own funds. We do not ask them for their political ideology. If they are running as a Republican in a target race and they are working, we will fund them. For instance, at the state convention anybody that runs for any party office is grilled on his or her political ideology. We don't do that. We just figure if they are running as a Republican they are going to be better than the other guy. Plus we need the majority.

We have given money to good candidates and were involved in recruiting candidates back in the days when you couldn't find them. Now they are coming out of the woodwork. We do not take part in primaries at all. We don't endorse one candidate over another. The winner of the primary comes in and makes a presentation to the candidate committee of ART, which is quite large, sometimes fifty or more people. Then we vote on how much money we want to give each candidate.

Obstacles

Please Don't Use My Name

ANN WALLACE, FORT WORTH & AUSTIN

It was either 1959 or 1960. I would go to luncheons and events for Nixon or for Tower. I would be seated at a table and feel a tap on my knee. The first time, I kind of wondered what was going on. I put my hand down, and here was a hand with folded money. In those days, it didn't matter because it wasn't against the law. No one wanted to be known to be against Lyndon Johnson. But here was a little money, and I had a notebook where I would very carefully write this down. It was always cash. They would say, "You know what this is for?" I did, and that is where it went. They didn't want a paper trail. We ran that entire campaign in Tarrant County on less than $3,000.

I kept those records for I don't know how long. I did relay to John who had given after he was elected. He needed to know. I would write just a note that said "it was so good to see you" and copy John on it. I was scared to death that, if Lyndon really got fired up, he would track me down and I would be the source revealing where all of the money came from.

SITTY WILKES, AUSTIN

I had a list—it was years ago—of the millionaires in Austin. It was only like twenty-something. We had a Lincoln Day dinner, and we would sell tickets. I remember even going to Mildred Moody—she was former Democrat governor Dan Moody's widow—upstairs to her bedroom. Sometimes, there would be $500. She would buy a ticket from me. She was a conservative. There were people who were hidden that didn't like the socialist ideas of the Democratic Party but who couldn't afford to be a front person.

NANCY LOEFFLER, SAN ANGELO & SAN ANTONIO

People weren't used to giving money to candidates, particularly Republican candidates. That was the biggest challenge.

FRAN ATKINSON, LUFKIN & SAN ANTONIO

A lot of people gave money as long as I didn't use their names. That was before the days when you had to report everything. I couldn't do that now. Back in those days, I could cash checks and just turn the money in. People would give me cash.

> *Secrecy assisted you when being a Republican was not acceptable. If you were required to report contributions then as you are today, it would have been a deterrent?*

Oh, yes!

The Candidate

FRANCIE FATHEREE CODY, PAMPA

I got a whole room full of people to pay $50 to have lunch with Tower after he got elected. As soon as he finished talking, he went straight to his room. I had told them they would get to meet him and shake hands. I was furious with him. I went down and pounded on the door and said, "Now, Senator Tower, you have got to come back. I have already told them that you are going to visit with them." He did, but he wasn't that thrilled. It hurts you in your fundraising. It hurts you when you drag these people out and make them pay. Back then $50 was a pricey luncheon. These were people I was counting on for money for other elections.

Competition for Fundraising Dollars

JANE JUETT, AMARILLO

One thing that hurts locally is every week we get maybe two requests from the state party and two from national for money. I am sorry, but what I can give to them is such a drop in the bucket. We support our local candidates. In a way, they have made people so mad with all of their letters and phone calls. People consider it wasted money to do that. If I received a letter a few times a year rather than one every week, I would be a lot more inclined to donate. We get one addressed to W. E. Juett. One addressed to Mrs. Jane Juett and one to Mr. and Mrs. W. E. Juett, and then sometimes we get one addressed to Mr. Juett. We have told them about all of these duplications. They say it is cheaper to send them than it is to correct the list. That does not leave a good impression.

RITA PALM, FORTH WORTH

When Bush ran for Senate in 1970, we had John Tower over to our house one Sunday afternoon. We invited people over and got him a little money for his next campaign. We also made sure he knew that in Tarrant County, at least, it was going to be balanced if Bush won. It was not a threat to him.

When Bush ran for president in 1988, I was chairing that campaign. The sheriff candidate came down with a couple of the legislators and judges that needed help. The swell was going for

Bush pretty heavy here. I said, "Listen, if you all would get behind us to get Bush 61 percent of this county, you all will go in without having to spend a lot of money." They had never thought about that. We sold the coattail effect. There was no bickering or complaining that, "I didn't get my share." We had everybody out at all of the big sports events and outside the fence at General Dynamics. They could hand out their literature, but they had to hand out Bush literature. We had somebody out there handing out literature three shifts a day for the fourteen days prior to the election. We had to have the help of the local candidates because there were not enough of us. We had parades, and they all carried Bush banners. It was a joyous campaign with minimum antagonism.

NANCY PALM, HOUSTON

Let's face it, the fact is the state party is an absolute necessity, but in the major metropolitan counties they are not as necessary as they are out in the rural counties. I objected to them coming in constantly and raising big money out of Harris County to be used in other counties.

How did you balance the need for money in the late 1960s and early 1970s?

There wasn't much balance. They were able to collect large sums of money out of Harris County. We went with direct mail to small donors, which was sort of innovative. Volunteers made up for a lot money. We did our own polling. Why couldn't they see that a local person running locally helped the individual running a statewide race?

HALLY CLEMENTS, VICTORIA

The thing I dislike the most is the Republican National Committee running in and sending out all these little flyers first, before you get an opportunity to work your traps. I could name people who would give $1,000 or $500, but they receive a letter asking for, say, $500, $200, or $100. I think they need to let the individual workers do their bit and then pick up the pieces later on.

CHAPTER 18

We Won! Now What?

"Lots of candidates have high aspirations and expectations that
they are going to change the world." —MARJORIE VICKERY

*F*ighting uphill battles year after year, longtime Party workers
*could easily see an election victory as an end in itself. Yet, after
each victory, the now–former candidate had to find a way to
make the transition to the new role of elected official. Election
day victories were a new beginning not only for the candidates
and workers but also for Texas. Republicans now had an
opportunity to put their philosophy into action.*

*As newly elected officials or as their staff, women made a
lasting imprint on Texas and the nation. They found that, as
with elections, passing new law was not an end in itself. Laws
needed proper implementation and revision or repeal if they were
not producing the desired results. The boards that run Texas government required conscientious men and women as members, and the
newly elected or appointed Republican boards worked to wrestle
power from the entrenched bureaucracies that administered
programs on a daily basis. Some women from Texas also served
on a national level in the legislative and executive branches.*

*Beginning in the 1960s through today, women politicians
tried to make government operate with the best interests of all
citizens in mind. Women also found a new source of power.
After years as credible, loyal, and trusted campaign and Party
workers, they became both informal and formal advisors to state
and national members of both the legislative and executive
branches. At last, women influenced the Texas and national governments in the ways they had so humbly worked for since the 1950s.*

They helped secure a two-party political system in Texas and, as either Republican elected officials or their advisors, women endeavored to assure that our governmental bodies be honest, responsive, and fiscally responsible.

What was the responsibility of those early Republicans once they got elected?

ANNE ARMSTRONG, ARMSTRONG

We always hoped they would help give a boost to other Republicans. Most did. There was a great feeling of camaraderie not just among the women but also in the whole Party. Senator John Tower was a model for helping other Republicans. He was not the world's best glad-hander, but he did believe in the Republican Party of Texas and the two-party system. He would help other candidates. Frankly, and I won't name names, there were even times when I and other state leaders didn't want certain local candidates to be associated with some of our stronger candidates. We felt that they were so weak they would drag other candidates down. This is one of the eternal problems of politics. You make hard decisions.

Elected Officials

What did it feel like the day after you won a seat on the city council and reality set in?

KATIE HECK, MIDLAND

It was amazing. All of a sudden I was one of the "stupid set" — elected officials. It was discouraging. I can see why good people tend to have better things to do than run for office these days.

The day after the election for county judge that you weren't supposed to win, what did you do?

BARBARA CULVER CLACK, MIDLAND

[*Party official*] Payton Anderson gathered up Bill Davis, who won a seat in the legislature, and me and took us to Dallas for an

SREC meeting. There was a handful of Republican local candidates who won that year. We were there for the SREC to look at successful candidates.

During the campaign—I wouldn't say it was a dirty campaign— the state district judge here, being a partisan Democrat, sort of got caught up in the race toward the end. Some things that he reputedly said, of course, got back to me. I wasn't in the mood to go down there on January 1st along with the other Democrats and have him swear me in. So our little campaign organization got Julius Neunhoffer, the Kerr County judge, to come out from Kerrville. We had a luncheon and a celebration, and he swore me in. That was sort of my revenge or something. I don't think that got me out on the right foot, but it felt good to celebrate with my constituents this occasion of being the first Republican in the courthouse.

How did you build a consensus with the Democrats on the court?

They realized that I was going to be there four years, and we might as well work together.

When you look back on it now, what was the difference for the county to have you, a Republican judge, as opposed to another Democrat?

I don't think any. I just probably brought a few little new ideas, but everyone does. Nobody likes officious females so I didn't try to boss them around. I tried to make sure that the county commissioners got all of the glory and all of the blame. I presided and did not take an active part in the deliberations unless they asked me. They finally realized that I wasn't on a glory ride and that they could trust me. I was a lawyer, which helped.

MARJORIE VICKERY, COPPER CANYON
Lots of candidates have high aspirations and expectations that they are going to change the world. I had those expectations, and I do think I was able to accomplish a lot of things, but I didn't accomplish all that I wanted to. All I needed to do was take a

speed-reading course. We had mountains of things to read to be ready for each state board of education meeting. One of the goals that I was able to accomplish was, I wanted mandatory kindergarten for children. At that time, it was optional for school districts to have kindergarten. Another thing I wanted was for every child to learn a second language from kindergarten on up. If a child learns that from six years on up, it is not as difficult. I was co-chairman of the curriculum committee. We went all over Texas having hearings on this. As it worked out, we got a second language to be optional.

CYNDI TAYLOR KRIER, SAN ANTONIO

I am a classic Republican in the south, who Governor Lamar Alexander from Tennessee identified in the '80s as running for office for the first time because they were against whatever the Democrats in the office were doing. Then they got elected and realized they couldn't just be against everything. They were responsible for governing. That took programs that worked and commitments and philosophies of how to build things up, not just tear them down. I felt fortunate that Lamar and some other national Republicans at that time organized a group that invited local legislators and local officials from states across the south to Tennessee twice a year. We focused on local and state issues and how we could come up with legislation, and we exchanged ideas. I became committed to how we could control state spending and control the growth of taxes that had just exploded right before I got to the state senate.

I filibustered in the senate in 1991. I called attention to the fact that Texas was ignoring the constitutional amendment that limited the growth of state spending to the growth in the state population and the inflation rate. If they wanted to spend more than that, they had to disclose to the public what they were doing and they had to take a vote specifically to exceed that cap. The amendment had been adopted at a time in the '70s when we had more money than the legislature knew what to do with. The case ended up being taken to the Texas Supreme Court. While the court ruled that we were too far down the way in the budgetary process, I think it is significant to every taxpayer in Texas that in every budget since, the law has been followed. It is important for Texas and state spending, but I think it is more important for good government. If government doesn't follow the rules and play by them, it's hard to expect the public to.

The differences that I have made aren't the big differences, such as the bills that were passed—like reforming the workers compensation system, which was absolutely about to die, or casting a decisive vote on indigent health care, which now needs fixing again. Those aren't the things I think of when I look back. I think of the one-on-one personal differences I've made through constituent casework. For example, the little girls who had PKU, a disease that I had never heard of. It is really a dietary problem where they couldn't digest normal food and had to live their lives on a dietary supplement. With it, they could live fairly normal lives. The state didn't treat that dietary supplement as a medication. It's very expensive and the family couldn't afford it. So I worked with the health department in getting medical professionals involved and getting the rule changed, not just for that family but for all the families. That's what makes me feel good.

I keep these boxes that I call small harbors. It's after a poem I read one time that goes loosely "we all have small harbors in our soul where we may go and rest a while." Whenever I am really frustrated and think I'm not accomplishing anything, I just go and open one of those boxes and pull a note out, and I am reminded of all those little things that made a big difference in people's lives.

MARY DENNY, DENTON

The first week or two is just so awesome. Truly awesome. Just walking into the state capitol and realizing, my gosh, I have been elected to the legislature. Am I really going to be up for the task? I had some self-doubt and insecurity starting out. It is not the warmest, friendliest place to just go into. Republicans in the house and senate don't have a mentoring program in place for new members. For real basic stuff, there is an orientation, but it doesn't tell you a lot that is real practical and that you need to know. Members themselves, because of the very nature of the competitiveness of dealing with legislation, don't share a lot. The Democrats, on the other hand, have put in place a better farm club. We Republicans have been watching them over the past four to five years to see how they do with the new freshman. You'll see that happen this next session when some of the more senior members will take new ones under their wings. We will give them pieces of legislation, something that we know is going to pass, and shepherd them through the whole process so that they learn how to do all this. I'm not sure that women haven't helped speed the process along or bring it to full service, and now the men even realize, well, yes, we could do a bit better job of this.

NANCY JUDY, DALLAS

The main thing as a public official is to think defensively every minute of every day. Before you ever open your mouth, every time you are asked a question you think, "What can somebody make of this?" It makes a difference in how you phrase your response. It is instinctive if you want to prevail. You think about what you're going to say and how it will come out in the paper.

I had very good press coverage. I had good rapport with the reporters. If I ever felt they were not getting in the story the proper reflection of what I had said, I would never hesitate to call them. They respected me. I was not intensely political. I had to ask for people's votes, but when I had the job [*as Dallas county commissioner*] I addressed the issues at face value. I did my homework, and I voted my conscience.

LIZ GHRIST, HOUSTON

I was asked to fill a one-year vacancy on commissioners court. I wish people understood the power of commissioners court. I could have probably gone into the office with the intention of just holding the seat until the election, but I was an activist commissioner. My attitude was, "Let's find out what we think should be done, and we've got eleven months to get it done." I hired three women and one male. I said that I wanted everything wound up by the time I left office.

Was one of the people you hired Molly Pryor?

Yes. Molly probably could have run this county with one hand tied behind her back. I asked her to be my administrative assistant. She knew how to reach people and how to make people feel good about doing their jobs correctly. She could also take factions and make them work together. She had been John Tower's executive assistant here in Houston.

You can't do it without a good staff. If everyone doesn't pull his weight, you are defeated before you start. The secret to success is finding people that are smarter than you are. My philosophy is never compromise on quality.

SHAROLYN WOOD, HOUSTON

The federal courts were going to take over the state judiciary. The Democrat officeholders at the top were going to let it be done. In September 1988, the attorney general's office [*of Democrat Jim Mattox*] called a meeting of the judges in metropolitan counties, and a lot of us were Republicans. They looked around and said, "I don't know if any of you guys are going to be here, because there is this suit in federal court [*for voting rights violations*] and they are going to win." Of course they had a grin on their faces, telling all of the Republicans their days were numbered. Dallas judge Harold Entz, Houston judge Bill Powell, Vinson and Elkins partner John Golden, and I started looking into it. We found that maybe it was not that clear-cut. In lawsuits about voting rights, there is a [*state*] violation and then there is the [*federal*] remedy. The remedy was to put judges into the state rep districts. We knew exactly what would happen there. We felt we were fighting for the independence of the judiciary. In February, it was very clear that we had things in place, including the support of Governor Bill Clements. As soon as Jim Mattox found that out, all of a sudden the plaintiffs dropped the Governor as a party in the lawsuit. When they dropped him as a party, the judges lost our only champion.

My husband and I talked it over and decided that if I didn't do it, nobody would. There was no judge in Dallas that would agree to put his name on it. I decided to do it and called the law firm that I knew to have a fantastic federal court securities litigator, Porter and Clements. Senior partner Gene Clements agreed to handle it. They hoped they would be able to recover their attorneys fees somehow, and I committed to raise the money to pay the $150,000 in expenses. I did raise that, but the $750,000 in attorney's fees it took for my lawyers to prevail in that lawsuit were totally unpaid. Vinson and Elkins assisted with the expenses. Bracewell and Patterson assisted with manpower. When we got to trial, the attorney general's office didn't argue. Everyone thought we lost. We won on appeal. We won it twice in the Fifth Circuit. We half won in the Supreme Court, and it came back and we won it again twice in the Fifth Circuit. It took us a lot of years. The reason that there are Republican judges today in Texas is because we did that.

GWYN SHEA, IRVING

My district elected me to the legislature not to pass another law but to kill all of the bad ones that we could. They also wanted me to correct the legislation that was not working. It was basically a conservative philosophy.

Agendas happened to wind up on your desk because of your committee assignments. I was the first female to be appointed to the ways and means committee, which put me right in the middle of every business issue in the state because it deals with taxes or revenue. I served all five sessions on the house insurance committee and was the only female elected to the national conference of insurance legislators. I also served on the county affairs and house administration committees.

In 1987, the largest tax bill in the history of the state was proposed. We did not need a tax increase. We had a surplus, but the Democrats were in control. We were able to not pass that tax bill out of committee when it came. The speaker, who was of course a

Democrat, took the tax bill out of the ways and means committee and put it in one of his friendly committees. They didn't pass as large a tax as they would have, but they did pass a tax bill. That was probably one of the biggest battles that we have ever been in. Of course, the next session, myself as well as all of the rest of us were eliminated from that committee and didn't sit on it again.

Later, in 1993, I was appointed by commissioners court to fill an unexpired constable term. I thought of all the things that I might do after I left the legislature, this certainly was not on my radar screen. After I was there six months, I thought I may have something to contribute. So I enrolled in the police academy. It was an intense study of all the codes—the alcohol beverage code, the family violence code, the vehicle code, the code of criminal procedures, the penal code, and all of those things that we deal with in law enforcement. I remember thinking, "Gee, I was there when we wrote this. We meant for it to do this but in the real world of application, it is not working."

So interestingly enough, in 1995 I went back to the legislature as a quasi-lobbyist. We spoke to those things that needed to be changed. We changed five areas of the codes in order to make them serve the public better and help law enforcement at the same time. My professor at the police academy said, "We have never had this perspective. You can tell us what was happening at midnight on the floor of the house when this crazy bill in the vehicle code was passed regulating roller skates." I have been back on occasions as a guest adjunct instructor at the academy, to give a legislator's perspective on how some of this crazy stuff gets done.

PATRICIA LYKOS, HOUSTON

After I became a judge, I had no friends who were lawyers. It is terribly isolating to be a judge if you behave appropriately because you are cut off from your friends. You can not ever have a sense of impropriety. I demanded the lawyers be prepared. It is appalling to me that lawyers think they can walk into a court with criminal jurisdiction, when you are talking about life and liberty, and be very cavalier in their approach.

I was able to do a lot in the way of policy. Judges have a tremendous responsibility. We don't just sit there and say "sustained" or "overruled." If there is a problem out there that you ascertain from your presiding, then it is your duty and obligation to do something about it. For example, I got the first residential center here for probationers. It took a long time to get twenty-some other judges into agreement and to get the funding for it. We also got community service and required urine analysis for probationers. I asked them when the plea was over when was the last time they used drugs. If they used the night before, I wasn't going to punish them for telling me the truth, but I needed to know what their problem was so that we could create these programs. There is a lot a judge can do to make the world a better place and not violate any ethical standards.

DORIS WILLIAMS, LAKE JACKSON

Everyone knew that I was a Republican when I was mayor. I still participated in my partisan politics on a regular basis. It never hurt me. You can not bring partisan politics into city politics. About the only thing that you can bring there is your conservative philosophy. I really took care of people's money, probably better than I took care of my own money. I believe in not raising taxes. All those things in your Republican beliefs are good with local politics.

ANITA HILL, GARLAND

You have to prove yourself as a woman member of the legislature. You have to prove that you are not emotional. As long as you carry part of the load and you don't fall back on "poor little ol' female me," they respect and help you. One time, I went to the Citadel Club at the Driskill Hotel. I was told to go up to the second floor and wait outside the door to the Club. I sat there and sat there and sat there, and finally I was going to go in. I started in, and this woman rushed up. I told her I needed to meet with members of the Garland city council. She wouldn't let me go in. We moved the meeting downstairs. I was just boiling and steaming inside because my people were being punished. I believe in the private club concept, but not when it receives tax benefits and public officials, male or female, can't come in. I was furious. When I got back to the capitol, I went right up to the press table. A lot of the well-known names, like [*liberal commentator*] Molly Ivins, were there. Word got out to my colleagues, and one of them got up and proposed a resolution that no one use the Citadel and the Driskill until I had been apologized to and everything had been resolved. On Friday night, MCI [*telecommunications company*] had a dinner and reception scheduled for the Driskill Hotel and they cancelled it. I didn't do anything aggressively at all except to get it out of my system, but the Citadel did offer an apology.

At the time that it happened, the president was asked about it and he said that women were a distraction and they sounded like a gaggle of magpies. I still don't know how a gaggle of magpies sounds, but the day after I was kicked out there was a luncheon held. Carole Kneeland with Channel 8 in Dallas passed the mike around the tables, and it was very loud. There were only three or four women and all of these men. They played that back on the late news, my publicity machine was working by accident. After I calmed down a little bit, I got to thinking, "What about my colleagues who are minorities?" One of the most outstanding members of the house was Wilhelmina Delco from Austin. I asked her about getting inside the Citadel. She said she would have to go up the fire escape just to get in.

But the episode did give some attention to that issue.

KAY BAILEY HUTCHISON, HOUSTON & DALLAS

In the '70s and even in the '80s, we still had to prove that we were credible, tough, capable of handling the job, and reliable. When I ran for the legislature in the '70s, I ran as and was a conservative woman. I was told later, after I served a term, that everyone was so surprised because I was really conservative. They had never had a conservative woman so this was a new phenomenon.

How did that help you when you came to the U. S. Senate?

Each experience certainly helped me succeed in the next experience. Certainly my legislative experience made me able to cope with the ebb and flow of politics. But it also helped that I knew state government and that I knew enough to be able to have a platform. Legislative experience allowed me to make a smooth transition into the Senate because I understood the give-and-take and the rough-and-tumble. I understood losing. I understood compromising. I understood, pretty much, parliamentary procedure because it was similar.

In what areas have you been able to have the biggest impact legislatively or otherwise as a public official?

In each of the positions I've held, I have had a different kind of impact. In the state legislature, I focused on a few big things and I won those. I passed the first mass transit bill for Texas. I reorganized the highway department to include mass transit in the highway system. I created county historical commissions because I thought it was so important to preserve our Texas heritage. I, along with the other women members together in a coalition, passed the bill that would put Texas in the forefront of fair treatment for rape victims, which was the forerunner for addressing violence against women. We also passed equal credit rights for women in Texas.

In the state treasurer's office, I was successful in holding the state income tax back, which I think will have far-reaching consequences for Texas. We passed a 5 percent ceiling on state debt. I think that will keep us in a good financial situation. Then in the Senate, I feel I have been effective for Texas, but I have also had an impact in the foreign policy arena. In national defense issues, I have been very active and now serve on the Helsinki Commission. I have also allowed homemakers to have equal IRA's [*individual retirement accounts*] with those who work outside the home. I have been able to pass anti-stalking laws. I broke the impasse in welfare reform by getting a formula that was fair to all of the states. In each area where I have served, I have picked certain issues that were important to me and tried to make an impact, and I think that I have.

Staff Members

MARTHA CROWLEY, DALLAS

I volunteered in Bruce Alger's Washington office in 1955. My husband, Frank, was his administrative assistant. They kind of split the duties. Bruce did the homework. He studied issues thoroughly, and Frank handled the office for the most part. They would consult if it was a controversial issue coming up for a vote. Pretty much I think they were in agreement.

In the office, I learned how to use the roto-typer. I just did the nit-picking things that no one else wanted to do. I was pretty much acting as the hostess. I would take constituents sightseeing and tour the Capitol. That way, it gave him some time. He didn't have to stop and do the same things over and over with constituents. I had them for dinner. I just did unofficial entertaining. If they needed any work to be done themselves, I would often help. If they needed to contact somebody, I would write and find out where.

CAROLYN BACON, DALLAS

I was the first woman administrative assistant. To be honest, I really didn't face any obstacles. Before Senator Tower named me, I thought I would. When he told me that was what he wanted to do, I said, "You ought to think very carefully about whether or not you should have a woman in this position." In fact, there were three men in Texas to call and see if they approved. He told me that he called and they all approved. It wasn't long before there were other women named administrative assistants.

How did you develop the expertise in the various committee areas that the Senator was involved in?

I had worked for Bruce Alger. It is amazing how much legislation is the same year after year after year. I worked in Tower's state office with Honey Alexander. I did casework and some legislative work. Then, when I went to Washington and was working directly with his administrative assistant, I got involved in all of the different areas.

So many have said John Tower voted right. What importance did you have as his administrative assistant to keep him on that track?

When you look at his legislative career, he was a man who worked from a very strong philosophical base. On the big issues he knew exactly what was the right thing. There were always many smaller issues, and that is when the role of the staff is to make sure the Senator has all the data he needs to make the right decision on that vote. So it is in some ways a research operation. Gathering the data, presenting it to him in the most objective fashion as possible, and then looking at it and making a decision.

Why do you think Tower was willing to hire you to be his critical staff person and Nola Gee to be his critical campaign person when it was uncommon to hire women?

It was the mark of Senator Tower. He was really a wonderful person to work for because he delegated very well and yet was always the first one to step up and take responsibility. When you look at his staff, you will see that it was really remarkable; he had very little turnover. When people left the staff it was because they were going to a higher position. He had no gender bias. He had no ethnic bias. We always had a good mix of women and minorities in the top positions. When I left he named David Martinez, a Hispanic, as administrative assistant. He looked for ability, loyalty, and dedication. Gender and other things were not a part of his criteria for making decisions. When you look at the Tower staff, he launched many wonderful careers by being an exceptional mentor to his staff.

JOANNE POWELL, SAN ANGELO

The job that I have working in Lamar Smith's office is getting to meet the constituents. Of course, it doesn't matter who walks through that door, whether they're Democrats or Republicans, Congressman Smith is their representative if they live in the Twenty-first Congressional District. Lots of times, the people who come to this office for help are on their last leg. They don't know which way to go and maybe have had the door slammed in their faces before. If it's something that deals with a federal agency, I will tell them up front that we can't change or influence a decision but we can make sure that they have been given every proper consideration. Sometimes their problem is just bogged down in red tape. Sometimes they just want people to listen.

CINDY BROCKWELL, BOERNE

As chief of staff for State Senator Wentworth, I am responsible for the capitol office and the San Antonio district office and the office in San Angelo. I am responsible for everything. I hire and fire. I am much more involved in the legislative process in Austin. The district offices don't get involved at all in legislation. We have only three legislative staff members in the capitol office. Some of the bills were mine. When you work a bill, it means it's yours. You work with the constituents or lobbyists whose idea it was. You go to the hearings. The Senator has bill books, and you write his remarks to lay out the bill before the committee. You answer possible questions the committee might have. You have to think of what objections or what questions they might have, then come up with answers. If you get it through the committee, you write his floor remarks. If it passes, then you coordinate with the house member who's going to carry that bill. Give them your bill books so they have every bit of information on that bill and do not have to reinvent the wheel. You coordinate with the house member's staff to get the bills through the house. Then if it passes and it is a big bill and you want a bill signing with the governor, you coordinate with the governor's staff to get a time and slot.

Every morning when I walk in the capitol, I think I am the luckiest person in the world. They are paying me to do this! I like Texas government. There are only thirty-one members in the Texas Senate. In Congress, there are 435 House members. Surely you can make more of an impact as one of thirty-one than in Congress. I just like to be a part of it.

CATHERINE SMYTH COLGAN, DALLAS

I worked in Jim Collins's congressional office in Dallas for years. I ran the volunteer program there, keeping up with the mailing list. We had what we called our hotline. There was another lady named Tera Mae Carson. We kept up the mailing list. We worked one day a week in the office for a number of years. He used it for his newsletter, where he communicated and corresponded with all of his constituents. From that list we pulled volunteers and campaign workers. We did solicitations for funding. It was primarily a communication line with his constituents for all purposes.

Appointees

RUTH SCHIERMEYER, LUBBOCK

We had sixty-some appointees from Lubbock County under Governor Clements. It doesn't just happen. You have to be very proactive. As county chairman, I worked very closely with the chamber of commerce. Every time I had someone that we wanted to have or wanted an appointment, I would call the chamber and get their support and contact our senator and both of our state reps. The chamber organized a committee on political affairs with an appointments subcommittee. They met regularly and looked at all of the appointments that were coming out, and I served on that committee. That helps the governor and the senators or state reps if people are out there actively looking for people that represent the views of the governor. You know then that his philosophy is being carried through those boards and commissions. If the people being appointed do not represent that philosophy, then the governor is simply a figurehead and has no strength.

JANE ANNE STINNETT, LUBBOCK

From my perspective in watching the Bush appointments, they have been extremely diligent to make sure people have a real interest in the position that they are being appointed to, know something about it, and are dedicated to show up at the meetings and take an active role. Clements did the same thing. The people who were on the task force that I was on were all people who were leaders in agriculture. I think that both Bush and Clements were more into—of course, I'm probably prejudiced because I'm Republican—appointing people because of their abilities. There are plenty of women and plenty of minorities who are extremely capable and do a great job.

All Kinds of Influence

SHIRLEY GREEN, AUSTIN & SAN ANTONIO

A wonderful opportunity came to be appointed Director of Public Affairs for NASA at headquarters in Washington. I went to start my space career, which was three unbelievable, wonderful years except the [*space shuttle*] *Challenger* blew up in my first month on the job. It was the biggest public affairs disaster of the century.

The first week that I got to NASA, I had a meeting with the fellow immediately above me. NASA is a very nonpolitical agency. There were only five political appointees in the whole structure nationwide. He was looking at my resume and he said, "Well, I see that you have been deputy press secretary for the vice president, and I am sure that was very heady stuff but it was a very small office. NASA is known for managing big programs. You will be judged at NASA on your management abilities. Do you feel like you have that kind of background?" He asked this in the most patronizing tone. I looked at him and I said, "You're right, we do come from very different backgrounds. I am sure that the things from my political life don't have very much meaning for you. I ran a headquarters with all volunteers where I kept ten phones manned, three shifts a day, and had more than 100 people working for me everyday. And they were all volunteers. They could all leave if they didn't like my management style. You learn something about managing people."

How in the world did you hold it together when you were
watching the Challenger lift off that day and continue to do
your job?

It was unbelievable. At the launch control center down at the
Kennedy Space Center, there is one console for the agency's director of public affairs and the Kennedy Space Center's director of
public affairs. We had monitors of the three network television
stations and NASA television and headphones where we could
talk back to the press center on our own loop as well as hear the
mission commentary. The console was by big glass windows. Chuck
Hollingshead, who was the director of the Kennedy Space Center,
was sitting by the window.

I can still see it. I had only seen one other launch. When the
big puffball of smoke and flames happened and then the boosters
started falling off, all I could think was, I don't remember this happening before. Surely, it's just because I'm so inexperienced that I
don't know. There was not a sound in launch control. Finally, I
realized as Chuck turned around that I had been gripping his shoulder. When he turned back, of course we both had on our ear-
phones. We couldn't hear each other, but I said to him and he
could read what I was saying, "Is it gone?" I have never seen a look
of such horrible sadness in a face in my life. He was just shaking
his head and said, "Oh, yes, it is gone." Then as I looked back
through the tiers of consoles in launch control, everybody was just
staring at their blank computers. It was just dead quiet. It was just
the most shocking, sad, and difficult situation.

Every part of the NASA family, every element of its management structure, has contingency plans. I would always sit and read
my contingency plan carefully all night in my hotel room the night
before. The first thing on my mind was that, if the administrator
was not there, get in touch with the administrator. On our console, I had one outside line. I grabbed the phone to place a call to
Washington immediately to get him on the line, at which point,
all of the other contingency plans started kicking in. One of them,
for the whole launch control center, was to cut all outside phone

lines so that phone calls couldn't come in. This one phone line that I had open was the only phone line that we had open for several hours. By the time I had gotten through to headquarters, they were saying that [*spokesman*] Larry Speaks at the White House was trying to reach me. So they patched him through and I told Larry what we knew, which was of course absolutely nothing, because he had to go out and file a brief. It was just unbelievable.

That day we had credentialed over 650 reporters for the launch. It was the largest one for a long time because of the teacher [*on board, Christa McAuliffe*]. By that night, we had nearly 1,100 reporters at the Cape not counting the ones in Washington or Houston. By the next morning, we had 1,300 reporters. Our phones at the press center recorded nearly 4,000 lost phone calls because of busy signals. Every news organization in the world was either calling or getting on a plane and arriving. We put our public affairs people on 24-hour duty at both Kennedy Space Center and Johnson Space Center in Houston and at headquarters and Marshall [*Space Flight Center in Huntsville, Alabama*]. We had around-the-clock shifts for six weeks because some news agency from somewhere in the world on some other time frame was on filing deadline all the time.

> *If you can make it through that as a public affairs officer, you can make it through anything?*

I had several gripping moments before, which were good preparation. When Bush was elected vice president [*in 1980*], I was his deputy press secretary and was with him in Fort Worth the day President Reagan was shot [*in Washington, D. C.*]. We had only been in office two months. I had not been traveling that much. That kind of attention was new, and we had a lot of press on the plane that day. That proved to be an interesting dry run for one of the things that I learned—anytime things start happening in a crisis, start taking notes because later you can't remember the times and places. Reporters always want to know what time did Alexander Haig call? What time did the Vice President get the word? What time did you all land?

I did that the day of the *Challenger* accident. I immediately grabbed a yellow pad and started jotting down when I first talked to the White House, when I talked to the administrator, when we said we'd set a briefing. I've gone back and looked at some of those notes and can't read them. Obviously, I was just scribbling like a mad woman.

When the Marine barracks was bombed in Lebanon and killed 250 Marines, the Vice President went over on a secret mission. We were smuggled out of the White House. Nobody even knew that we were out of town. That was, I thought at the time, probably the hardest day that I would ever spend working professionally. They had recovered all but I think thirty-five or thirty-eight of the bodies when we got there about thirty hours after the bombing.

So I had several very, very difficult and dicey times. The thing about *Challenger* that was so extraordinary was that as gripping as the first twenty-four hours were, it didn't end for six months. The evidence was all buried under three hundred feet of the Atlantic Ocean. As soon as they got the salvage operation going, it was every day and every night—what have the ships found? The leaks about where we were in the investigation, the impounded material that you couldn't get out of impoundment—the press was killing us, charging us with hiding evidence and not being straightforward. The presidential investigation was doing its thing and the Congress wanted to do its thing and NASA was trying to do its thing. It was just around-the-clock horror stories for six months.

How do you keep your integrity in that kind of situation, with the endless contact and all of those different groups asking questions and making requests?

Well, you try and do the best you can. Our record was pretty spotty. There have been a lot of books written about the *Challenger* accident and round tables addressing how you plan for crisis, how you build a good contingency plan, and what should be included in the plan. We did a lot of soul searching, and we did a better job than we were given credit for at the time. There was a rush of the media to want answers and want them now. It led to the assumption that if you didn't give the answer now you must be withhold-ing evidence. I used to say to public affairs groups that scientists and engineers are not like you and me. They are accustomed to subjecting everything to peer review to ascertain its authenticity. If they brought up a piece of what they thought might be the right solid rocket booster, which is what blew up, reporters with their long camera lenses would think, "That is the booster." We couldn't confirm that it was part of the booster, and they would put the story out about what they thought "but NASA won't confirm it." They would take another hit on us, but the scientists and engi-neers would want to take that piece of debris and examine it and ascertain for sure. So it was a push-pull between the scientific need for accuracy and the public affairs desire to tell what we knew, even if we weren't sure. There was a lot of internal conflict that made it very difficult.

BERYL MILBURN, AUSTIN

Governor Clements appointed me to be the chairman of the University of Texas coordinating board [*now the Texas Higher Edu-cation Coordinating Board*]. I was the first woman to do that. I didn't even know what it was when he asked me to do it. He had already promised me that he would name me a regent when the time came. To him, being on the coordinating board was a more powerful position. Well, he just didn't have any idea what a plum a regent appointment was. So more than a year later, when I was serving as the chairman of the coordinating board, he appointed me to the board of regents. At the coordinating board you were a referee, and nobody likes a referee. Being a regent was just fascinating, and I loved every minute of it. It was a lot of work, and I gave it a lot of time because I had the time. I was chairman of the land and in-vestment committee for four years, which was in charge of all the millions of acres out in West Texas, the Permanent University Fund, and the investments.

After I retired as state vice chairman of the Party, I was ap-pointed vice chairman of the Texas Constitutional Revision Com-mission in 1973. We did all the research, rewriting, and recommendations. Then we presented that document to the constitutional convention, which was composed of the legislators and the senators sitting as one body. They did not adopt any of it. It turned out to be an exercise in futility. Who knows why? I think they had high hopes that it was going to go, but it didn't.

GWYN SHEA, IRVING

My first appointment after I left the legislature was as a member of the Texas Workers' Compensation Insurance Facility. The Governor's instruction [*George W. Bush*] at that time was get in there, clean it out, and shut it down. I said, "Yes, Sir." You get in there as a governor's appointee with a board that has been appointed by the former governor. It doesn't take a brain surgeon to count votes. I sat there quietly like all good freshman should and learned the program and process. When I said yes to this appointment, I had already said no to four others. I knew the workers' compensation insurance facility because I was there when it was created in the legislature. I knew that it had a date it was supposed to go out of existence. I couldn't remember exactly when, but I said, "I can say yes to this because it'll be a short-term deal."

Finally, we got enough board members that we had enough votes to exactly follow the instructions that had been given. In the meantime, I realized that instead of cleaning it out and closing it down, why don't we privatize it and sell this piece of business to the private sector? So I went to the Governor and said, "What would you think about it?" He said, "Sounds great to me." We privatized that facility and sold it to the largest reinsurer in the world. That was a real feel-good kind of accomplishment.

One of the things that everybody talks about is that the governor of Texas is a weak governorship. What they fail to realize is that government really rests at his appointees' feet. His appointees are probably the most powerful thing that he has going for him. The philosophy that you bring to the arena is paramount because they make major, major decisions not only about how state dollars are spent but about the day-to-day mechanics of how that agency ought to respond to things. That is one of the things both Democrats and Republicans give George W. Bush big marks for—making really meaningful appointments to boards with people who are very grounded in what their responsibilities are going to be.

ANNE BERGMAN, WEATHERFORD

Governor Clements appointed me chairman of the community development board in Austin. The first year, we worked with capital development grants and loans for sewers and water supplies, infrastructure that people needed in small towns. There's a certain amount of federal money that comes to the state and is administered within the region. We had oversight of the grants. Staff did most of the work. Appeals came to our board. Sometimes cities appealed when they got ranked below another. The Democrats were political. They would cave in to somebody because they liked him or because of a consideration that shouldn't be given. It was supposed to be on the merits only. It was all ranked. It never occurred to me to be political.

DEBORAH BELL, ABILENE

I was appointed by Governor Clements to the Brazos River Authority. I was the first woman ever appointed. I kept saying, "What do I know about water?" He said, "You are going to learn about water." The river authorities in general had had a bad name. The way we're structured at BRA is that we get $100 for a meeting, which is not a fortune, and we get reimbursement for our expenses. I spend about forty days a year either in committee meetings or board meetings or going to a national water resources meeting. When I came on the board, the median age was like sixty. There had been people on the board that had been serving twenty-five years with no turnover, no fresh ideas, and no new thoughts. River authorities are very arrogant because they are quasi-governmental. We get our revenue from the municipalities, counties, and individual customers. We don't have to come to Austin begging.

When I came on this board I was in my thirties, and men were in shock. It was a very "yes" board. They would stay within their own confines and committees. I went to every committee meeting even though I was only a member of the lake management committee. I could see the workings of the board rather than having them come to me at the quarterly board meeting and give me the lowdown. When Clements started making appointments, we changed the BRA from a "yes" board to a "wait a minute, is this the best thing for the Brazos River?" board. Now the board is active and forward thinking. What I was doing with Governor Clements was changing the way river authorities are run. It was going to be the board telling the general manager what to do and not the other way around.

DEBBIE FRANCIS, DALLAS

Governor Clements appointed me to the Texas Developmental Disability Board Planning Council. I served, I guess, ten years. I have worked over the years on disability-related issues because our youngest son was in a near-drowning accident when he was almost two. Bo turned twenty last week. He is severely brain damaged and handicapped. For a number of years, I have also done political work, but I really had somewhat of a more specialized calling. But that's also taught me a lot about government—state government, federal government, their programs, and how money really filters down. I don't think there is a person alive that pays taxes and minds helping somebody who can not help themselves—particularly somebody with mental disabilities. Part of my goal is, if everybody can be more responsible and better educated, then hopefully they will need less government dollars and more government dollars will be spent on a child who will never be able to function as an adult.

Both elected officials and citizens have a responsibility. I have the responsibility to pick up the phone and call their office and ask the legislative aide who deals with the issue. I have done some of that. They have a responsibility to have a staff that is going to cover all areas of government and be knowledgeable. I will tell you, if there was a book put out that had nothing but one page that said, "You won't believe the difference you will make if you will take the time to write or call". . . Most of us never write, and most of us never call. We never give any input other than to vote if we vote. Because I'm close to certain legislators or certain other government officials, I know the impact. Officials will tell me they received a letter, and they didn't know anything about the issue. It may have been one person who wrote, called, or went by the office. They are more moved by that than a lobbyist. It's just that lobbyists are mostly who they hear from. When an individual does do it, they are very moved because not that many individuals give sincere input on issues.

NADINE FRANCIS, ODESSA

I worked for the Governor's Office for Volunteer Services. I was the field coordinator. I helped various departments learn how to recruit volunteers. I had contacts all over the state. Our secretary was a holdover in that office when we went in. After I had been there for a little while, she came in one day and she said, "I don't understand why people would volunteer like you are asking them to. Why don't they get out and get a real job if they are going to give their time like that?" When I went to Austin, I didn't know people didn't know that you volunteer or how to use volunteers. They were afraid that if a volunteer could do their job then they would lose their job. I couldn't see why they didn't know that when they needed somebody to help out in Timbuktu and didn't have anybody out there, they could call. Well, we had somebody in all of these places.

PATTILOU DAWKINS, AMARILLO

I went to Austin and so many times I would think, "What's a little girl like me doing in a place like this?" It was an ego trip. I'll tell this story—it was a part of me I didn't like. The mental health and mental retardation department had a commissioner. He was an M. D., a psychiatrist. It takes someone with business experience to run a department like that. The previous legislature had realized that we needed a business manager and had changed the law saying that the head man did not have to be an M. D. I was appointed in June of '87. It took a lot of time to come up to speed.

Clements appointed me chairman in November. He called me into his office. James Huffines, his appointments chairman, was there. He said, "I want you to be chairman. Can you handle it?" "If you are asking me if I have the ability to be chairman of an organization, the answer is yes. If you're asking me if I know or have the knowledge of MHMR, the answer is no. I can learn it, though, and I can be a good chairman." Clements said, "Well, I want you to be chairman, and there is one thing that I want you to do." He said, "James has done your work for you, and we've got the votes to fire the commissioner. You are the swing vote, and you've got to vote against him." In MHMR, the chairman only voted to break a tie. He said, "Can you do that?" and I said, "Sure, I can do that."

I got back to my hotel room—I get emotional every time I think about it. I thought, that's not right. You can't vote against that man. You don't know him that well. I felt like the most un-Christian person on earth. I felt like, "This is what power has done to you, Patti." I hated myself. The governor's office is the most awe-inspiring place. The whole ambiance is so powerful. I was in there and I was caught up in it and I hated myself. I knew it was wrong. It was *wrong* for me to vote against that guy.

The next morning I called James Huffines and I said, "James, I can't vote against him. I don't know of anything bad that he has done. Let me go talk with him and see if I can get him to resign. Let's go at it another way." He said, "You told the Governor that you would." I said, "Well, I can't, James." He said, "Can you get him to resign?" I said, "I don't know. What can I offer him?" He said, "Well, I don't know, maybe three months severance pay." I said, "Let me go visit with him." So I went in and said, "I'm sure that you have gotten wind the Governor wants you replaced." He said, "Yes, I know." I said, "I think that he has the votes. If I can get you a good severance package, would you resign?" He said, "Yes, I'll do that." I said, "What do you want?" He said, "Six months." So I called James back and I said, "James, he wants six months, but he will resign." He said, "Well, let me talk to the Governor."

We had a board meeting that Friday and this was like Tuesday. He called me back Thursday. He said, "The Governor wants to talk to you." I talked to Governor Clements and said, "Governor, the man has young children. He probably can get a job back in Houston, and I think it's even going to take six months to find somebody to get transitioned. Please do six months." He was real disappointed with me and said it often. Finally, he said, "Okay, you have six months." I called the commissioner that night and said, "You've got six months. Please write a letter in the morning." So that Friday at our board meeting, I presented his letter of resignation.

I look back and I will never forget the power that people have over other people's lives. I thought, I will never, ever again do anything like that. I hated myself. I think of it whenever I think of power—the abuse of power there would have been if I had voted against that guy. You just feel omnipotent. Several years later, James and I discussed that conversation. It was a very defining moment in my service to my government. It made me so aware. I see that happening with people when they get elected or get appointed to something. It's so easy.

CAROLYN PALMER, SAN ANTONIO

In the '80s, the commissioners mostly let the organization tell them how they should work. That was the way it was on the library commission [*Texas State Library and Archives Commission*] in 1989 when I first started. They didn't have a clue as to what was happening in the libraries, and I don't think they even really cared. When I was appointed by Governor Clements, I didn't know a thing about libraries. But I did want to serve on a commission. So as we would go around to various cities, I would call the library and go and talk to whoever would talk to me and learn the language. One time I was in Houston and I finally realized they were rolling out the red carpet. I talked to the head librarian and said, "What is going on? I can't give any speeches. I am trying to sneak in the back door and learn something." He said it was because I was the only commissioner that had ever stepped foot in the library that they knew of. Now, you can't keep the commissioners out. They work very hard with the legislature. I think that appointments are no longer being made as a reward for having given money or your time for helping the governor get elected. You only get appointed if you are going to work.

One would think, as I did, that getting appointed to a commission like the library commission is going to be very quiet. I could not have been more wrong. One of the rules that we set is about who handles the records and how, and where and which records of state government are kept—which ones can be destroyed and which ones can not. Sometimes we don't help the governor. For instance, I got a call when Ann Richards was governor from the state librarian. He said, "I need some help. I got a call from the Governor's representative from Houston. They want me to write a letter saying that it was okay to destroy some of the records that she had destroyed." I said, "Don't write the letter. Let me find out what is going on." What had happened was the Governor had destroyed some telephone records. This was right before Kay Bailey Hutchison was going to go to trial [*on charges of misuse of state employees*]. It was a Monday. I talked to my husband about it. He didn't react like I thought he should react. I thought, well, maybe I am just over reacting.

It was now Thursday. Rick Perry [*then agriculture commissioner*] joined us for hunting, and I said to him casually, "I want to tell you this story." He said, "You are kidding me, of course." I said, "No. This is happening right now. The Governor is in Houston. She wants us to okay that she did this." He said, "What have you done?" I said that I had been trying to get somebody to give me some advice and to react the way I think they should be reacting because I thought this was wrong. Then he called [*political operative*] Karl Rove and all of these phone calls and faxes started. It was just an unbelievable experience. The newspapers got a hold of it and, as a result, the following Monday Kay Bailey Hutchison's trial was dropped. It was because the Governor had just done what they were trying to say that Hutchison had done. The Governor did not get the kind of letter that she wanted. She got a letter, but it stated that there had to be some further investigation. So in that respect, a commission can help or not help the governor.

CLAIRE JOHNSON, ABILENE

I don't think I am nearly as partisan as I may appear. As Governor Bush says, we work for the people of Texas not for either party. In doing that, you have to be willing to listen to what the other side has to say. There are certain issues where the person you expect least likely to agree with you will show you that he is right. You may be wrong because you didn't have the right information. You have to learn to put your ego away and listen to what people have to say.

JANIS LOWE, FRIENDSWOOD

I was appointed to the Board of Pilot Commissioners for the Ports of Galveston County. According to the statute, the pilots work directly for the governor. The governor has got to have the board in order to ensure safety in the ports. He expects the commission to make recommendations as to who are the best qualified pilots.

We have been a hands-on commission, and with all respect to the gentlemen I think it is because there are three women on the commission. We went out on the ships to see what in the world we were setting policy for. I have boarded many a ship at sea when it is ten miles out. You go out on the pilot boat and the boat and the ship run right together. A very talented pilot boat operator will just kiss the big ship and never stop. You climb up a ladder sixty feet in the air that can swing. To let go of the boat and put both hands on the ladder and climb—I was so exhilarated that I had done it. I appreciate what pilots do in inclement weather because I am a fair weather commissioner. It was really scary, but it gave me an appreciation for what they do. The skills they have to possess—because when they are called, they don't get a choice of not going. It is a male world, and the three of us women have pushed our way into it.

CAROLE WOODARD, HOUSTON & GALVESTON

When Bush was elected governor, he appointed me to the Texas Board of Human Services. I feel like we have been able to accomplish some things that have made a difference. We brought out the Lone Star Card—it's used to purchase groceries like a credit card. We implemented programs to bring mothers off welfare. We supervise welfare, the elderly, Medicaid, food stamps, nursing homes, and homeless care agencies. We try to push forth Bush's agenda—every citizen being held accountable and those people that are able to work having opportunities to work. We also push his agenda for welfare to work.

CYNTHIA TAUSS, LEAGUE CITY

When I got in there, I quickly realized that the perception of the parole board as dealing only with violent murderers and pedophiles is incorrect. The really violent offenders are only a small, small percentage. The rest is drugs, credit card theft, and burglary. Back in the early '90s, they were letting everybody out. The Governor has changed a lot of the laws. Those truly violent people do not get out. The State of Texas, whether it be through mandatory release or discharge of sentences or parole, has to maintain a 15 percent release rate or we will be back in court. Fifteen percent every year! No matter how full the prisons are, I know that the Governor is never going to ask us to release anybody that we are not ready to release.

Victims' groups used to despise the parole board. Now the parole board is supported by all of the victims' organizations. Contrary to what the media says about us being a secret organization, we are not. All of the members meet regularly with the victims groups, with family members, and even with inmate groups. We try to communicate with everyone in the process.

Did you seek this appointment?

After the election [*of Governor George W. Bush*], everyone talked about appointments. When I was in high school, I made a list of goals for myself. One of them, and I don't know where it came from, was to be on the Texas Board of Pardons and Paroles. So when this opportunity came up I applied. I worked very hard for it. I got letters of recommendations from my senator, some police departments, the NAACP, and Democrat elected officials. I went everywhere to show support and to get the position. Some of the people that I work with on the board who were Ann Richards' appointees said, "You applied?" There didn't seem to be any application process at that time. When people ask me, I tell them to call the appointments office and have them send you a green sheet. Fill it out and send it in. It is very open.

What kind of goals were set by the president when you held an appointed position?

ANN WALLACE, FORT WORTH & AUSTIN

Actually, you are pretty much left without anybody saying "this is what you must do." When I went to Washington, I sort of sat there thinking, "Okay, where's the word? What do I do as director of the United States Office of Consumer Affairs?" I found out after about a month that there wasn't a guidebook. Concern about privacy issues had started at this point because of the ability of computers to compile data. So that was one of the things we dealt with. We published a handbook and gave the name and address of almost every major corporation in the United States, along with who to write and a sample letter of how to complain. We dealt with various complaints. You try and serve the president as best you can.

I was head of the delegation to go to the Organization of Economic and Property Development—OEPD. The headquarters were in Paris. You'd go to these meetings and come out in the hall and all these people were saying the Bush administration doesn't pay any attention to us. It would really irritate me. I told the White House one time, "I've got a woman, an ACLU [*American Civil Liberties Union*] lawyer, who is pretty reasonable, and I'm going to put her on my official delegation to go to the OEPD meetings." There was dead silence. I said, "Check it out, but I think this would be a wise thing to do." Finally, somebody called me back and said,

"Well, it's your game." I almost had an ulcer over the thing. I did that two or three times with people who were really very vocal against the administration. All of them thanked me for being included in the delegation and thanked me for allowing them to speak. They would bring up their issues, which was all right in my opinion because at least I was giving them an arena to express things, which sort of somehow had the blessing of the President. They couldn't very well bad-mouth him.

When I first got there I said, "Give me the name of everybody that is out there against us." The top person was Ralph Nader. I sent word out to all of them that I wanted them to come over for a brown-bag lunch. My staff thought I'd lost my mind. I said, "I don't want any of you all there because I don't want to be able to pull on a resource. I want one person there to take notes." Ralph Nader did not come but Joan Claybrook did. They all came because they were very curious about this. We had a very good meeting. They wanted to know what my agenda was. I said, "I don't have one. I want to know what your agenda is." I said, "I've got somebody over here taking notes because at my age I don't remember everything." So at least I was on speaking terms with everybody and knew where our enemies were, so to speak.

BERYL MILBURN, AUSTIN

I served on the U. S. delegation that observed the El Salvador elections. We rode with armed guards everywhere we went. I remember taking a helicopter ride to go to one of the remote villages to observe the election. We flew high enough that we couldn't be hit by a rifle but low enough to be able to see the countryside. While we were gone, there was a firefight in the mountain behind our hotel.

It amazed me that you would see people walking for miles to go and vote. Then they would dip their finger or thumb in some kind of ink to show that they had voted. They had to walk home knowing that some of their neighbors might shoot them. The opposition was very vehement about trying to stop the election. People stood in line for hours to vote, and they had walked for hours to get there. But the trouble with an official delegation like that is there are really three parts to an election—registration of the voters, casting the ballots, and counting the ballots. All we observed was the voting. The first part and the last part we didn't participate in, so how could we tell whether it was an honest election? You really couldn't.

ESTHER BUCKLEY, LAREDO

My husband told me on a Friday that on Sunday we were going to Washington. On Monday I went through interviews all day long. At the end of the day, they told me to go back to my hotel and "we will let you know." That night, they called me back and said that I was going to be appointed to the Commission on Civil Rights.

My job was to enforce the Bill of Rights, to study the issues of discrimination as to race, color, creed, ethnic or national origin, and to look at all laws and all agencies. We had monitoring responsibilities on all the agencies. The commission is an advisory board to the president. We met once a month except for July or August. It could be either two days or four days, and we would have hearings all over the country. I was very lucky because my school superintendent was extremely progressive. When I got appointed, I came back and said, "They want me to travel maybe two to four days a month." My superintendent said, "Every time you go, you do more for the 22,000 children in our school district than if you stay in the classroom."

Did it make a difference that you were appointed to the commission as opposed to a Hispanic Democrat?

It was of value in the community in the sense that the Democrats had been here for so long they really didn't have a Laredo Hispanic woman out there. I was on the stage with Reagan at the rallies in Dallas and in Austin. It made Democrats look again. It made them think, maybe we are in the wrong place. Plus, I am convinced that a lot of women got recognition in the Democratic Party because they had to compete with the Republican Party for a change. If Clements or Tower appointed somebody, they needed to do something to match it because they were losing. For a change, they were actually having to do something for this area [*South Texas*], whereas before they were taking us for granted. It's the way the system works. We were getting discretionary money from Clements for this area so the Democrats were going to have to do something. They were going to have to deliver some of what they had promised because now there was somebody else who could deliver. Having money coming in during the Reagan years, we got a lot of things done with housing grants and urban development grants that wouldn't have come in otherwise.

As a member of the commission, I did not get what I wanted as far as putting out reports on Hispanic issues. But I read every single report that came out during my nine years. I did a lot of editing. We looked at some issues that I think were important. In 1988, we were looking at the fact that the minority population in Texas is going to be a majority, and we had better do something about their education and work skills. If 40 percent of our Hispanic kids are dropping out of school, and they're one of the larger groups, it doesn't take a very efficient mathematician to know this is serious. There will be 40 percent unemployment and more in the Hispanic community. A lot of what I learned I brought back. Education is the answer, and anything that we do for education is going to make a difference.

Influencing Public Policy

As a woman dedicated to politics and agriculture your whole life, did you ever have an opportunity to affect public policy?

NITA GIBSON, LUBBOCK

Have you ever heard of the PIK program? That was my idea. In 1982, the first part of Reagan's administration, we were in a very, very serious economic slump. Farmers were going broke. Every time I'd walk, my mind was full of agriculture. What can we do? Everything you can point your finger at, we have a surplus. Prices are zilch, and here we are getting ready to raise another bin-buster.

We lived out of town a couple of miles, and I used the Hobbs Highway to go into Seminole to the cotton co-op office. It was a four-lane highway, and the side going into town was torn up. Have you ever seen these machines that tear up the old asphalt and run it through a little deal, then they run it back through and press it and it is brand new highway? The second day I watched this I thought, why can't we recycle our crops back to ourselves? Why do we want to just keep producing when there isn't a market and go further in debt? It was a custom of mine to try my wild ideas out on friends and some enemies every once in a while. You know you have got to get the truth. I asked about five farmers that were big in Gaines County. What if we agreed to set aside 50 percent of our land this year and not plant? In lieu of that, we get back an equal amount from last year's crop. They said, "You know, it might work." As it happened, a friend called me and said, "The National Cotton Council is having a producers' steering committee meeting in Lubbock. Are you going to go?" She said, "I wish that you would."

The meeting started at nine o'clock. I was the only female, which was not unusual, except for the reporter at the *Avalanche Journal*, Kathleen Harris. She and I sat at the very back. They knew who I was, and at coffee-break time, I went up to the chairman of the committee and said, "I've got an idea. I have a copy of it here. Would you like to see it?" So I gave it to him and to the others that were standing around. After the coffee break, I sat down with Kathleen. First thing you know, I heard my name. The delegate from California stood up and said, "This cotton pool, what is this cotton pool?" So I explained it.

I said the whole idea is PIK—Payment In Kind. Instead of us raising 100 percent of our production capability, let us produce only 50 percent of it and receive equal amount from storage—because it is in the bins—as a payment in kind. Old Charlie Cunningham was in the audience from the USDA [*U. S. Department of Agriculture*]. There were some soybean and corn people there. That was like 9:30 or 10:00 in the morning and by noon that idea was in Washington D. C. Within ten days time, I was called to come to the White House because President Reagan was going to announce this program. I said, gosh darn, I don't have the money to fly up there. So Charles and I drove to Dallas, and Reagan came to Dallas and announced it at the Farm Bureau convention.

How do you think that your involvement in politics helped you have the confidence to present your idea?

People need to realize that their involvement in politics is one of the best ways to grow. I remember the first time I had to introduce somebody I was shaking all over. Just scared absolutely to death to make any kind of public announcement. You have the challenges, the opposition, the confrontations, and you grow. You don't get cynical and get mad and get all bent out of shape. You just work with it and roll with the punches.

Have you seen women have an impact on policy on an informal basis?

DORIS WILLIAMS, LAKE JACKSON

Sure. Once they get to know you, they listen to you. I've had many candidates call me up and ask me about my opinion on things before I was elected mayor. They believe in your judgment and if you say things, you're going to follow through. Republican women through the years have a very good reputation and get very much respect from the elected officials because they realize that these people have helped them in many ways. Maybe they want to just call and get some grassroots information on what is happening. Through the years you do get to know people real well, and you are important to them.

LUCILLE ROCHS, FREDERICKSBURG

The people that I have supported, like Jeff Wentworth, Harvey Hilderbran, and Lamar Smith, are people that I have checked out and gotten to know personally. I was in Washington this March with the Child Welfare League of America. We spent an afternoon on Capitol Hill. I was in nine congressional offices and talked to aides. I have gone up for the last three years to do this. We have been able to get legislation through Congress to improve the lives of families and children. We got new legislation passed this year for children who are in foster care and will be graduating from high school and becoming independent. They were not allowed to have more than $1,000 in assets. What were they going to live on? We got that changed from $1,000 to $10,000. We have gotten other benefits for kids who do not have family to support them but who really want to get an education or a job or vocational training.

My advice is to get to know the elected officials' aides. Attend their functions and introduce yourself. If there are bills before the House or before the Senate, get people involved in letter writing and phone calling so they know that we out here in the grassroots know they are there and have some things that we would like for them to consider and support. I have not done this alone. I have done this because I know a lot of people and am very involved in the community. I am just the spark plug.

CHAPTER 19

Where Now?

"A lot of other people just say, oh, politics is a dirty game.
It's very sad. They are giving up their right to control their own
destiny by not participating!"   —MARY LOU WIGGINS

*he Texas Republican Party now has the opportunity to take
advantage of the organization and victories of the past fifty
years and develop into a party that can dominate the Texas
political landscape for the next fifty years. The Party must find
ways to attract youth and minorities to the Republican philosophy the way it did in years past. To rid the state and nation of
apathy, the Party must effectively communicate the ways in
which politics affects our daily lives. People of all generations can
fulfill their dreams and breathe political life into their ideas
through their actions and with their money.*

The Changing Role of the Party

ANNE ARMSTRONG, ARMSTRONG

Things have changed a lot since I was so active in politics.
The Party is far less important now. I remember the columnist in
Washington, David Broder, who I came to respect even though he
is much more liberal than I am. When I went up to Washington as
co-chairman of the Republican National Committee, I was proud
that with the help of others we got the female part of the pair
designated as co-chairman, not vice chairman, and I was elected
instead of just appointed by the male chairman. It gave me my
own constituency and my own strengths for the women. David

Broder told me and subsequently wrote often on how the parties were diminishing in power. He was very sorry about it. I was sorry then and a little miffed to think that the Republican National Committee was going to diminish in importance, but it has and so have the state parties.

I say that media is the main reason. With television now, the candidates can build up their constituencies in a way that was impossible before. But the main thing, I think, is that the media has taken the place, in many ways, of the state party and its importance in backing candidates. It's more like a referendum now than it is a regular election. There is not the filtering anymore of a party. In some ways, that is bad. We make mistakes. Maybe if we had had a larger, wiser Democratic Party, it would have checked more on William Clinton. But he was awfully good on the tube, and the public liked him. There weren't the old back-room party checks and rechecks on candidates they were going to offer to the public.

It's fun to relive the Party the way I saw it was, or wished it were, in the past. We need to face reality about the campaigns of President George Bush or Senators Kay Hutchison or Phil Gramm. They want the Party. They need the Party. They treasure the Party. They don't want to get at odds with the Party. But their clout today, compared to what it would have been in the '60s, is far greater than it was back then. The individual candidates whether a legislator or a Senator—and the higher up the rank you are the more clout you get—have independence from the Party because they can command the media.

Organizational Priorities

Passing the Torch

THEO WICKERSHAM, SAN ANTONIO

Mary Morton Jackson [*precinct organizer and SREC member*] told me you can never retire until you have someone to follow in your footsteps.

GAIL WATERFIELD, CANADIAN

My bottom line thinking, and I tell my kids this, is that I worked during my younger years and I have contributed and now it's *your* turn. You're the ones that are going to have to go through the educational system with children. You're the ones that are going to have to go begging on the streets for medical care. I'm financially secure, and I've got insurance. You go solve it. I think that the forty-year-old and younger generations are very disillusioned.

I think there are so many people who truly say to themselves, "I can't do anything about it. I can't make a difference." Whereas my generation never thought we couldn't make a difference. We weren't smarter. We weren't brighter. My children are both very successful. They just don't have any interest in politics. I think they will one day, maybe. I hope so.

SURRENDEN ANGLY, AUSTIN

One of the deepest concerns that I have is watching my children and their families and their friends. They are all married, and they all live in Austin. Even when the mother stays at home, the husband doesn't get home until 7:30 or 8:00 o'clock at night. There are a lot of driven and well-educated people with good ideas that can't possibly take on a political role in anything. They can barely take on a PTA meeting. It is very disturbing to me how much this generation, let's call it thirty-plus, works. Many of them have fabulous ideas, but they are exhausted. We were not that way. I am concerned that this is going to cut down on good potential candidates of any kind.

MARTHA WEISEND, DALLAS

I will spend my time to help groom the younger generation. We have some very bright young men and women, young professional people who are very capable, to lead our party by being elected to office or just by simply giving of their time and energy. I think that will be my challenge. What I've learned I can put in a thimble, but I want to share that thimbleful of what I know with younger, wiser people who are coming along. They care about Texas, and they care about what is happening to our country. When you look at the television, we are very blessed to be Americans. If that's silly or a little weird, I don't care because I believe that, and unless we keep telling our story it is going to fade.

Challenges of Governing

ANN LEE, HOUSTON

It is easier to be knocking on the door trying to get in, because you mind your p's and q's more, but when you get in and dominate things it's scary. We have to be very careful. It is very disheartening for me to realize that not all Republicans wear a white hat.

MARJORIE ARSHT, HOUSTON

The Republican Party has to learn how to govern. They are learning it at the state level. But the fact of the matter is that today, with the wealth of elected people that we have, it's up to them now not to be intimidated and to stop feeding the kitty with money. We have a man here [*a political consultant*]. He intimidates people. "If you don't give me $10,000 or $25,000 then I will run someone against you." They have all fallen for it. With the 1998 Republican sweep [*of statewide offices*], I hope that they are not going to be as intimidated as they have been in the past. Our future lies with our elected officials now. I used to believe in the power of the people, but I don't anymore because well-rounded people have lost interest. We were after the Holy Grail. We were idealists. We were going to change Texas, change the world. I think people have lost faith in that.

Minorities and Youth

NANCY PALM, HOUSTON

We have got to find some way to deal with the ethnicity that is here. One of the media came to me about the Asian community not too long ago. They said, "Nancy, you are the only one that I remember back in the '70s who was talking about the fact that the Asians had to be brought into the political process." We did have an Asian candidate, and she is now on the council and ran for countywide office and we almost elected her—Martha Wong. That to me is the biggest problem this Party faces—that and not allowing litmus tests. I will be blunt about it—the homosexual situation and the abortion situation. I am about as firm against abortion as a human can be. My husband [*a doctor*] would come home and talk to me about these little babies. He came close to thinking that it was murder to kill one of them. That affected me a great deal. But we can not let two issues determine the future of this party.

RAQUEL GONZALEZ, LAREDO

We have to go to the grassroots to reach Hispanics. We have to educate people. We have to have leaders who are willing to go out there and, like anything else, start converting people, like a religion, and start communicating what Republicans stand for. It's going to be a big effort. We have to invest money in the process.

BILLIE PICKARD, RAYMONDVILLE

We tend to lump Hispanics as though they are a homogenous group. I would go after the better-educated people because they have more in common with the Republican Party. Their goals and aspirations are more like the Republican Party. I would not pursue the vote of the Hispanics who are used to having their vote bought, being carried to the polling place, and being told how to vote. That was one of the mistakes that I saw during my time of involvement. There were Hispanics who were desirous of getting into your pocket. So they would go to the campaigns and say, if you will give me money to do this and money to do that then I will put on this event for you and we can bring x-number of votes. History shows that they couldn't and didn't. Yet it was a natural thing for the candidate or the organization of the candidate to want to believe that they could deliver.

If I were building the Party, I would contact people like our upstanding local federal judge and ask him for names of young, promising Hispanics who have similar conservative views and work with them. Whether Anglo, Hispanic, or whatever, they need to be people that can be respected. They will bring other people along with them.

ANNE SHEPARD, VICTORIA & HARLINGEN

Give Hispanics opportunities for fundraising and helping. Give them opportunities to come into the Party and be a part of it as far as organization. When you are having a fundraiser, invite new people to help. When you're having a Republican function and have different officeholders to town, be sure and include them in the organization process. Include new people. It doesn't matter if they are male or female, old or young—you just need a mix of people working. When you have the same old group, whether it is five of you or twenty but it is the same people, you have a clique and people are uncomfortable in a clique. It is common sense and it is courtesy.

CAROLE WOODARD, HOUSTON & GALVESTON

The best way to reach African Americans is to constantly keep the education process going among the black professionals who think for themselves and are basically Independents. There are many, many, many blacks in Houston that are independent thinkers. They don't vote party, but they vote who is going to do the best for them. Those are the people that you have to target and pull into the Party. The more information that you give them, the more knowledgeable they become about the two parties and candidates. There are poor candidates in both parties. There are some Republicans that I would not vote for, but overall the Republican platform and the Republican Party is where you'll find most of the professional people and that is where most of them are voting. The problem is you can't count them because they live in neighborhoods where the boxes are predominantly white. Unless you're out there doing an exit poll, you do not know that black people are voting Republican. If the polls show that you got 27 percent of the black vote, it is probably much higher. The neighborhood that I live in is mostly white. I'm probably counted as a white vote.

How can you reach black children?

It has to be done through the churches and organizations like Jack & Jill and Links. Organizations and churches where children are taught to be independent thinkers. I don't think you tell them to be one party or another but just not to be brainwashed.

JAN CLARK, HOUSTON

The Greater Houston Council of Republican Women has gotten involved with immigration and naturalization. We just had a day passing out the Republican philosophy in six languages. I put a welcome sheet on there with my phone number. We actually got our first phone call. We are trying to put together things that these people really need when they become new citizens or come to a new country. Of course, some of them have been here for a while. We're trying to pull together some things that they really are interested in to get them involved with us. Job opportunities, health, doctors they may need to know about, that sort of thing. We have an outreach chairman, and she has six people under her—a Filipino, a Chinese, two blacks, and a Hispanic who has been through immigration herself. The Filipino does a radio program every morning. She works to get them to vote. They will call her and ask who to vote for. They opened a Hispanic Republican headquarters here in town. They try to pull them in and get them active. Get them to vote. Make them Republicans.

DIANA RYAN, SAN ANGELO

The young people probably don't see themselves as contestants at all in the arena because they don't think they have what it takes. Words are cheap and unless you have the money you can't buy a place in it. One thing that may be good is the computer age. People can bypass high-dollar giving and get to issues and someone's position. The information superhighway may prove to be able to include people across the land like we have never been able to do before. It's getting so you can get any kind of information you want, and it is not jaded by what ABC or NBC says. Television is kind of a catch-22. People turn on the TV, and if it is broadcast it is believable. We as a nation have not learned to say, "Wait a minute. I don't believe that." People are the key to everything. People caring about one another.

CINDY BROCKWELL, BOERNE

Young women can form school clubs through the schools' government classes. Some take field trips to county commissioners court so they can see personally what kind of decisions elected officials are making. When I talk to kids, I just remind them that government affects everything you do. What age do you get your driver's license? Do you have to wear a helmet riding a motorcycle? What age can you drink alcohol? How fast can you go on the roads? They can see, yes, it does affect me.

CATHY McCONN, HOUSTON

I see the future of the Republican Party growing brighter because the young people who I meet, particularly in the Young Republicans—the young marrieds and the young singles—are very enthusiastic about our message. They are every bit as conservative if not more than those of us who have been at it for a longer time. They understand that it helps the family. There was a recent survey that identified the Republican Party as the Party of family values. It is about individual freedom and letting people do what they know they can do if the government would just get out of the way and stop taxing them so heavily. All those things the young people understand.

LAVERNE EVANS, EL PASO

I taught for a quite a while and worked to get young people involved in the political process. I always stressed that it was a privilege and a responsibility to be involved in the political process and to know what is going on. If you know where a candidate stands, you have a pretty good idea of what they are going to do once they are elected. You need to follow up to see if they fulfilled their promises. I even got to take them to the airport when President Reagan came. When Congressman Jim Collins came, the students interviewed him. They got to go to several of the election-night campaign headquarters and see what the process is of winning and losing. It was just a process that I got them involved in so that when they got older they would vote.

ANN HARRINGTON, PLANO

I read patriotic stories to my grandchildren that you can hardly find anymore, if you are not an old book collector like I am, since they have changed the history books. We put out a flag, and we respect the flag. I think it is just being a good citizen in general. You have to start treating people the way you like to be treated.

What advice would you give a girl today who wonders if she could be an outspoken woman of principle?

PATRICIA LYKOS, HOUSTON

First of all, search for a virtuous life. You are going to die, and you know it, so you have got two choices in life. You can live a life of honor and dignity or you can make it an existentialist absurdity. Then you make the decision that you're going to live your life with honor and you're going to be in search of a virtuous life. You determine what your principles are. You live them. It is sort of like religion. I subscribe to Saint Matthew's theory that you pray in private. Or like they say in Texas, that you walk the walk because there are a lot of people who talk the talk. You have got to be able to look in the mirror and respect yourself. I despise the word self-esteem. That is such an oxymoron anyway. How can you esteem yourself? You esteem others, but you can respect yourself.

So the first thing is to live your life so that you have self-respect. You start out with that as your premise and your foundation. You gain as much knowledge as possible. I encourage girls to be as athletic as possible. Not only is it healthy, but competition hones those skills. Whatever you decide to do, be passionate about it. Politics manifests itself in many ways. Some people are campaign managers, others are strategists or run for office. There are just so many ways to participate in politics, but the important thing is that you do participate. If you care, do something.

SUSAN WEDDINGTON, SAN ANTONIO

The Republican Party has got to take a more serious look at today's technology, especially to reach our young people. The Internet is a wonderful vehicle for accessing the youth. The other thing is to increase our visibility on the college campuses. It is hard to keep a consistency to that organization because young people move in and out of school. In the near future, the state party needs to take a more active role to be sure that that auxiliary is more consistent and more active on the campuses. Our leaders need to spend more time going into classrooms. We need to be more actively engaged. We also need to cast a vision to the local communities, either through the local Republican Women's Clubs or through the county organization or both, to develop outreach programs that will include younger people in various activities and events. There is so much we can do at the local level to include young people. The vision and emphasis need to come from the top leadership.

How about the minority community?

The model of the last four years is fairly good to continue, which is personal outreach. In the past, outreach programs have consisted of touring the minority areas just before the campaigns and establishing a Hispanics-for-whomever and really never hearing from us again. Governor Bush along with our other statewide candidates in '98 really went all out going to areas that had been traditionally Democrat and spending a lot of time there. The fruit of that was the number of Hispanics voting Republican was substantially increased, with the Governor winning some counties that had never been won before by Republicans. What it takes is commitment. The SREC followed up on that and took our meetings out of Austin for the first time in twenty years. We went to McAllen, El Paso, and Beaumont. We got great coverage because the question was, "Why are you bothering to come to areas that are Democrat strongholds?" To show people that we truly want them to have an opportunity to participate in our Party and get to know us. It is important for us to go to where the people are and not ask them to come to us.

How did Jacque Allen influence you when you were young and thinking about getting involved in politics?

CAROLYN NICHOLAS, WICHITA FALLS

Jacque was the Republican Party not only in Wichita County but also in the entire area. When I first became interested in the Party, Jacque had been the county chairman and on the state committee. She commanded the respect of people because she had knowledge and she was effective. Even when we were young, she was always a political mentor. She didn't exclude us. She made a special effort to invite us to special things. It was fascinating to see her interact with people because it was always about the issues and the races. It was never a front for her to promote herself. But for me, especially, it was the respect that Jacque seemed to command from everybody.

Get Rid of Cynicism and Vote

MARY LOU WIGGINS, DALLAS

It is so important to vote. A lot of other people just say, oh, politics is a dirty game. It's very sad. They are giving up their right to control their own destiny by not participating! They don't have that sense of mission. They are willing to compromise and let it happen.

CAROLE RAGLAND, LEAGUE CITY

People are complacent and don't want to be bothered. They don't want to rock the boat. They'd rather stay home and watch television than go to the precinct conventions, or go sail than go to the county conventions.

JUANDELLE LACY, MIDLAND

I know and I hope that others realize how important politics is—the process of it, not necessarily politics itself. Without it we would not have our freedom. I don't think that so many young people or baby boomers realize the price that has been paid and what we've got. All wars are political. I have been all over the world, and there is truly nothing better. We have lots of faults, but our process is the best there is.

LOIS WHITE, SAN ANTONIO

You are in politics whether you know it or not. It is a part of life. Dirty people make dirty politics. I learned way back when that you always voted. Even when you didn't vote, you voted, because by not voting you helped whoever win. You helped the bad guys win by not voting so you have voted. It's hard day after day to keep on doing what people see as change. But if I had been in a state that was all Republican and there were no Democrats, I would have said, maybe we need a second voice here.

I am accustomed to being a minority. It taught me some things, too. I know how you have to survive in a majority. Republicans here don't know that—how to survive as a minority. They have never been a minority in anything else. There are certain ways a minority has to survive. You believe in your righteousness—I am on the side of right. Even though there is one person here, I am worth more than 2,000 or 3,000. It doesn't get you the office but it doesn't stop you from trying to jump on out there.

Openness

BETTE JO BUHLER, VICTORIA

I don't think there is a question but what we all have the responsibility to maintain openness, morality, and conservatism without a capital "C." We've got to maintain our interest in the entire population. We get the reputation for being kind of a closed party for only the elite. I don't know how we earned that.

Every piece of mail that I get stresses how serious they are in getting your opinion. We all raise our eyebrows because down at the bottom there it is—the question, will you give $100, $500, or $1,000? You feel that that is the ultimate purpose.

You have got to choose a candidate locally that convinces people. We have to have people working for the Republican Party on the volunteer staff and the women's clubs who are totally open and not discouraging and unwilling to listen.

CAROLYN NICHOLAS, WICHITA FALLS

There is always a group that comes along and thinks they invented the Party. About every decade it seems. The biggest thing is to co-opt that group. So often they come in as an opposition group. Get them interested in, not a single issue and not a single candidate, but in the Party. I have been told that those days are numbered, but to survive as a Party, that is what we have got to do.

BILLIE WHITEFIELD, HOUSTON

They can not squabble and get too compartmentalized. Some of the women would be diametrically opposed to each other on certain issues and yet if their candidate got the nomination I worked for them because he was Republican. If we can continue to keep that as our objective, we will grow. In other words, sure, I'm going to work for a candidate that reflects my views and others will work for another candidate, but philosophically we agree 75 percent maybe 80 percent. Decide that winning the election is the main thing. I feel like, if after the primary our candidate is elected, and I helped elect him, then even though we may not agree on everything I have more influence and more input. He is still more likely down the line to vote my way on something than a Democrat.

GAYLE WEST AND ISABEL GRAY, PASADENA

West: Disagree, have your differences in your precinct, but don't hold grudges.

Gray: We had to work with all different kinds of people. Any Republican would be better than a liberal Democrat as long as they aren't immoral. You can't win if you are fighting each other. We had battles in the SREC, and after it was over we didn't dislike each other, we worked with each other. Some people think that there is just one issue and they will stick with it no matter what. We are losing our country! They can't see the forest for the trees. I'm not for abortion, but some people just can't understand. The only thing they think about is abortion. There is more than one issue—taxes, crime, and national defense. I truly don't believe that you can legislate morality. If a person is going to have an abortion, they will find a way.

West: It's definitely power. We have a lot of that in the local organization.

Preserve the Grassroots

PAT JACOBSON, FORT WORTH

You have to get people involved to get them to the polls. When [*President Bill*] Clinton won, very few people went to the polls. That means not very many people were involved. When Reagan won, just look at the people that he drew. Ronald Reagan was the grassroots guy. He believed in people being involved. I think that's why he won. I'm not saying that you don't need money. That would be foolish to say. But it is more important that you have people involved. You can't win a race unless you have people voting.

ESTELLE TEAGUE, HURST

The biggest responsibility Republicans have is to listen to their constituents. If you don't listen to your constituents, you don't know what is going on. As long as they continue to listen to their constituents, they will continue to be reelected.

JESS ANN THOMASON, MIDLAND

I have had some disappointing fundraisers for incumbent candidates where donors felt "we got them elected and they've forgotten us." I would put things together the next election, and people would say, "Well, I have already supported him. He has forgotten who I am, and I was his best friend the last time." So the candidates don't stay in touch with their donors and contributors. That really hurts worse than anything.

They need to come into Midland or other cities, like Senator Teal Bivens does. He will bring different candidates in and have a luncheon. It's called the 31 Club. Then you follow that with a little reception say at five o'clock and serve Diet Cokes and Sprites. Just spend thirty minutes telling them what is happening in Austin or Washington. You have the Republican Women on the phones calling people to get them out for it, or you send postcards. They show up. They want to be remembered.

MICKEY LAWRENCE, HOUSTON

We have got to get back to grassroots campaigning, and we have got to get back control of the grassroots in the Republican Party. It belongs to big-money interests and special-interest PACs. Different PACs are trying to get the word out and recruit candidates. One thing we are trying to do is to get information out to the Republican activists about this process. I have been giving talks on how PACs work, how they get their money. I accumulated all of the different articles that have been written in the last three or four years. Usually, when people walk out of my talk and are active Republicans, they say, "We didn't know all of this was going on." It is a matter of educating people about how this system really works.

The bottom-line message that I am trying to give is grassroots Republicans have to take back control of their Party. Now, it is large-money interests, and a lot of the large-money interests are nothing more than candidates on a slate pooling all of their money into a PAC, which is nothing more than a political consultant handling twenty-five different candidates who are contributing to the political consultant's action committee. The literature all comes out as if there is a PAC endorsing all of these candidates. Really, it is not the support of individuals like you and me. It is from the campaign funds of all of these candidates that pool their money.

People don't even realize that. People need to know the truth. The truth is not getting out. A lot of times, when people do hear the truth, they are very uncomfortable with confrontation. They hear the truth, but it is sort of a silent truth.

Role of Candidates

ANDY BEAVER AND NANCY STEVENS, CORPUS CHRISTI

Stevens: It might take longer for Nueces County to be a two-party county, but we carried for Governor Bush last time.

Beaver: Even in my precinct. In 1968, seven voted in the primary, but in the 1998 general election we carried it. Now we can be the election judges.

Stevens: If your precinct goes Republican, then you get to be election judge. We went from 20 election judges to 63, and there are 122 precincts in Nueces County. When you have an election judge, you don't have to pay a poll watcher. You know the election is going to be run better.

JAN KENNADY, NEW BRAUNFELS

Having qualified candidates who will run is our next challenge. We have a real dearth often of candidates who are qualified. It's from the local level on up. The life of a politician is not very easy. I know so many people who would be wonderful elected officials who wouldn't touch it. That is certainly true on the local level. That is one of our greatest challenges.

RUTH SCHIERMEYER, LUBBOCK

I ran a campaign for an Independent. Our sheriff died, and because of the timing the parties had to put someone on the ballot. The executive committee met and put someone on the ballot that had been forced to resign from two other counties. I had the man that I knew needed to run put his name on the ballot as an Independent. Then I volunteered to run his campaign. Everyone said that you could not win a campaign as an Independent. The Republican vote was too strong. Roughly 35 percent of the people in Lubbock County vote straight party. We won with 87 percent of the vote. Everything that could be against us was. Straight party votes did count, so we had to educate voters that they could vote for him. From the party side, he is a Republican. He voted Republican thirteen years and is a Hispanic Republican.

They asked him if he was going back to the Republican Party the night he was elected. He said, "I never left." The other Republican had not voted in one of our primaries. It was just a power play. It puts a lot of responsibility on us. I am Republican through and through, but as Republicans, if we become as strong as the Democrats used to be, it is our responsibility to be absolutely certain that the Republican candidates are the best candidates. That is not what we had done in this case.

Role of Volunteers

ANNA MOWERY, FORT WORTH

I really do dislike the fact that we're using paid phone banks, even away from the state. We're having people that can not pronounce the names of the candidates making the phone calls. I realize that it is very difficult to get the volunteers necessary to run a phone bank, but Mike Waldron, my phone bank chair, never has had a problem with it and I have never had a problem. The fact that you have a dedicated person making the phone call for their friend [*the candidate*] is very effective to me. I hate that we're getting away from it. Politics is local—everybody knows that. Anytime we replace volunteers with paid staff, there is a problem. Volunteers defend you at the coffee shop. When you're having coffee and people start saying that the person who's running for office is a stupid idiot, you have someone who will say, I don't think so. I know this person and they have bright ideas. You have armies out there, going where they go everyday besides being at the headquarters.

BILLIE PICKARD, RAYMONDVILLE

TV is now the dominant factor. I look back at Clayton Williams, and his [*gubernatorial*] campaign was primarily a TV campaign. The first one I can remember. They made some effort locally but did not have the state and county organization that candidates like Bill Clements had. So when Williams stubbed his toe, he didn't have people in a local area that had made the commitment to his campaign there to say, "Oh, he shouldn't have done that, but . . ."

JANE NELSON, FLOWER MOUND

In today's world, you need money to win a campaign. There is no doubt about it. The beauty of volunteers is that these are people who know you. They live in your community. They each have their realm of people that they live with and go to church with and work with. No message that comes across on television relates to people like somebody in their community saying, "I know this lady and she believes in what we believe in and she will make it happen." The value of volunteers is immeasurable. I could never have won my election without dedicated volunteers. But you still need some money.

CATHERINE SMYTH COLGAN, DALLAS

If you take the people out of politics, you lose. There is an old saying that involvement breeds interest. When you involve the people, they become interested in the candidate and interested in the race. They will get out and work.

Special Interests

Do you think you made a difference being elected as a Republican rather than as a Democrat?

SHAROLYN WOOD, HOUSTON

Yes. I don't know if it is true for people coming in today because of a more mature Republican Party. But definitely in the '80s, we could come in without special-interest groups wanting a piece of us. I have watched my Democrat judge friends have to go out to the special-interest groups in their Party and stand up and eat all of their principles and try to walk a tightrope without compromising their principles to stay in office. Their special-interest groups are pretty well known and identifiable. It concerns me that I see Republican special-interest groups following the natural paths.

In my election speeches, I have said repeatedly that the most wonderful thing about running as a Republican was that you didn't have special-interest groups wanting to litmus test you. I think that is changing today. There are a lot of people on the bench today to whom I said, "Run as a Republican—it is not like being over there in the Democratic Party where there are all of these people that you have to kowtow to. Come to the Republican Party because the Republican Women are there and they will not hold you up for money. They are good honest people that just want good honest public servants." That is our selling card, and it is what we ought to stay with as a Party. We have been successful and should not forget that.

Stay True to the Mission

PATTILOU DAWKINS, AMARILLO

The TFRW has been a real influence. That is a wonderful organization if they'll stick to their knitting. One of the most influential books in my life was *What We Must Know about Communism, [former FBI director]* J. Edgar Hoover's book. I read that book, and one of the questions asked of Mr. Hoover was, "How do we know if our organization is being infiltrated by Communists?" That was real important in the early '50s. Of course, now we do not have the Communist threat, but his answer was to make sure that your organization sticks to its mission statement and its purpose. If somebody starts wanting your organization to move away from its mission, be leery. It would be like going to a ladies' golf association meeting and somebody standing up and wanting the ladies' golf association to get involved in a bicycle run to cure lupus. It may be a very worthy project, but it's not the purpose of the ladies' golf association. Well, that is the way I am looking at TFRW right now. We had better really stick to our mission statement or we're going to be off on some tangent that has nothing to do with electing Republicans and women in politics.

Civics Education

DOLLY MADISON McKENNA, HOUSTON

What I have seen from my last ten years in politics is that you really have both parties pulling very much farther to the right and to the left in terms of the activists within the organizations. The people who are working in primaries, who are volunteering, and who are choosing the candidates are the ones that are coming from some issue-oriented group. Now, in the Democratic Party, it may be unions or environmental groups. In the Republican Party, it may be the gun people or the anti-abortion people. Those are the ones that have gone out and taught their people how to participate in the political process—that have had training sessions on going to precincts, taking over meetings, organizing ways to get issues on platforms, and that kind of thing. Meanwhile, the average person doesn't even know that this process exists.

I think in the whole state of Texas maybe 75,000 people participate in both parties' precinct meetings combined. They are the ones that are determining the issues that will go to the platform. People are so turned off about politics because they see harshness from these groups running the parties and they don't want to participate. And yet when they don't, the parties are more like these groups that they don't like. So the more they participate, the more they will like the process because the process will look more like them.

Don't Sit on Our Laurels

What do you think your mother, Henrietta Armstrong, would

*say if she were alive today and could see how far the Republican
Party has come in Texas?*

ILLA CLEMENT, KINGSVILLE

I think she would be very pleased but would say it is never
safe to think that just because it is this way now it's going to stay
that way. There are a lot of places in the country that are not this
way. Maybe we ought to be giving them money. Maybe the Republican Party leadership ought to be saying, you know, the place
that needs your money is so-and-so; if you are satisfied with what
is going on in your state, if you have any money, you can send it to
these people. It's going to take money to do anything.

JAN CLARK, HOUSTON

The Republican Party rests on its laurels and gets over confi-
dent. This is our greatest danger. Okay, we have all of this success—let's sit back. That is when you need to worry. When you're
on the top of the hill, somebody wants to knock you off badly.
Now we have to start working harder than we ever have and keep
this together because it is not going to be easy.

The Role of Women

POLLY SOWELL, McALLEN & AUSTIN

We see more women holding office. They're usually a little bit
older and have kids at least in college and not under foot. So this gives
them something to do with the second half of their lives. I think
it's great, and they ought to get into politics because they know a lot.

SUSAN WEDDINGTON, SAN ANTONIO

There is nothing but good news for women in the Republican Party. In the last two years, the Republicans have had more
females on the general election ballot for statewide office than the
Democrats. We currently have more female officeholders statewide than the Democrats ever had in their strongest years. We

have women in positions that are traditionally held by men, for example, agriculture commissioner and comptroller. The fact that my election as the first female state chairman of either major party in Texas speaks volumes about the Republican Party being a party that is looking for leadership first, whether it is male or female. When I talk to the press and tell them the facts—that the Republicans have actually had more females on the general election ballot and we have more women in office today than the Democrats ever did—it shocks them. Women have changed. They have a more diverse group of interests. Our Party has got to be able to meet the interests of women today. No one-shoe-fits-all.

CAROLE KEETON RYLANDER, AUSTIN

Women have a very bright future in the Republican Party. You hear talk of the so-called gender gap. There is a gender gap in Texas, but it is in the Democrat Party not the Republican Party. We now have nine women in statewide elected office in Texas. The Democrats have none.

I can remember when I switched parties some very outspoken Democrats said you will be leading women in the opposite direction. I said I will be leading women in the right direction. We are role models for others. Bottom line, women are concerned with families, budget, paychecks, jobs, education, and all of the same things that men are concerned about.

Fundraising

PETER O'DONNELL, DALLAS

First thing they have to do is write their own checks. Many of them are well able to do it, but they are not used to doing it. Then call on others. No one is stopping you from going out and raising money. If you think you can do it, why, saddle up. I don't know of anyone saying we don't want you raising money around here because you are a woman. That is crazy. We have some outstanding women that raise money for charitable purposes, but I haven't seen them utilize that talent for political purposes. Nancy

Brinker is a good fundraiser for both. Women, in my opinion, are still not drawn to fundraising. Not too many people are.

PATRICIA LYKOS, HOUSTON

Women need to open up their checkbooks. I have been at functions where women were discussing going to Tony's for lunch, then they turn around and write a check for twenty dollars and think they have done something big. I also know people who are on very modest incomes that when they write out a twenty-dollar check it is something extremely significant for them. So if you care and if you believe, then you write that check.

Money gives you access. If there are issues that you care about, how are you going to get your candidate to address them rather than just give them lip service? The media is, I would say, 90 percent liberal Democrat. It takes money to get those critical ads out there, which is free speech. Free speech in the media is very expensive. It is like a war. It takes money to buy the materials, the uniforms, and the troops. You need a treasury to finance it. If you don't have great financial resources then give what you can and volunteer your labor.

DEBBIE FRANCIS, DALLAS

We were having a fundraiser for Susan Combs, and it was less of a fundraiser than getting people out to see her and get that vote out. I made the comment to Susan that I was glad she was having another fundraiser that was going to be a bigger hitter, because all of the women I asked to come to this luncheon were also being asked to work the phone banks, get out the postcards, and attend volunteer activities. Most of the men are not being asked to do all that. They have just been asked to give some money. But you're asking all of these women to do all of this stuff. There is kind of a limit on how much money you can also hit them for. With most of the men, you are not asking them to do five things. You're asking them to do one thing, write that check.

She said, "Oh, gosh, do you think we should do the event at all?" I told her we would have no problem having a wonderful event at a lesser price. But if we're going to go up into the hundreds of dollars just for a woman's event in the middle of the day it's not going to fly.

POLLYANNA STEPHENS, SAN ANGELO

It is kind of a joke out here. People always tend to visit my husband, Steve, in his business to get his support. He will come home and tell me so-and-so came by today and I gave him such-and-such. Never once did they ask for *my* vote or *my* support. A lot of times, if it was somebody that I knew, I would say, "Well, tell him that he's going to have to ask for my vote or my support before he gets it." I've had some call me and talk about it. Of course, it was all done kind of tongue in cheek. But I find that interesting. They would always go to him, and they would always expect that I would support whatever he supported.

Now, people really do realize that women voters have a lot of say-so, a lot of strength. They have a lot of money to contribute, and candidates are out seeking their support now a lot more than they used to. I did it jokingly for a long time, but in the back of my mind I'm thinking, "I wonder why they just take it for granted that whoever Steve supports I'm going to support."

DIANE RATH, SAN ANTONIO

Fundraising is the next step we have to conquer in politics because that does get you into a different level of decision-making and a different level of appointments. You do have governors or senators with national appointments and governors with state appointments where the major appointments usually go to men, and I think we are seeing that change. They're being much more diverse with those appointments, but they normally go to major donors and women just haven't been there.

JANE ANNE STINNETT, LUBBOCK

A few years ago, mostly the men raised the money. That was the deal. Women did the work—the invitations, nametags, and refreshments—and men raised the money. I don't think that's true today. Our mayor, Wendy Sitton, raised $90,000 to run, practically by herself. I think women now, particularly women in business, are more in tune with asking for money themselves. Women will give money. I don't think that they give it as well as men. In the old days, you always sent the fundraising letter to the man's office because you didn't want the wife to open it and say, "Oh, that would be a new dress for me." Women can raise money and do raise money. Certainly, the big fundraisers around the state are women. Sylvia Nugent and Jeanne Johnson Phillips are two.

CATHY McCONN, HOUSTON

There is a feeling among women, if you don't own your own business and you are a mother and a wife, it's almost like it's the man's job to give money. The school asks for money for a fundraiser, and they will write out a $50 check or a $100 check, no problem. But when it comes to a candidate, they either feel like "my amount is too small," which of course no amount is ever too small to make a commitment, or it's not something they focus on. As a couple we give, but I sign the checks. My husband lets me decide who we should support. I have gotten thank you notes back several times to my husband. Not even to me. I signed the checks! The very least they could do is figure it was from both of us and send a thank you note to both of us. I would write this nice little note and say, "If you ever want to get money from me again, you ought to thank the person that sent you the money."

DEBORAH BELL, ABILENE

Women can raise more money than men can. If I believe in a person, I am not afraid to call anybody and try to raise money for that candidate. I really think women have a leg up on men. The polls show women are playing a bigger and bigger part in the elections. Women can bring other women in. It is important not to overlook other women and just go straight to men. Women are in business now and have just as many contacts and different kinds of contacts that men can not touch.

KAY BAILEY HUTCHISON, HOUSTON & DALLAS

When I first started running, it was very difficult to get women to give money because they weren't used to it. Women have come into the system, and they have come into the system of giving money. Not as much as men because they are not used to writing the big checks as much, but it is a lot better than it used to be. It *is* important because if you care about an issue, the way to have an impact is to get *your* candidates elected. That takes elbow grease and money. We do have to encourage women to get involved.

Communicating Our Message

MARY DENNY, DENTON

You know, generally, when women are involved in politics people assume that they are Democrats or that they are liberals or moderates certainly. But that is just not true. I am really pleased that Republican women are getting more and more involved because it helps break that stereotype. We have worked with our Democrat counterparts to enact a lot of good legislation dealing with women's issues. I even hesitate to call them women's issues, although when they are about women's health, that's really what they are. I would like to be successful in breaking the stereotype that women in elected office are moderates or liberals. It's amazing to me that, across the country, when I'm sitting on an airplane and people ask me what I do and I tell them [*a state representative*], they assume right away that I'm a Democrat and then are somewhat surprised to find out that I am a conservative Republican. I've never been in a "class" that fit a stereotype until now. We have some work to do in that area.

BECKY FARRAR, HICO

Republicans don't do a very good job of making their case to the people. They need to package their message in a better way. The Democrats are masters at that. They have the message of the day. If Bill Clinton says something one day, you hear that same message coming from congressmen, Democrat chairmen, office-holders, legislators, and candidates. The Republicans are not like that. People are listening, and if they hear the same message over and over and over, they begin to remember it. This to me is why the Democrats have been so successful. This second level is where we have got to get to—the heart not just the brain. The Republicans are cerebral and academic. Our message is often directed to the brain not the heart. Voters who are not activists respond to heart messages not brain messages. So we have to learn somehow to talk about the heart issues, whether it is safe children or good schools or protect Social Security. It is hard for Republicans because we are not offering the moon. We're not offering them free health care or government giveaways. Republicans have to have the right message and we have got to package it in such a way that it hits the heart. We need to learn how to campaign with integrity but still win the election and the war.

CHAPTER 20

The Legacy

"Women of that generation have left a legacy of having accomplished
a great deal, but don't stop there. Keep going. The sky's the limit."

—DIANNE THOMPSON

*O*ne must only look at the election results of the late 1990s to
realize the legacy left by the thousands of women working in
Republican politics through the years. The election of Republican
candidates is not the only legacy they leave us. Their work in
Texas is a model for grassroots political organization in the U. S.
as well as in former Eastern Block countries and Latin America.
It also shows us that anything worth accomplishing is worth
whatever time and effort it takes to accomplish it. In today's
hurry-up world, these Texas heroines show us that patience,
hard work, and determination remain character traits to be
admired and instilled in future generations. They also prove
that good government does not develop independently. It exists
only when the citizenry actively involves itself in government,
works to elect qualified candidates, then holds them accountable.
Simply put, participation protects the American system of
government and ultimately our way of life.

Created Something New

JOCI STRAUS, SAN ANTONIO

It's a challenge to build something from scratch. It's people oriented and I love people. It's been a learning experience the whole way. I have learned so many things that I have been able to apply elsewhere. I couldn't begin to tell everything I have learned about people or about how to be convincing about something that you believe in strongly, how to raise money, and how to write your own press releases. The successes were so beautiful that you forget the times that you have not been successful. We had an opportunity, which I think is critically important, to build from the bottom up a competitive system which is the root of our whole American philosophy.

You've got a daughter who is in her early teens. What do you think that your mother, Bobbie Biggart, would want her to know about what she and her friends did for Texas?

LEE BIGGART, DALLAS & AUSTIN

She would be the proudest about the odds they were up against. They started off organizing, supporting candidates, making phone calls, and getting their groups organized. They didn't expect to win. When they finally pulled off a few victories, they were upset victories. They never had the consensus on their side. They took such a long view. Nobody's going to win this year or in the next decade. It was an incredibly patient approach. What they decided was, if you didn't have a Republican governor of Texas you couldn't win the national election. Talk about a stretch—to say "We're going to elect the first Republican governor so we can get the president." That's moving pretty far uphill. That's what they were doing when everyone was saying about Bill Clements, we're going to win this one. From that base, we are going to elect Reagan. Texas Republican women got to see it go from nothing to the full banana in their careers. Some died ten years before it happened, and their kids got to see it. But these women, by and large, got to see finally the fruits of their labors. I think they were all politically satisfied because when it was finally said and done, whatever they contributed, they saw success in ways they couldn't have believed. My mother was enthusiastic about politics and had enough good victories, I think, there at the end. She saw plenty of defeats too. But they just kept plugging away. The result was the statewide slate of Republican candidates that we elected in 1998. How did this happen? Well, it didn't happen over night.

Made Texas a Role Model

ANNE ARMSTRONG, ARMSTRONG

Our state from the beginning gave women true leadership roles in finance. I remember the patronage committee, early on, that I was put on. The powerful things that counted in politics— Texas women had those jobs. All states are glad to have us lick the envelopes and put out the yard signs, but in Texas we were right at the fulcrums of power. I felt that it was a very good example to set. I use John Tower as an example. Nola Smith ran three of his campaigns. We put a woman up for the Texas Supreme Court, Barbara Culver Clack from Midland. Then Tower had a woman as his chief of staff, not as a constituency person or liaison to women or something like that, in his office. Carolyn Bacon ran that office. Many Senators still haven't gotten that message. We set examples not just for the rest of the South but for the nation.

Someone said you used to say, "Okay, girls, let's go save the country."

GWEN PHARO, DALLAS

Everywhere I would go in the country I would run into Republican politicians. They'd say, "You have got to tell us how you all do it." We would sit down and say there is nothing pleasant about it. It is just hard work. Step one leads to step two and two to three. It is just a standard way that you win elections. Number one, you go and ask for the votes.

CATHERINE SMYTH COLGAN, DALLAS

In Texas, it was, "Why not try it?" Many of us who learned in

Texas have carried our knowledge on to other places. Shirley Green, Mary Lou Grier, and I all ended up in Washington at the same time. We had a fantastic old-girls network on the national and international levels. I can remember talking to Jim Baker on the phone one day when he was chief of staff [*to President Reagan*]. We were talking about the questions of the day on the phone. My comment to him was that international politics was a piece of cake after you have survived the back alleys of Texas.

Sense of History

DIXIE CLEM, PLANO
Our children need to know history. Our people need to know that the state of Texas did not always have a Republican governor and our county did not always have a Republican county judge, or our city a Republican mayor. They need to know what the Republican Party stands for. They don't really know. The kids need to know what they're standing up for. What they believe.

Provided Inspiration to Other Women

SHEILA WILKES BROWN, AUSTIN
The women who were involved then have stuck with it. The Anne Armstrongs, the Rita Clements, the Polly Sowells, the Beryl Milburns. They are still doing it. Bobbie Biggart did it till the day she died. I guess maybe that is the generation of the '50s as opposed to the '60s or the '70s. Once they got started down that path, they just never gave up, and they are still doing it today. I think that is probably why they have been successful. Persistence. They have it.

DIANNE THOMPSON, BOERNE & HOUSTON
Women of that generation have left a legacy of having accomplished a great deal, but don't stop there. Keep going. The

sky's the limit. That's the legacy. It says, "You can do this. Don't stop here. Reach for the stars."

*W*here are the stars that you want to reach? What do you want to accomplish for your family, education, or business? How does the government affect your life? Women asked these same questions in 1952 before they got involved in Republican politics and the Texas Republican Party. Instead of saying "we face insurmountable odds" they said "this is a challenge we need to embrace," and they persisted until the job was done. Did they get discouraged when their friends and family thought them foolish for pursuing their political interests? Perhaps. But they did not let these reactions dissuade them from their ultimate goal of honesty and responsiveness in government and a two-party Texas. Their dedication gives us all a real example of the power of grassroots political action.

Each of us has the opportunity to face the challenges of today with the same long-term, optimistic approach that our mothers and grandmothers, friends and neighbors used yesterday. Their legacy to us is a grassroots model which will help us make things happen in politics. Let's use it!

Acknowledgments

*T*he women featured in *Grassroots Women* and those they represent provided a constant source of motivation. Many times when facing an obstacle I asked myself, if these women faced the same challenge, how would they approach it? Their examples of creative problem solving led the way.

Research would be almost impossible without access to public libraries, and we have one of the best here in Boerne, Texas. Louise Foster, Library Director, and John Powell, Reference Librarian, helped track down even the most obscure fact or figure.

Just like many grassroots women who were influenced by their parents, I am a better person because of mine, Sue and Dave McKain. They taught all five of their children—Carolyn, David, Kathy, John, and me—our responsibilities as citizens. In addition, Mother's sharp eye and Dad's view of the big picture made immeasurable contributions to the book.

Grassroots Women would not have been written without Mary Lou Grier. From the moment the book was envisioned, she did whatever she could to see it come to fruition whether recommending women for interviews, reading through multiple initial drafts and making suggestions, or acting as a sounding board. She is the true inspiration for this book. Kitchen cabinet members Fran Atkinson, Polly Sowell, Beryl Milburn, Sally McKenzie, Pam Hodges, and Susan Block, with their enthusiastic support from inception, bolstered me while I found my way through the research and book-development maze.

Shannon Davies understood the concept of *Grassroots Women* from our first conversation. She believed in fully telling this slice of Texas history and encouraged me to keep the original plan although others advised fitting it to the publishing industry mold. Shannon edited this oral history and its numerous speaking styles with ease and insight. George Lenox made this book look as graceful and full of life as the women whose story is conveyed on the pages. He is a gifted designer whose knowledge and experience enhanced the finished product in more ways than design. Thank you to Carla Giammichele for her expertise and concern for the quality of the book. Many of her ideas were touchstones for the marketing and distribution of *Grassroots Women*.

Jim Grier deserves my deepest gratitude. In addition to being a wonderful husband and best friend, his levelheaded approach to life keeps me on track. I wholeheartedly agree with Marguerite Binkley, who said, "Many husbands gift their wives with jewels; my husband indulged me the greatest gift a man can accord his wife: my time."

Finally, I thank God and my family at St. Mark Presbyterian Church for the courage to envision and complete this undertaking, and for carrying me over the bumps in the road along the way.

Photo Scrapbook

The Dallas delegation to the 12th Annual Republican Women's Conference, with Congressman Bruce Alger (*left*) and Senator John Tower in Washington, D. C., April 1964. Courtesy Babs Johnson

Joci Straus (*second from left*) takes the family to Washington to visit Congressman George Bush. Courtesy Joci Straus

Ruth Mankin and John Tower staffer Tom Cole celebrate the 1966 Senate election with a "We Kept Tower" bumper sticker. Courtesy Ruth Mankin

Dwight Eisenhower supporters at the Dallas County precinct 56 convention in 1952. Photos such as these helped seat the Eisenhower delegation at the 1952 Republican National Convention in Chicago. Courtesy Martha Crowley

A candidate for state legislature in the 1970s, Leon Richardson (*left*) rides on Melinda Paret's horse-drawn buggy at a campaign fundraiser.
Courtesy Leon Richardson

Theo Wickersham speaks to the McAllen Rotary Club about the importance of being politically educated.
Courtesy Theo Wickersham

Barry Goldwater visits with Mary Lou Grier before a fundraiser in San Antonio in the early 1960s.
Courtesy Mary Lou Grier

Pasadena
Republicans pull
out all the stops
with a booth for
Jack Cox at the
1962 Pasadena
Rodeo. Courtesy
Marion Coleman

Louise and Jim Foster
register voters in Austin.
Courtesy Louise Foster

Many precinct
organizations took
root at neighbor-
hood coffees.
Senator Tower
visits with voters as
his wife, Lou, walks
to greet them in a
living room in
Lubbock. Courtesy
Nita Gibson

From second left: Babs Johnson, president of the Dallas County Council of Republican
Women's Clubs; Rita Bass (Clements), state committeewoman; Flo Kampmann
(Crichton), national committeewoman; and Barbara Man, TFRW president are guests of
the Bruce Alger Weekly Report with Melvin Mudd (*right*). Courtesy Babs Johnson

Anne Armstrong while serving as a counselor to President Richard Nixon in 1973.
Courtesy Anne Armstrong

Flo Kampmann Crichton (*left*) and then husband, Ike Kampmann, dance alongside Republican National Committee Vice Chair Bertha Adkins and Ed Mayer, a state committeeman, in 1957. The Bexar County Republican Party welcomed Adkins to a celebration of the important role played by women in the Texas GOP.
Courtesy Flo Kampmann Crichton

Robin, from the TV show *Batman and Robin,* lands at the 1966 Harris County Republican Convention for a surprise respite during a long night of hardball politics. Courtesy Ruth Mankin

Polly Sowell chats with President Gerald Ford in 1975 while former Governor John Connally listens in. Moments earlier, Connally, a 1976 vice presidential hopeful, made a Freudian slip and introduced Sowell as the vice president —not the vice chair— of the Republican Party of Texas. Courtesy Polly Sowell

Opposite page, from left:
Ruth Fox, Barbara Kaufman, and Estelle Teague on the floor of the 1988 Republican National Convention in New Orleans. Courtesy Ruth Fox

Barbara Culver Clack and Bill Shaner unveil the sign for Midland County Republican Headquarters. Courtesy Douthea Shaner

Babs Johnson (*left*) presents Liz Strickland, president of the Dallas County Women's Republican Club, founded in 1920, with a plaque naming the club Club Emeritus of the Dallas County Council of Republican Women's Clubs in 1963. Courtesy Babs Johnson

At the 1967 National Republican Women's Convention, Marguerite Binkley, Anna Claire Rice, Jarvis Jenkins, and other members of the Houston delegation were guests of Senator and Mrs. John Tower and Mrs. Clair Shenault at her home in the Watergate in Washington, D. C. Courtesy Anna Claire Rice

Members of the Canyon Lake Republican Women's Club participate in a Fourth of July parade. Courtesy LaVerne Cudabac

The Inner-City
Republican Women's
Club in San Antonio
hosts an event.
Courtesy
Lois C. White

Members of the West Memorial Republican Women in Houston visit State
Representative Milton Fox and his wife, Ruth, in the capitol. Courtesy Ruth Fox

Lou Tower (*far left*) and John Tower
visit with Nita Gibson (*second from left*)
and Terry Tapp in Lubbock.
Courtesy Nita Gibson

From left: Betty Cunningham,
Jodi Salzman, Alice Koonz,
and Anna Claire Rice welcome
Lou Tower (*second from left*)
to Houston as she campaigns
for Senator Tower.
Courtesy Anna Claire Rice

Bill and Ginny Elliott of Houston
celebrate his corner-turning election to
the city council in 1968. Ruth Mankin
was Elliott's campaign manager.
Courtesy Ruth Mankin

John Tower campaigns with Marjorie Arsht
in her 1962 run for state legislature.
Courtesy Marjorie Arsht

From bottom: Martha Weisend,
Congressman Steve Bartlett,
Roger Staubach, Eddie Chiles,
Cipriano Guerro, Fran Chiles,
General Dick Cavazos, and
Beryl Milburn accompany
Governor Bill Clements
(*bottom right*) as he flies around
the state during the 1986
campaign.
Courtesy Martha Weisend

Mary Lou Grier with the
other Republican statewide
candidates in front of the
"GOP Voteswagon" in 1974.
Courtesy Mary Lou Grier

Lucy Saenz (*left*) and Alicia Vela Cantu along with her children, Arnold and Leticia, pick up senatorial candidate George Bush at the Laredo airport for a campaign event in 1970. Courtesy Alicia Vela Cantu

Barbara Bush and LaVerne Cudabac make calls for President George Bush's reelection campaign at a phone bank in New Braunfels. Courtesy LaVerne Cudabac

Pat Jacobson hands out a Ronald Reagan bumper sticker to a telephone lineman in the "Pioneers for Reagan" tour of East Texas in 1980.
Courtesy Millie Teas

Jean Baker of San Antonio works a phone for Clements in 1978.
Courtesy Teddy Peterson

George and Barbara Bush visit with 1970 Senate campaign volunteers Teddy Peterson and Lane Vaughan in San Antonio. Courtesy Teddy Peterson

Pattilou Dawkins, with B. R. Barfield, introduces a grateful Governor Clements to an Amarillo crowd after a record-setting voter turnout in the 1986 election. Courtesy Pattilou Dawkins

An example of creative fundraising: Bob Overstreet, candidate for state representative, and Marion Coleman prepare for Donkey Softball, pitting the Young Republicans against the candidates. Courtesy Marion Coleman

New Braunfels Republican Women raised record amounts for candidates at their annual Wurstfest food booth. Courtesy Bucky Smith (*far left*)

George W. Bush campaigns for his father in 1988 in San Antonio with (*from left*) Teddy Peterson, June Deason, and Caroline Ellwood. Courtesy Teddy Peterson

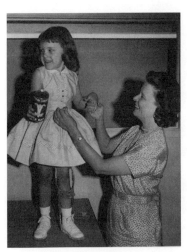

Barbara Culver Clack, as Midland County Judge, promotes an Easter Seals fundraiser. Courtesy Barbara Culver Clack

State Senator Betty Andujar is sworn in as governor-for-a-day on May 7, 1977, while her husband, Dr. John Andujar, looks on. Official program courtesy Fran and Vic King

Community Development Committee chair Betty Sterquell and city commissioners Jerry Ammerman and Houston DeFord listen to a grant request presentation in Amarillo. Courtesy Betty Sterquell

State Representative Kay Bailey (Hutchison) speaks to the 63rd Texas Legislature
in January 1973. Courtesy Texas State Library and Archives Commission

Henry Bonilla cuts the ribbon and opens his 1992 Campaign for Congress in Laredo.
Courtesy Bebe Zuniga

About the Participants

This is a brief description of the political activities that each participant discussed in the interviews. It is intended to introduce the people speaking in the book and not intended to be a full biography detailing their years of political work. Most of the women who were interviewed held many positions in the state and local Republican Women organizations. Only the office of club president is noted when the women discussed that position. The interview date follows each name.

ART *Associated Republicans of Texas*
TFRW *Texas Federation of Republican Women*
NFRW *National Federation of Republican Women*

Nancy Abdullah, Dalhart, *March 28, 2000:* County chair, campaign worker.

Jacque Allen, Wichita Falls, *April 20, 1999:* County chair, campaign manager, state committeewoman, County Chairman Association organizer.

Helen Anderson, Houston, *March 24, 1999:* Party activist, campaign worker.

Penny Angelo, Midland, *August 19, 1998:* Campaign worker, candidate's wife.

Surrenden Angly, Austin, *March 15, 1999:* Campaign manager, TFRW president, candidate's wife.

Anne Armstrong, Armstrong, *May 13, 1999:* State and national committeewoman, co-chair Republican National Committee, advisor to Presidents Nixon and Ford, ambassador to Great Britain, fundraiser, campaign chair.

Marjorie Arsht, Houston, *February 23, 1999:* County vice chair, candidate for state legislature, fundraiser.

Fran Atkinson, Lufkin & San Antonio, *October 31, 1997:* State committeewoman, deputy state vice chair, fundraiser, ART board, campaign worker.

Carolyn Bacon, Dallas, *March 7, 2000:* Congressman Bruce Alger's staff, Senator John Tower's administrative assistant.

Margaret Baird, Houston, *August 17, 1999:* Party activist, campaign worker.

Barbara Banker, San Antonio, *August 31, 1998:* Fundraiser, campaign worker.

Libba Barnes, San Antonio, *July 20, 1998:* Precinct chair, fundraiser, state committeewoman, campaign staffer.

Andy Beaver, Corpus Christi, *June 4, 1999:* Party activist, Republican women's club president.

Deborah Bell, Abilene, *November 19, 1998:* Fundraiser, campaign worker, Brazos River Authority appointee.

Joy Bell, Dallas, *August 18, 1999:* Party activist, campaign worker.

Norma Benavides, Laredo, *April 5, 1999:* Party activist, elected school board member.

Anne Bergman, Weatherford, *September 22, 1998:* Precinct chair, campaign worker, TFRW president, Texas community development board appointee.

Lee Biggart, Dallas & Austin, *September 15, 1998:* Son of Dallas party activist Bobbie Biggart.

Joan Biggerstaff, Plano, *May 4, 1999:* Party activist, campaign worker, Texas board of health appointee.

Marguerite Binkley, Houston, *July 6 and August 2, 1999:* Party activist, rules expert.

Mary Bodger, Corpus Christi, *June 6, 1999:* Republican women's club president, party activist.

Robbie Borchers, New Braunfels, *October 1, 1998:* State committeewoman, campaign manager, candidate's wife, Republican women's club president, county chair.

Betty King Boyd, Waco, *March 1, 2000:* County vice chair.

Jayne Brainard, Amarillo, *September 2, 1999:* Republican women's club president, rules expert.

Janie Brock, San Angelo, *August 19, 1998:* Campaign worker, precinct chair.

Cindy Brockwell, Boerne, *October 9, 1999:* Campaign manager, State Senator Jeff Wentworth's chief of staff, state committeewoman.

Lou Brown, Midland, *August 19, 1998:* TFRW president, campaign worker, county vice chair, NFRW third vice president.

Shelia Wilkes Brown, Austin, *August 13, 1998:* Campaign staffer, Governor Bill Clement's staff.

Patty Bruce, El Paso, *October 17, 1998:* Campaign worker, county vice chair, state committeewoman.

Dona Bruns, New Braunfels, *February 4, 2000:* Campaign worker, party activist.

Esther Buckley, Laredo, *March 2, 1999:* County chair, U. S. Commission on Civil Rights appointee.

Jane Bucy, Lubbock, *November 20, 1998:* Campaign worker, fundraiser, party activist.

Bette Jo Buhler, Victoria, *April 7, 1999:* State vice chair, state committeewoman, fundraiser, campaign worker.

Penny Butler, Houston, *March 24, 1999:* National committeewoman, fundraiser, campaign worker.

Barbara Campbell, Dallas, *February 3, 2000:* TFRW president, campaign worker, party activist.

Judy Canon, Houston, *September 20, 1999:* Party activist, Women for Reagan organizer.

Alicia Cantu, Laredo, *April 12, 1999:* Candidate for school board, campaign worker, party activist.

Vera Carhart, Richardson & Houston, *February 23, 1999:* TFRW president, party activist, campaign worker.

Hardy Childress, San Antonio, *September 11, 1998:* Husband of party and TFRW activist Beulah Childress.

Fran Chiles, Fort Worth, *September 24, 1998:* National committeewoman, fundraiser, campaign worker.

Barbara Culver Clack, Midland, *August 18, 1998:* Elected first Republican woman county judge in Texas, Texas Supreme Court appointee.

Deanne Clark, Lubbock & Dimmitt, *August 17, 1999:* County chair, campaign worker.

Jan Clark, Houston, *May 28, 1999:* Campaign worker, Republican women's club president.

Gloria Clayton, Dallas, *June 15, 1999:* County vice chair, campaign worker.

Dixie Clem, Plano, *May 4, 1999:* State committeewoman, county executive director.

Illa Clement, Kingsville, *May 13, 1999:* Fundraiser, state committeewoman, ART board.

Hally Clements, Victoria, *April 7, 1999:* Fundraiser, campaign manager, party activist.

Rita Clements, Dallas, *June 14, 1999:* Fundraiser, national committeewoman, national Goldwater door-to-door campaign chair, wife of Texas's first modern Republican governor.

Dee Coats, Houston, *August 18, 1999:* Campaign worker, party activist.

Amelie Cobb, Beaumont, *February, 25, 1999:* Fundraiser, state committeewoman, campaign worker.

Francie Fatheree Cody, Pampa, *August 28, 1999:* State committeewoman, campaign worker, fundraiser.

Marion Coleman, Pasadena, *February 23, 1999:* County area chairman, campaign worker.

Catherine Smyth Colgan, Dallas, *September 24, 1999:* TFRW president, campaign staffer, county vice chair, appointed Canadian embassy cultural affairs officer.

Mary Anne Collins, Dallas, *September 23, 1998:* State party staffer, county vice chair, campaign worker.

Susan Combs, Austin, *May 12 and September 15, 1998:* Elected state representative and Texas Commissioner of Agriculture.

Lisa Compton, Clyde, *November 18, 1998:* Party activist, campaign worker.

Becky Cornell, San Angelo, *August 17, 1998:* Fundraiser, party activist, campaign worker.

Margaret Cosby, Boerne, *October 29, 1997:* Precinct chair, campaign worker.

Nadine Craddick, Midland, *September 20, 1999:* Party activist, candidate's wife.

Flo Kampmann Crichton, San Antonio, *October 2 and 28, 1998:* State vice chair, national committeewoman, national finance committee member.

Dorothy Crockett, Odessa & Marble Falls, *February 16, 1999:* County chair, campaign worker, Republican women's club president.

Nancy Crouch, Houston, *March 26, 1999:* Campaign worker, party activist.

Martha Crowley, Dallas, *September 25, 1998:* Party activist, campaign worker, Congressman Bruce Alger's staff, candidate's wife.

LaVerne Cudabac, Canyon Lake, *December 12, 1999:* Party activist, campaign worker, Republican women's club president.

Pauline Cusack, Houston & Willow City, *March 25, 2000:* Fundraiser, campaign worker, county chair.

Linda Custard, Dallas, *September 24, 1998:* Precinct chair, campaign worker.

Kay Danks, Galveston & Austin, *September 15, 1998:* State committeewoman, campaign worker, fundraiser.

Anita Davis, Hemphill, *February 24, 1999:* Party activist.

Nancy Canion Davis, Galveston County, *August 18, 1999:* County chair, state committeewoman.

Pattilou Dawkins, Amarillo, *July 25, 1998:* Party activist, candidate for state legislature and county judge, appointed mental health and mental retardation board chair.

Dottie De La Garza, Dallas, *September 11, 1999:* Senator John Tower's Senate and campaign staff.

June Deason, San Antonio, *February 16, 1998:* Party activist, campaign manager.

Holly Decherd, Austin, *August 10, 1998:* Campaign worker, state party secretary, fundraiser.

Mary Denny, Denton, *July 27, 1998:* County chair, elected state representative.

Becky Dixon, Waco, *February 21, 2000:* Party activist, campaign worker, State Senator David Sibley's staff.

Dorothy Doehne, San Antonio, *August 9, 1998:* State vice chair, state party secretary, state committeewoman.

Mary Donelson, Amarillo, *July 22, 1998:* Party activist, campaign worker.

Linda Dyson, Houston, *February 23, 1999:* Party activist, campaign staffer.

Virginia Eggers, Wichita Falls & Dallas, *September 30, 1999:* Campaign staffer, deputy state vice chair, state vice chair.

Wanda Eidson, Weatherford, *September 22, 1998:* County chair, state committeewoman, fundraiser.

Laverne Evans, El Paso, *February 3, 2000:* Party activist.

Becky Farrar, Hico, *February 2, 2000:* Candidate for state legislature, county chair, campaign worker.

Barbara Foreman, Odessa & Dallas, *May 4, 1999:* Candidate's wife, state committeewoman.

Louise Foster, Austin, *March 15, 1999:* Party, TFRW, and NFRW activist.

Ruth Fox, Houston & Austin, *August 10, 1998:* TFRW president, candidate's wife, campaign manager.

Debbie Francis, Dallas, *September 24, 1998:* Party activist, campaign worker, Republican women's club president.

Nadine Francis, Odessa, *September 27, 1998 and June 16, 1999:* Party activist, Governor Bill Clement's staff.

Joan Gaidos, Dallas, *August 18, 1999:* Party activist.

Gaynor Galeck, Amarillo, *July 23, 1998:* Party activist.

Mary Garrett, Danbury, *February 1, 2000:* Party activist, state committeewoman.

Liz Ghrist, Houston, *March 25, 1999:* Fundraiser, party activist, commissioners court appointee.

Nita Gibson, Lubbock, *November 20, 1998:* Campaign worker, candidate for county judge, state committeewoman.

Taffy Goldsmith, Dallas, *June 16, 1999:* Party activist, campaign worker, precinct chair.

Raquel Gonzalez, Laredo, *April 12, 1999:* Party activist.

Isabel Gray, Pasadena, *March 23, 1999:* Party activist, campaign worker.

Shirley Green, Austin & San Antonio, *August 12, 1998:* Campaign manager, Vice President George Bush's deputy press secretary, NASA public affairs officer, Governor Bush's staff, TFRW staff.

Fay Surrett Greenwood, El Paso, *August 24, 1999:* Party activist.

Mary Lou Grier, San Antonio & Boerne, *September 1, 1997:* Campaign manager, county vice chair, appointed deputy director National Park Service, candidate for Texas land commissioner.

Frankie Lee Harlow, Del Rio, *February 29, 2000:* County chair, campaign worker.

Ann Harrington, Plano, *February 19, 2000:* Party activist, campaign worker, candidate's wife.

Jayne Harris, San Antonio, *February 11, 1999:* Campaign manager, candidate's wife.

Katie Heck, Midland, *August 18, 1999:* State committeewoman, campaign manager, elected city council member.

Bette Hervey, El Paso, *October 17, 1998:* Party activist, campaign worker.

Anita Hill, Garland, *September 30, 1999:* Elected state representative.

Chris Hoover, Corpus Christi, *February 3, 2000:* County vice chair, candidate's wife.

Annette Hopkins, San Angelo, *August 17, 1998:* Party activist, campaign worker.

Barbara Howell, Fort Worth, *September 7, 1999:* Party activist, campaign worker, fundraiser.

Becky Husbands, Waco, *February 8, 2000:* Party activist.

Kay Bailey Hutchison, Houston & Dallas, *October 21, 1999:* U. S. Senator, elected Texas Treasurer, elected state representative, fundraiser, candidate for Congress.

Pat Jacobson, Fort Worth, *September 8, 1999:* Fundraiser, campaign worker.

Mary Jester, Dallas, *June 17, 1999:* President Dallas County Council of Republican Women's Clubs, party activist.

Babs Johnson, Dallas, *September 23, 1998:* President Dallas County Council of Republican Women's Clubs, campaign worker.

Claire Johnson, Abilene, *November 19, 1998:* Party activist, campaign worker, governor's appointee.

Barbara Jordan, Kingwood, *August 30, 1999:* Campaign worker, TFRW activist.

Nancy Judy, Dallas, *February 1, 2000:* Elected county commissioner and school board member, candidate for Congress, party activist.

Jane Juett, Amarillo, *July 22, 1998:* Party activist, campaign worker, fundraiser.

Beverly Kaufman, Houston, *June 12, 1998:* Precinct chair, TFRW president, elected county clerk.

Jan Kennady, New Braunfels, *December 12, 1999:* Elected mayor, TFRW president.

Vic King, Fort Worth & Boerne, *June 5, 1998:* Precinct chair, elected county commissioner.

Carolyn Knight, Austin & Marble Falls, *August 13, 1998:* Party activist.

Cyndi Taylor Krier, San Antonio, *September 29, 1998:* Senator John Tower's staff, elected state senator and county judge.

Juandelle Lacy, Midland, *August 18, 1998:* Party activist, Republican women's club president, campaign manager, candidate's wife.

Betsy Lake, Houston, *March 23, 1999:* County chair, campaign worker, fundraiser.

Claudette Landess, Amarillo, *July 23, 1998:* Campaign worker, party activist.

Mickey Lawrence, Houston, *October 1, 1999:* Party activist, candidate's wife.

Ann Lee, Houston, *March 24, 1999:* Precinct chair, campaign worker.

Tony Lindsay, Houston, *November 12, 1999:* Campaign manager, candidate's wife, elected judge.

Wilda Lindstrom, Houston, *May 26, 1999:* Precinct chair, state committeewoman.

Nancy Loeffler, San Angelo & San Antonio, *July 31, 1998:* Fundraiser, party activist, campaign worker.

Tom Loeffler, San Antonio, *June 28, 2000:* Former U. S. Congressman.

Harriet Lowe, Dallas, *June 15, 1999:* County executive committee member, campaign worker.

Janis Lowe, Friendswood, *March 4, 1999:* Elected city council member, Port of Galveston pilots board appointee.

Patricia Lykos, Houston, *October 5, 1999:* Party official, elected judge.

Barbara Man, Wichita Falls & Dallas, *October 14, 1998:* TFRW president, national committeewoman.

Iris Manes, Houston, *August 24, 1999:* State committeewoman, campaign worker.

Ruth Mankin, Houston, *October 22, 1999:* Candidate's wife, party activist.

Wendy Marsh, Amarillo, *July 24, 1998:* Party activist.

Judy Jones Matthews, Abilene, *April 19, 1999:* Party activist, fundraiser.

Janelle McArthur, San Antonio, *March 30, 1998:* TFRW president, fundraiser, campaign manager.

Lila McCall, Austin, *February 19, 1999:* Party activist.

Pat McCall, Houston & Uvalde County, *May 27, 1999:* Party activist, Pachyderm Club organizer, county vice chair.

Cathy McConn, Houston, *August 25, 1999:* National committeewoman.

Glenna McCord, Dallas, *November 12, 1998:* County vice chair, campaign worker.

Kathryn McDaniel, Borger, *July 24, 1998:* State vice chair, state committeewoman.

Ruth McGuckin, Houston & Washington County, *October 4, 1999:* State committeewoman.

Dolly Madison McKenna, Houston, *October 22, 1999:* Candidate for Congress.

Sally McKenzie, Dallas, *October 24, 1997:* Fundraiser, party activist, West Point board of visitors appointee.

Beryl Milburn, Austin, *November 4, 1997:* Candidate, party activist, fundraiser, TFRW president, university coordinating board and University of Texas board of regents appointee.

Mary Ellen Miller, Austin, *March 15, 1999:* Political consultant.

Carolyn Minton, San Angelo, *November 9, 1998:* Party activist, campaign worker.

Ruth Cox Mizelle, Corpus Christi, *October 20, 1999:* Campaign manager, party activist.

Winnie Moore, Lubbock, *November 20, 1998:* Party activist.

Birdie Morgan, Abilene, *April 19, 1999:* Party activist.

Anna Mowery, Fort Worth, *September 8, 1999:* Elected state representative, county chair, candidate's wife.

Jane Nelson, Flower Mound, *November 4, 1999:* Elected state senator, campaign worker.

Florence Neumeyer, Houston, *October 4, 1999:* Party activist, campaign manager.

Carolyn Nicholas, Wichita Falls, *April 20, 1999:* County chair.

Louise Nixon, Fredericksburg, *April 4, 2000:* Party activist.

Barbara Nowlin, Houston & Friendswood, *March 5, 1999:* Party activist, Republican women's club president.

Sylvia Nugent, Dallas & Amarillo, *July 24, 1998:* Party activist, candidate for state legislature, campaign manager, congressional staff, fundraiser.

Ana Ochoa, Laredo, *April 12, 1999:* Party activist, elected college board member.

Peter O'Donnell, Dallas, *January 27, 2000:* State chair, national committeeman.

Nancy Palm, Houston, *May 28, 1999:* County chair, county vice chair, state committeewoman.

Rita Palm, Fort Worth, *September 7, 1999:* Fundraiser, campaign manager.

Carolyn Palmer, San Antonio, *April 9, 1999:* Party activist, library and archives commission appointee.

Martha Parr, Amarillo, *July 23, 1998:* Party activist, county party staff.

Mayetta Parr, Amarillo, *July 22, 1998:* Young Republicans activist.

Barbara Patton, Houston, *March 27, 1999:* Goldwater Texas campaign staffer, county party staff, fundraiser, campaign worker.

Ann Peden, Hondo, *June 27, 2000:* County chair, County Chairman Association president, state committeewoman.

Teddy Peterson, San Antonio, *September 29, 1998:* Campaign and congressional staff, party activist, Republican women's club president.

Gwen Pharo, Dallas, *June 15, 1999:* Fundraiser, campaign manager, party activist, congressional and presidential staff.

Billie Pickard, Raymondville, *October 12, 1999:* State committeewoman, fundraiser, campaign worker.

Caroline Pierce, Houston, *August 19, 1999:* Republican Women activist, campaign worker.

Billijo Porter, El Paso, *October 17, 1998:* County chair, campaign worker.

Ruth Potter, Dallas, *September 21, 1999:* Party activist.

Joanne Powell, San Angelo, *August 17, 1998:* Party activist, campaign worker, congressional staff.

Poolie Pratt, Victoria, *April 7, 1999:* State committeewoman, campaign worker.

Ann Quirk, Austin, *August 17, 1999:* Young Republicans activist, campaign worker, State Senator Drew Nixon's staff.

Jean Raffetto, Houston & Seabrook, *May 27, 1999:* Party activist, campaign worker.

Carole Ragland, League City, *March 22, 1999:* Precinct chair, campaign worker.

Diane Rath, San Antonio, *May 14, 1998:* State committeewoman, campaign worker, fundraiser, appointed Texas workforce commission chair.

Nora Ray, Fort Worth, *September 22, 1998:* Precinct chair, county vice chair, campaign worker.

William Rector, Wichita Falls, *April 20, 1999:* State committeeman.

Carol Reed, Dallas, *September 24, 1998:* Political consultant, fundraiser, Senator John Tower's campaign staff.

Dorothy Reed, Amarillo, *July 22, 1998:* County vice chair, campaign worker, Republican women's club president.

Glenda Reeder, San Antonio, *July 14, 1998:* Republican women's club president, state committeewoman.

Anna Claire Rice, Houston, *May 26, 1999:* Republican Women activist, campaign worker.

Leon Richardson, Nederland, *February 25, 1999:* Precinct chair, candidate for state legislature, campaign worker.

Lucille Rochs, Fredericksburg, *March 22, 2000:* Party activist, campaign worker.

Doris Mayer Rousselot, Sonora, *November 9, 1998:* Party activist, campaign worker.

Betty Ruminer, Seabrook, *March 23, 1999:* Precinct chair, campaign worker.

Ken Ruminer, Seabrook, *March 23, 1999:* Party activist, campaign worker.

Diana Ryan, San Angelo, *August 23, 1999:* Party activist, fundraiser.

Carole Keeton Rylander, Austin, *July 11, 2000:* Elected Texas Railroad Commissioner and Texas Comptroller of Public Accounts.

Dottie Sanders, Houston, *May 27, 1999:* Precinct chair, campaign manager, Republican Women activist.

Ruth Schiermeyer, Lubbock, *November 21, 1998:* Campaign manager, county chair, Brazos River Authority appointee.

Katie Seewald, Amarillo, *July 23, 1998:* Party activist, campaign manager, fundraiser.

Ellie Selig, Seguin, *January 28, 1999:* Fundraiser, Republican Women and party activist.

Bill Shaner, Midland, *August 18, 1998:* County chair.

Douthea Shaner, Midland, *August 18, 1998:* Precinct chair, campaign worker.

Gwyn Shea, Irving, *September 18, 1999:* Elected state representative, appointed and elected constable, Texas workers compensation insurance board appointee, Representative Bob Davis's staff.

Anne Shepard, Victoria & Harlingen, *February 8, 2000:* State committeewomen, campaign worker.

Bucky Smith, New Braunfels, *October 1, 1998:* Party activist, campaign worker, fundraiser.

Idalou Smith, Waco, *September 7, 2000:* Party activist, campaign worker.

Mary Jane Smith, Houston, *May 27, 1999:* County party staff, campaign manager, political consultant.

Reba Boyd Smith, Odessa & Abilene, *November 18, 1998:* Party activist, candidate for county treasurer, campaign worker.

Polly Sowell, McAllen & Austin, *August 12, 1997 and September 30, 1998:* Deputy state vice chair, state vice chair, campaign manager, Governor George W. Bush's staff.

Diana Stafford, Irving & Amarillo, *July 24, 1998:* Campaign manager, fundraiser.

Pollyanna Stephens, San Angelo, *August 17, 1998:* Candidate's wife, fundraiser, San Angelo State University board appointee.

Betty Sterquell, Amarillo, *July 23, 1998:* County chair, fundraiser, community development committee appointee.

Nancy Stevens, Corpus Christi, *June 4, 1999:* County chair, candidate for county clerk.

Jane Anne Stinnett, Lubbock, *November 21, 1998:* Campaign manager, political consultant.

Joci Straus, San Antonio, *February 16, 1998:* Campaign manager, fundraiser, precinct chair, presidential appointee.

Betty Strohacker, Kerrville, *July 13, 1998:* Party activist, campaign worker, Upper Guadalupe River Authority appointee.

Cynthia Tauss, League City, *March 5, 1999:* County chair, Texas board of pardons and paroles appointee, candidate for county commissioner and state representative.

Estelle Teague, Hurst, *June 15, 1999:* State committeewoman, TFRW activist.

Millie Teas, Dallas, *February 11, 2000:* Campaign worker.

John Tedford, Sonora, *August 20, 1998:* Colleague of state committeewoman Maxine Browne.

Mary Teeple, Austin, *August 13, 1998:* Campaign worker, fundraiser.

Jess Ann Thomason, Midland, *August 24, 1999:* Fundraiser, campaign worker.

Dianne Thompson, Boerne & Houston, *November 19, 1997:* TFRW president, campaign manager, NFRW fourth vice president.

Lou Tower, Wichita Falls & Dallas, *September 23, 1998:* Wife of U. S. Senator John Tower.

Patti Rose Trippet, Waco, *March 3, 2000:* Party activist.

Linda Underwood, Houston, *March 26, 1999:* Young Republicans activist, campaign staff.

Julia Vaughan, Midland, *August 18, 1998:* Candidate for appeals court judge.

Margaret Vickery, Fort Worth, *August 25, 1999:* Party activist.

Marjorie Vickery, Copper Canyon, *July 23, 1998:* Party activist, elected state board of education member.

Kris Anne Vogelpohl, Galveston, *March 4, 1999:* County vice chair, campaign worker, fundraiser.

Ann Wallace, Fort Worth & Austin, *August 10, 1998:* Campaign manager, fundraiser, state committeewoman, U. S. office of consumer affairs appointee.

Zubie Walters, Yoakum, *October 11, 1999:* Party activist.

Gail Waterfield, Canadian, *August 14, 1998:* Party activist, campaign manager, candidate's wife, fundraiser.

Susan Weddington, San Antonio, *March 7, 2000:* State chair (a first for a woman of any major political party in Texas).

Martha Weisend, Dallas, *May 4, 1999:* Campaign manager, fundraiser, state committeewoman.

Gayle West, Pasadena, *March 23, 1999:* State committeewoman, fundraiser, candidate's wife.

Lois White, San Antonio, *June 9, 2000:* Party activist, candidate for state legislature.

Billie Whitefield, Houston, *March 25, 1999:* Party activist, candidate's wife, campaign worker.

Theo Wickersham, San Antonio, *July 14, 1998:* State committeewoman, campaign worker, fundraiser.

Mary Lou Wiggins, Dallas, *September 25, 1998:* Campaign manager, party activist.

Sitty Wilkes, Austin, *August 12, 1998:* Party activist, fundraiser, elected school board member.

Doris Williams, Lake Jackson, *October 1, 1999:* Party activist, elected mayor.

Irene Cox Wischer, San Antonio, *June 4, 1998:* TFRW president, fundraiser, party activist.

Joan Wood, Waco, *February 28, 2000:* State committeewoman, campaign worker.

Sharolyn Wood, Houston, *March 26, 1999:* Elected judge.

Carole Woodard, Houston & Galveston, *June 9, 2000:* Party activist, campaign worker, candidate for county clerk, Texas board of human services appointee.

Bebe Zuniga, Laredo, *April 12, 1999:* Party activist, campaign manager, fundraiser.

Additional Interviews:

Tom Anderson, Houston, *March 24, 1999*

Anne Crews, Dallas, *September 13, 1999*

Caroline Emeny, Amarillo, *July 23, 1998*

Mamie Proctor, Houston, *May 21, 1999*

State Republican Executive Committee Women Members, 1952–1989

1952-53

NATIONAL COMMITTEEWOMAN:
Mrs. Carl G. Stearns, Houston

VICE CHAIR:
Mrs. Buck West, San Antonio

DISTRICT COMMITTEEWOMEN:
1 Mrs. George Hamilton, Texarkana
2 Mrs. Charles L. Bacheller, Kilgore
3 Mrs. Fred W. Graves, Jacksonville
4 Mrs. R. D. Holloway, Port Arthur
5 Mrs. Gertrude Leek, Livingston
6 Mrs. J. M. Sloan, Palestine
7 Mrs. I. L. Elam, Edgewood
8 Mrs. Sam Whitaker, Paris
9 Mrs. Jack Adamson, Honey Grove
10 Mrs. Rebecca Brune, Anna
11 Mrs. H. W. Roberts, Dallas
12 Mrs. Ben Ballard, Jr., Hillsboro
13 Miss Nettie Turner, Rockdale
14 Miss Henrietta Fricke, Brenham
15 Mrs. Elma Allen, Hallettsville
16 Mrs. R. H. J. Osborne, Houston
17 Mrs. James Hadcock, Galveston
18 Mrs. James Lawrence Wood, Refugio
19 Mrs. C. R. Guibor, Seguin
20 Mrs. Mildred F. McNab, Bertram
21 Miss Mollie Ann Nelson, Clifton
22 Mrs. E. H. Barnhart, Denton
23 Mrs. W. C. Witcher, Wichita Falls
24 Mrs. L. S. Howard, Roscoe
25 Mrs. William Schroeder, Fredericksburg
26 Mrs. Verlie H. Cowan, San Antonio
27 Mrs. Beatrice D. Frase, Donna
28 Mrs. Charles L. Renaud, Fort Worth
29 Mrs. John Darden, Midland
30 Mrs. Bertha Helen Kerr, Lubbock
31 Miss Ruthelle Bacon, Amarillo

1954-55

NATIONAL COMMITTEEWOMAN:
Mrs. John R. Black, Dallas

VICE CHAIR:
Mrs. Frank T. O'Brien, Amarillo

DISTRICT COMMITTEEWOMEN:
1 Mrs. Sam Whitaker, Paris
2 Mrs. Nan Bacheller, Kilgore
3 Mrs. Fred Graves, Jacksonville
4 Mrs. Jack Love, Orange
5 Mrs. Travis Moore, Crockett
6 Mrs. R. H. J. Osborne Jr., Houston
7 Mrs. Romer Bullington, Tyler
8 Mrs. Allie Mae Currie, Dallas
9 Mrs. H. M. Dyer, Commerce
10 Mrs. Jack D. Brownfield, Fort Worth
11 Miss Henrietta Fricke, Brenham
12 Mrs. Miles Hastings, Jr., Waxahachie
13 Miss Nettie Turner, Rockdale
14 Mrs. Elmore R. Torn, Taylor
15 Mrs. Hargrove Smith, Eagle Lake
16 Mrs. Emmie K. Schroeder, Fredericksburg
17 Mrs. J. C. Overbaugh, Lake Jackson
18 Mrs. Richard M. Lucas, Beeville
19 Mrs. Dorothy L. Vance, Hondo
20 Lila Nichols, Kingsville
21 Mrs. Neal D. Terrey, Alice
22 Mrs. Christine Unger, Denton
23 Miss Enid Gossett, Wichita Falls
24 Mrs. Gertrude Surratt, Snyder
25 Mrs. R. S. Waring, San Angelo
26 Mrs. Tom Slick, San Antonio
27 Mrs. Paul Armstrong, McAllen
28 Mrs. Sadie Thomas, Ralls
29 Mrs. Percy Pogson, El Paso
30 Mrs. Curtis Traweek, Hereford
31 Mrs. Raymond W. Harrah, Pampa

1956-57

NATIONAL COMMITTEEWOMAN:
Mrs. John R. Black, Dallas

VICE CHAIR:
Mrs. Miles Hastings, Jr., Waxahachie

DISTRICT COMMITTEEWOMEN:
 1 Mrs. Sam Whitaker, Paris
 2 Mrs. Charles Bacheller, Kilgore
 3 Mrs. Paul Powell, Woodville
 4 Vacancy
 5 Mrs. Rachel Faulkner, Coldspring
 6 Mrs. John W. Martin, Houston
 7 Mrs. T. W. Benham, Mineola
 8 Mrs. Ralph W. Currie, Dallas
 9 Mrs. H. M. Dyer, Commerce
10 Mrs. Joseph Kennedy, Fort Worth
11 Mrs. Elizabeth B. Daugherty, Fairfield
12 Mrs. W. H. Getzendaner, Waxahachie
13 Mrs. Nettie Turner, Rockdale
14 Mrs. Elmore R. Torn, Taylor
15 Mrs. Hargrove Smith, Eagle Lake
16 Mrs. Emmie K. Schroeder, Fredericksburg
17 Mrs. J. C. Overbaugh, Lake Jackson
18 Mrs. Frank Buhler, Victoria
19 Mrs. Dorothy L. Vance, Hondo
20 Mrs. Thomas R. Armstrong, Armstrong
21 Mrs. Neal D. Terrey, Alice
22 Mrs. Christine Unger, Denton
23 Mrs. W. H. Lobaugh, Graham
24 Mrs. John DuMont, Abilene
25 Vacancy
26 Mrs. Robert Grice Maverick, San Antonio
27 Mrs. Paul Armstrong, McAllen
28 Mrs. L. H. Thomas, Ralls
29 Mrs. E. C. Bunch, Odessa
30 Mrs. Curtis Traweek, Hereford
31 Mrs. G. N. McDaniel, Borger

1958-59

NATIONAL COMMITTEEWOMAN:
Mrs. John R. Black, Dallas

VICE CHAIR:
Mrs. Frank S. Buhler, Victoria

DISTRICT COMMITTEEWOMEN:
 1 Mrs. Sam Whitaker, Paris
 2 Mrs. Charles L. Bacheller, Kilgore
 3 Mrs. Jack H. Wade, Lufkin
 4 Mrs. Fletcher Graham, Beaumont
 5 Mrs. Rachel Faulkner, Coldspring
 6 Mrs. John W. Martin, Houston
 7 Mrs. Uldene Hill, Grand Saline
 8 Mrs. E. D. MacIver, Dallas

 9 Mrs. H. M. Dyer, Commerce
10 Mrs. Peggy Floore, Fort Worth
11 Mrs. Elizabeth B. Daugherty, Fairfield
12 Mrs. George Benjamin, Cleburne
13 Miss Nettie Turner, Rockdale
14 Mrs. Malcolm Milburn, Austin
15 Mrs. Hargrove Smith, Eagle Lake
16 Mrs. Emmie K. Schroeder, Fredericksburg
17 Mrs. J. C. Overbaugh, Lake Jackson
18 Mrs. W. D. Welder, Vidauri
19 Mrs. Frank X. Vance, Hondo
20 Mrs. Thomas R. Armstrong, Armstrong
21 Mrs. Neal D. Terrey, Alice
22 Mrs. G. W. Ewing, Jr., Breckenridge
23 Mrs. W. H. Lobaugh, Graham
24 Mrs. John DuMont, Abilene
25 Mrs. Charles F. Browne, Sonora
26 Mrs. Robert Grice Maverick, San Antonio
27 Mrs. Paul Armstrong, McAllen
28 Mrs. L. H. Thomas, Ralls
29 Mrs. R. L. Waller, Midland
30 Mrs. Curtis Traweek, Hereford
31 Mrs. G. N. McDaniel, Borger

1961-62

NATIONAL COMMITTEEWOMAN:
Mrs. Ike S. Kampmann, Jr., San Antonio

VICE CHAIR:
Mrs. G. N. McDaniel, Borger

DISTRICT COMMITTEEWOMEN:
 1 Mrs. Sam Whitaker, Paris
 2 Mrs. Robert T. Reeves, Kilgore
 3 Mrs. Jack H. Wade, Lufkin
 4 Mrs. Stewart Last, Beaumont
 5 Mrs. Drew Jackson, Dayton
 6 Mrs. M. S. Ackerman III, Houston
 7 Mrs. Uldene Hill, Grand Saline
 8 Mrs. B. L. Kanowsky, Dallas
 9 Mrs. H. M. Dyer, Commerce
10 Mrs. Peggy Floore, Fort Worth
11 Mrs. Sue Hayes, Palestine
12 Mrs. Charles G. Murray, Whitney
13 Mrs. O. W. Hayes, Temple
14 Mrs. Malcolm Milburn, Austin
15 Vacancy
16 Mrs. Emmie K. Schroeder, Fredericksburg
17 Mrs. D. D. Napier, Richmond
18 Mrs. Lawrence Wood, Refugio
19 Mrs. Frank X. Vance, Hondo
20 Mrs. Thomas R. Armstrong, Armstrong
21 Mrs. Neal D. Terrey, Alice
22 Mrs. G. W. Ewing, Jr., Breckenridge
23 Mrs. W. H. Lobaugh, Graham

24 Mrs. A. K. Doss, Jr., Abilene
25 Mrs. Charles F. Browne, Sonora
26 Mrs. John H. Wood, Jr., San Antonio
27 Mrs. Virginia Armstrong, McAllen
28 Mrs. Gordon Treadaway, Lubbock
29 Mrs. William A. Heck, Midland
30 Mrs. Gilbert Lamb, Muleshoe
31 Mrs. G. N. McDaniel, Borger

1964-65

NATIONAL COMMITTEEWOMAN:
Mrs. Ike S. Kampmann, Jr., San Antonio

VICE CHAIR:
Mrs. G. N. McDaniel, Borger

DISTRICT COMMITTEEWOMEN:
 1 Mrs. Sam Whitaker, Paris
 2 Mrs. Robert T. Reeves, Kilgore
 3 Mrs. Jack H. Wade, Lufkin
 4 Mrs. Stewart D. Last, Beaumont
 5 Mrs. W. A. Walling, Jr., Huntsville
 6 Mrs. M. S. Ackermann III, Houston
 7 Mrs. Howard Hill, Grand Saline
 8 Mrs. Jo Kanowsky, Dallas
 9 Mrs. H. M. Dyer, Commerce
10 Mrs. John L. Wallace, Jr., Fort Worth
11 Mrs. George A. Hayes, Palestine
12 Mrs. Charles C. Murray, Whitney
13 Mrs. O. W. Hayes, Temple
14 Mrs. Malcolm Milburn, Austin
15 Mrs. Paul Henderson, El Campo
16 Mrs. Maxine Smith, Uvalde
17 Mrs. D. D. Napier, Richmond
18 Mrs. Frank S. Buhler, Victoria
19 Mrs. Gladys Strauss, Seguin
20 Mrs. Tobin Armstrong, Armstrong
21 Mrs. Alonzo Benavides, Laredo
22 Mrs. G. W. Ewing, Breckenridge
23 Mrs. W. H. Lobaugh, Graham
24 Mrs. A. K. Doss, Jr., Abilene
25 Mrs. Charles F. Browne, Sonora
26 Mrs. Edward T. Hill, San Antonio
27 Mrs. Richard Sowell, McAllen
28 Mrs. Charles Gibson, Lubbock
29 Mrs. H. B. Phillips, Kermit
30 Mrs. Curtis Traweek, Hereford
31 Mrs. Warren Fatheree, Pampa

1966-67

NATIONAL COMMITTEEWOMAN:
Mrs. J. C. Man, Wichita Falls

VICE CHAIR:
Mrs. G. N. McDaniel, Borger

DISTRICT COMMITTEEWOMEN:
 1 Mrs. A. C. Hoffman, Mt. Pleasant
 2 Mrs. Barton L. Owens, Longview
 3 Mrs. A. E. Cudlipp, Lufkin
 4 Mrs. Lamar Cecil, Beaumont
 5 Mrs. W. A. Walling, Jr., Huntsville
 6 Mrs. Hal Hazelrigg, Houston
 7 Mrs. Howard Hill, Grand Saline
 8 Mrs. Jo Kanowsky, Dallas
 9 Mrs. David Wells, Sherman
10 Mrs. John J. Andujar, Fort Worth
11 Mrs. George A. Hayes, Palestine
12 Mrs. Charles C. Murray, Whitney
13 Mrs. O. W. Hayes, Temple
14 Mrs. Malcolm Milburn, Austin
15 Mrs. Adele D. Larson, Cuero
16 Mrs. Maxine Smith, Uvalde
17 Mrs. Clara Slough, Texas City
18 Mrs. Frank S. Buhler, Victoria
19 Mrs. Gladys Strauss, Seguin
20 Mrs. Tobin Armstrong, Armstrong
21 Mrs. Alonzo Benavides, Laredo
22 Mrs. Oran Boyles, Wichita Falls
23 Mrs. Jack Maxfield, Wichita Falls
24 Mrs. A. K. Doss, Abilene
25 Mrs. Charles F. Browne, Sonora
26 Mrs. Edward T. Hill, San Antonio
27 Mrs. Richard Sowell, McAllen
28 Mrs. Charles Gibson, Lubbock
29 Mrs. J. T. Moorhead, El Paso
30 Mrs. E. R. Little, Dimmitt
31 Mrs. Warren Fatheree, Pampa

1968-69

NATIONAL COMMITTEEWOMAN:
Mrs. J. C. Man, Jr., Wichita Falls

VICE CHAIR:
Mrs. Tobin Armstrong, Armstrong

DISTRICT COMMITTEEWOMEN:
 1 Mrs. A. C. Hoffmann, Mt. Pleasant
 2 Mrs. Howard Hill, Grand Saline
 3 Mrs. Basil Atkinson, Jr., Lufkin
 4 Mrs. Dale Hager, Beaumont
 5 Mrs. R. A. Buchanan, Liberty
 6 Mrs. Abe Farrior, Houston
 7 Mrs. J. D. Boggs, Pasadena
 8 Mrs. Jo Kanowsky, Dallas
 9 Mrs. Blanche R. Martin, Denison
10 Vacancy
11 Mrs. Elmer Lindstrom, Houston
12 Mrs. Paul C. Coffin, Itasca
13 Mrs. Charles Hanson, Temple
14 Mrs. B. J. Smith, Austin

15 Mrs. Raymond Arsht, Houston
16 Mrs. H. K. Herbert, Dallas
17 Miss Estelle Tartt, Galveston
18 Mrs. Joe N. Pratt, Victoria
19 Mrs. Joe R. Straus, Jr., San Antonio
20 Mrs. James H. Clement, Kingsville
21 Mrs. Alonzo Benavides, Laredo
22 Mrs. John J. Andujar, Fort Worth
23 Mrs. R. L. Robinson, Dallas
24 Mrs. A. K. Doss, Jr., Abilene
25 Mrs. Charles F. Browne, Sonora
26 Mrs. Baxter R. Grier, San Antonio
27 Mrs. Richard Sowell, McAllen
28 Mrs. J. L. Pinkerton, Monahans
29 Mrs. J. T. Moorhead, El Paso
30 Mrs. Tom Suits, Petersburg
31 Mrs. Warren Fatheree, Pampa

1970-71

NATIONAL COMMITTEEWOMAN:
Mrs. Tobin Armstrong, Armstrong

VICE CHAIR:
Mrs. Bradley Streeter, Wichita Falls

DISTRICT COMMITTEEWOMEN:
 1 Mrs. A. C. Hoffman, Mt. Pleasant
 2 Mrs. Walter Judge, Mineola
 3 Mrs. W. L. Rehkop, Athens
 4 Mrs. Dale Hager, Beaumont
 5 Mrs. S. W. Kowierschke, Bryan
 6 Mrs. Abe Farrior, Houston
 7 Mrs. J. D. Boggs, Pasadena
 8 Mrs. Jo Kanowsky, Dallas
 9 Mrs. Jack Martin, Denison
10 Mrs. John S. Howell, Fort Worth
11 Mrs. Elmer Lindstrom, Channelview
12 Mrs. Paul C. Coffin, Itasca
13 Mrs. Charles Hanson, Temple
14 Mrs. Robert Farris, Austin
15 Mrs. Eugene Fike, Houston
16 Mrs. H. K. Herbert, Dallas
17 Miss Estelle Tartt, Galveston
18 Mrs. Joe N. Pratt, Victoria
19 Mrs. Joe R. Straus, Jr., San Antonio
20 Mrs. James H. Clement, Kingsville
21 Mrs. Warren Wagner, Crystal City
22 Mrs. John J. Andujar, Fort Worth
23 Mrs. Robert R. McCready, Dallas
24 Mrs. Mary Doss, Abilene
25 Mrs. Don Wolfenberger, Midland
26 Mrs. Edward T. Hill, San Antonio
27 Mrs. L. V. Mead, McAllen
28 Mrs. Jack R. Cook, Andrews

29 Mrs. J. T. Moorhead, El Paso
30 Mrs. Tom Suits, Petersburg
31 Mrs. Warren Fatheree, Pampa

1972-73

NATIONAL COMMITTEEWOMAN:
Mrs. Tobin Armstrong, Armstrong

VICE CHAIR:
Mrs. Malcolm Milburn, Austin

DISTRICT COMMITTEEWOMEN:
 1 Mrs. Bill Gaw, Marshall
 2 Mrs. Walter Judge, Mineola
 3 Mrs. W. L. Rehkop, Athens
 4 Mrs. Joe Richardson, Nederland
 5 Mrs. S. W. Kowierschke, Bryan
 6 Mrs. Abe Farrior, Houston
 7 Mrs. J. D. Boggs, Pasadena
 8 Mrs. Jo Kanowsky, Dallas
 9 Mrs. Jack Martin, Denison
10 Mrs. Richard Hewitt, Fort Worth
11 Mrs. Elmer Lindstrom, Channelview
12 Mrs. Paul C. Coffin, Itasca
13 Mrs. Charles Hanson, Temple
14 Mrs. Stuart Benson, Austin
15 Mrs. Eugene Fike, Houston
16 Mrs. H. K. Herbert, Dallas
17 Mrs. Jack Garrett, Danbury
18 Mrs. Lee Briscoe, Eagle Lake
19 Mrs. Edward Baker, San Antonio
20 Mrs. James H. Clement, Kingsville
21 Mrs. Bruce Foster, Hondo
22 Mrs. John J. Andujar, Fort Worth
23 Mrs. I. Ray Dunlap, Dallas
24 Mrs. Jack McGlothlin, Abilene
25 Mrs. Edgar Francis, Odessa
26 Mrs. Louis Doehne, San Antonio
27 Mrs. George R. Lipe, Brownsville
28 Mrs. R. S. Tapp, Lubbock
29 Mrs. John Root, El Paso
30 Mrs. Tom Suits, Petersburg
31 Mrs. Jack Hart, Gruver

1974-75

NATIONAL COMMITTEEWOMAN:
Mrs. Richard D. Bass, Dallas

VICE CHAIR:
Mrs. Richard Sowell, McAllen

DISTRICT COMMITTEEWOMEN:
 1 Mrs. Jack C. W. Martin, Denison
 2 Mrs. Walter Judge, Mineola
 3 Mrs. W. L. Rehkop, Athens

4 Mrs. O. J. Richardson, Nederland
5 Mrs. Lee Briscoe, Eagle Lake
6 Mrs. Elmer Lindstrom, Channelview
7 Mrs. Jack E. Brown, Houston
8 Mrs. Jo Kanowsky, Dallas
9 Mrs. M. J. Snell, Dallas
10 Mrs. Joe F. Teague, Hurst
11 Mrs. Lewis A. Rockwood, Houston
12 Mrs. John J. Andujar, Fort Worth
13 Mrs. Paul H. Till, Houston
14 Mrs. R. T. Roberts, Austin
15 Mrs. Charles E. McGuckin, Houston
16 Mrs. Charles A. Foster, Jr., Dallas
17 Mrs. Jack Garrett, Danbury
18 Mrs. Kenneth L. Jarratt, Edna
19 Mary Morton Jackson, San Antonio
20 Mrs. John B. Armstrong, Kingsville
21 Mrs. Edward Baker, San Antonio
22 Mrs. Jack L. Eidson, Weatherford
23 Mrs. I. Ray Dunlap, Dallas
24 Mrs. Jack McGlothlin, Abilene
25 Mrs. Robert S. Johnson, San Angelo
26 Mrs. Louis C. Doehne, San Antonio
27 Mrs. George R. Lipe, Brownsville
28 Mrs. Edgar B. Francis, Odessa
29 Mrs. John Root, El Paso
30 Mrs. John J. Kirchhoff, Plainview
31 Mrs. Jack Hart, Gruver

1976-77

NATIONAL COMMITTEEWOMAN:
Mrs. William P. Clements, Dallas

VICE CHAIR:
Mrs. Richard Sowell, McAllen

DISTRICT COMMITTEEWOMEN:
1 Mrs. Jack C. W. Martin, Denison
2 Mrs. George Pearson, Tyler
3 Mrs. W. L. Rehkop, Athens
4 Mrs. Howell Cobb, Beaumont
5 Mrs. Lee Briscoe, Eagle Lake
6 Mrs. Elmer Lindstrom, Channelview
7 Mrs. Jack E. Brown, Houston
8 Mrs. Jo Kanowsky, Dallas
9 Mrs. M. J. Snell, Dallas
10 Mrs. Bruce Jacobsen, Fort Worth
11 Mrs. Jack Boggs, Pasadena
12 Mrs. John J. Andujar, Fort Worth
13 Mrs. Paul H. Till, Houston
14 Mrs. R. T. Roberts, Austin
15 Mrs. Charles E. McGuckin, Houston
16 Mrs. Charles A. Foster Jr., Dallas
17 Mrs. Brockett Hudson, Seabrook

18 Mrs. Kenneth L. Jarratt, Edna
19 Mary Morton Jackson, San Antonio
20 Mrs. John B. Armstrong, Kingsville
21 Mrs. Burton Barnes, San Antonio
22 Mrs. Jack L Eidson, Weatherford
23 Mrs. I. Ray Dunlap, Dallas
24 Mrs. Jack McGlothlin, Abilene
25 Mrs. J. K. Dixon, Llano
26 Mrs. Louis Doehne, San Antonio
27 Mrs. Manning Dierlam, Brownsville
28 Mrs. Edgar Francis, Odessa
29 Mrs. John Root, El Paso
30 Mrs. John J. Kirchhoff, Plainview
31 Mrs. Jack Hart, Gruver

1978-79

NATIONAL COMMITTEEWOMAN:
Sen. Betty Andujar, Fort Worth

VICE CHAIR:
Mrs. Polly Sowell, McAllen

DISTRICT COMMITTEEWOMEN:
1 Mrs. Blanche Martin, Denison
2 Mrs. Juanita Broyles, Tyler
3 Mrs. Lila Rehkop, Athens
4 Mrs. Amelie Cobb, Beaumont
5 Mrs. Sue Briscoe, Eagle Lake
6 Mrs. Wilda Lindstrom, Channelview
7 Mrs. Randy Brown, Houston
8 Mrs. Barbara Foreman, Dallas
9 Mrs. Iris Snell, Dallas
10 Mrs. Pat Jacobson, Fort Worth
11 Mrs. Nancy Boggs, Pasadena
12 Mrs. Barbara Howell, Fort Worth
13 Mrs. Jacquelyn Till, Houston
14 Mrs. Mary Lee, Austin
15 Mrs. Ruth McGuckin, Houston
16 Mrs. Jennie Foster, Dallas
17 Mrs. Dottie Hudson, Seabrook
18 Mrs. Jayce Jarratt, Edna
19 Mary Morton Jackson, San Antonio
20 Mrs. Billie Pickard, Raymondville
21 Mrs. Libba Barnes, San Antonio
22 Phyllis Kay Babcock, Denton
23 Mrs. Peggy Wilson, Dallas
24 Mrs. Bette McRae, Waco
25 Mrs. Elizabeth Rohn, Kerrville
26 Mrs. Dorothy Doehne, San Antonio
27 Mrs. Peggy Rodgers, Edinburg
28 Mrs. Janelle Evans, Brownfield
29 Mrs. Patty Bruce, El Paso
30 Mary Ellen Cummings, Wichita Falls
31 Mrs. Ila Jo Hart, Gruver

1980-81

NATIONAL COMMITTEEWOMAN:
Mrs. John J. Andujar, Fort Worth

VICE CHAIR:
Mrs. Louis C. Doehne, San Antonio

DISTRICT COMMITTEEWOMEN:

1 Mrs. Jack C. W. Martin, Denison
2 Mrs. Emmitt Clem, Jr., Plano
3 Mrs. W. L. Rehkop, Athens
4 Mrs. Barbara Rush, Beaumont
5 Mrs. Sue Briscoe, Eagle Lake
6 Mrs. Elmer Lindstrom, Channelview
7 Mrs. Archie H. Manes, Jr., Houston
8 Mrs. Ed Foreman, Dallas
9 Mrs. Jack Sommerfield, Garland
10 Mrs. Bruce Jacobson, Fort Worth
11 Mrs. Jack Boggs, Pasadena
12 Mrs. John S. Howell III, Fort Worth
13 Mrs. Paul H. Till, Houston
14 Mrs. Clyde E. Lee, Austin
15 Mrs. Charles E. McGuckin, Houston
16 Mrs. Kay Bailey Hutchison, Dallas
17 Mrs. Marilyn Smith, Alvin
18 Mrs. Simon C. Cornelius, Victoria
19 Mary Morton Jackson, San Antonio
20 Mrs. Marshall Pickard, Raymondville
21 Mrs. Burton Barnes, San Antonio
22 Mrs. Virginia Upham, Mineral Wells
23 Mrs. W. W. Wilson III, Dallas
24 Mrs. James F. Wood, Waco
25 Mrs. Edward J. Rohn, Kerrville
26 Mrs. W. J. Pieper, Jr., San Antonio
27 Mrs. R. W. Rogers, Edinburg
28 Mrs. Mark Majors, Odessa
29 Mrs. H. L. Bruce, El Paso
30 Mrs. Jacque Allen, Wichita Falls
31 Mrs. Scott Nisbet, Pampa

1982-83

NATIONAL COMMITTEEWOMAN:
Mrs. H. E. Chiles, Fort Worth

VICE CHAIR:
Mrs. Louis C. Doehne, San Antonio

DISTRICT COMMITTEEWOMEN:

1 Mrs. Nancy Gordon, Avinger
2 Mrs. Emmitt Clem, Jr., Plano
3 Mrs. Jeannie Turk, Sour Lake
4 Mrs. Tommie Byrd, Beaumont
5 Mrs. Mildred Fike, Hempstead
6 Mrs. Elmer Lindstrom, Channelview
7 Mrs. Archie H. Manes, Jr., Houston
8 Mrs. Ed Foreman, Dallas
9 Mrs. Jack Sommerfield, Garland
10 Mrs. Bruce Jacobson, Fort Worth
11 Mrs. Jack Boggs, Pasadena
12 Mrs. Anna Mowery, Fort Worth
13 Mrs. Pat Black, Houston
14 Mrs. Kay Danks, Austin
15 Mrs. Ann Striegler, Houston
16 Mrs. Kay Bailey Hutchison, Dallas
17 Mrs. Nancy Canion, League City
18 Mrs. Simon C. Cornelius, Victoria
19 Mrs. Mary Morton Jackson, San Antonio
20 Mrs. Marshall Pickard, Raymondville
21 Mrs. Burton Barnes, San Antonio
22 Mrs. Virginia Upham, Mineral Wells
23 Mrs. Wanda Damstra, Grand Prairie
24 Mrs. James F. Wood, Waco
25 Mrs. Edward J. Rohn, Kerrville
26 Mrs. W. J. Pieper, Jr., San Antonio
27 Mrs. Dorothy McDonald, Pt. Isabel
28 Mrs. Janelle Evans, Brownfield
29 Mrs. Lisa Mercurio, El Paso
30 Mrs. Jacque Allen, Wichita Falls
31 Mrs. Sybil Daniels, Perryton

1984-85

NATIONAL COMMITTEEWOMAN:
Mrs. Fran Chiles, Fort Worth

VICE CHAIR:
Diana Denman, San Antonio

DISTRICT COMMITTEEWOMEN:

1 Mrs. Nancy Gordon, Avinger
2 Mrs. Jan Copas, Tyler
3 Mrs. Jeannie Turk, Sour Lake
4 Mrs. Tommie Byrd, Beaumont
5 Mrs. Katye Kowierschke, Huntsville
6 Mrs. Wilda Lindstrom, Houston
7 Mrs. Patricia Vanoni, Houston
8 Mrs. Virginia Steenson, Richardson
9 Mrs. Joan B. Wood, Waco
10 Mrs. Pat Jacobson, Fort Worth
11 Mrs. Nancy Canion, League City
12 Mrs. Anna Mowery, Fort Worth
13 Mrs. Iris Manes, Houston
14 Mrs. Kay Danks, Austin
15 Mrs. Nancy Palm, Houston
16 Mrs. Martha B. Weisend, Dallas
17 Mrs. Vicki Hapke, Houston
18 Ms. Sybil Daniel, Victoria
19 Mrs. Mary Morton Jackson, San Antonio
20 Mrs. Delores Price, Kingsville
21 Mrs. Robbie Borchers, New Braunfels
22 Mrs. Virginia Upham, Mineral Wells
23 Mrs. Ruth Rayner, Dallas

24 Mrs. Amelia Dixon, Llano
25 Mrs. Elizabeth J. Rohn, Kerrville
26 Mrs. Diane Rath, San Antonio
27 Mrs. Laura B. Duffey, Brownsville
28 Mrs. Janelle Evans, Brownfield
29 Mrs. Bette D. Hervey, El Paso
30 Mrs. Jacque Allen, Wichita Falls
31 Mrs. Lottie Eller, Panhandle

1986-87

NATIONAL COMMITTEEWOMAN:
Fran Chiles, Fort Worth

VICE CHAIR:
Diana Denman, San Antonio

DISTRICT COMMITTEEWOMEN:
 1 Nancy Gordon, Avinger
 2 Jane Yancey, Plano
 3 Marguerete Graves, Kirbyville
 4 Marguerite Foulk, Beaumont
 5 Katye Kowierschke, Huntsville
 6 Wilda Lindstrom, Houston
 7 Patricia Vanoni, Houston
 8 Virginia Steenson, Richardson
 9 Joan Wood, Waco
10 Pat Jacobson, Fort Worth
11 Gayle West, Pasadena
12 Darla Mortensen, Fort Worth
13 Iris Manes, Houston
14 Kay Danks, Austin
15 Nelda Eppes, Houston
16 Martha Weisend, Dallas
17 Vicki Hapke, Houston
18 Anne Ashy, Victoria
19 Katy Evans, San Antonio
20 Leona Knight, Corpus Christi
21 Robbie Borchers, New Braunfels
22 Vivian Millirons, Burleson
23 Patricia Taylor, Dallas
24 Amelia Dixon, Sunrise Beach
25 Ann Peden, Hondo
26 Diane Rath, San Antonio
27 Becki Olivares, McAllen
28 Janelle Evans, Brownfield
29 Bette Hervey, El Paso
30 Jacque Allen, Wichita Falls
31 Lottie Eller, Panhandle

1988-89

NATIONAL COMMITTEEWOMAN:
 Mrs. Fran Chiles, Fort Worth
VICE CHAIR:
Diana Denman, San Antonio

DISTRICT COMMITTEEWOMEN:
 1 Nancy Gordon, Avinger
 2 Jane Yancey, Plano
 3 Marguerete Graves, Kirbyville
 4 Marguerite Foulk, Beaumont
 5 Katye Kowierschke, Huntsville
 6 Wilda Lindstrom, Houston
 7 Jeanne Wilson, Houston
 8 Virginia Steenson, Richardson
 9 Sarilee Ferguson, Waco
10 Jane Burgland, Arlington
11 Gayle West, Pasadena
12 Jane Berberich, Fort Worth
13 Iris Manes, Houston
14 Holly Decherd, Austin
15 Nelda Eppes, Houston
16 Lynne Tweedell, Dallas
17 Penny Butler, Houston
18 Anne Ashy, Victoria
19 Mrs. Theo Wickersham, San Antonio
20 Leona Knight, Corpus Christi
21 Barbara Schoolcraft, Seguin
22 Vivian Millirons, Burleson
23 Patricia Taylor, Dallas
24 Helen Rutland, Belton
25 Cindy Brockwell, Boerne
26 Diane Rath, San Antonio
27 Mary Ann Rios, McAllen
28 Janelle Evans, Brownsville
29 Bette Hervey, El Paso
30 Jacque Allen, Wichita Falls
31 Bobbie Nisbet, Pampa

SOURCE:
Texas Almanac for the years 1952-1959;
1961-1962*; 1964-1989

*Although the *Texas Almanac* has consistently
been published biannually on even years, the
almanac was not printed in 1960. The biannual
publication resumed in 1964, therefore names
of some of the officeholders during this time
period are unavailable. Original state
committee rosters were unavailable from the
Republican Party of Texas.

APPENDIX 2

Women Delegates to the Republican National Conventions, 1948–1988

1948 (33 TOTAL DELEGATES)

AT LARGE DELEGATES /*Alternates*

Mrs. H. E. Exum, Amarillo
Mrs. Carl G. Stearns, Houston

DISTRICT DELEGATES /*Alternates*

 1 *Mrs. Ida Watson, Naples*
 5 *Mrs. H. W. Roberts, Dallas*
 7 *Mrs. Minnie W. Smith, Houston*
 8 *Mrs. R. H. J. Osborne, Jr., Houston*
 9 *Mrs. Mary Ann Marcak, Victoria*
12 *Mrs. Sarah M. Renaud, Ft. Worth*
15 *Mrs. Helen Sargeant, McAllen*
17 *Mrs. L. S. Howard, Roscoe*
18 Miss Ruthelle Bacon, Amarillo
20 *Mrs. H. A. Cowan, San Antonio*

1952 (37 TOTAL DELEGATES)

AT LARGE DELEGATES /*Alternates*

Mrs. J. C. Overbaugh, Lake Jackson
Mrs. Jack E. Bliss, Midland

DISTRICT DELEGATES /*Alternates*

 1 Mrs. Charles Bacheller, Kilgore
 5 Mrs. Allie M. Currie, Dallas
 8 Mrs. R.H.J. Osborne, Jr., Houston
   Mrs. Ralph Feagin, Houston
 9 *Mrs. R. S. Morris, Rosenberg*
10 *Mrs. E. R. Torn, Taylor*
   Mrs. R. L. Hatchett, Jr., Austin
12 Mrs. J. D. Kennedy, Ft. Worth
20 *Mrs. William Smith, Houston*

1956 (54 TOTAL DELEGATES)

AT LARGE DELEGATES /*Alternates*

Mrs. John R. Black, Dallas
Mrs. Frank Buhler, Victoria
Mrs. R. D. O'Callaghan, San Antonio
Mrs. Tom Armstrong, Armstrong
Mrs. W. A. Smith, Houston

DISTRICT DELEGATES /*Alternates*

 1 *Mrs. R. M. Head, Texarkana*
   Mrs H. F. McWilliams
 2 *Mrs. A. G. Natwick, Beaumont*
 3 Mrs. C. L. Bacheller, Kilgore
   Mrs. James W. Fair, Tyler
 5 *Mrs. E. D. MacIver, Dallas*
   Mrs. A. E. Swenson, Dallas
 6 Mrs. Eliz. Daugherty, Fairfield
 7 *Mrs. Sue Hayes, Palestine*
 8 *Mrs. John W. Martin, Houston*
 9 Mrs. J. Overbaugh, Lake Jackson
   Mrs. Hargrove Smith, Eagle Lake
10 *Mrs. Malcolm Milburn, Austin*
   Mrs. Virginia Dana, Austin
11 Mrs. Goodhue Smith, Waco
13 Mrs. W. H. Lobaugh, Graham
15 Mrs. Paul Armstrong, McAllen
16 *Mrs. R. M. Metcalf, El Paso*
17 Mrs. John Dumont, Abilene
   Mrs. Gus Ewing, Jr., Breckenridge
18 Mrs. G. N. McDaniel, Borger
19 Mrs. L. H. Thomas, Ralls
20 Mrs. Robert Maverick, San Antonio
21 *Mrs. E. K. Schroeder, Fredericksburg*
   Mrs. Charles F. Browne, Sonora

1960 (54 TOTAL DELEGATES)

AT LARGE DELEGATES /*Alternates*
Mrs. John R. Black, Dallas
Mrs. T. R. Armstrong, Armstrong
Mrs. I. Kampmann, Jr., San Antonio
Miss B. Blodgett, Corpus Christi
Mrs. Jane Smith, San Antonio
Mrs. Donald Cameron, Dallas

DISTRICT DELEGATES /*Alternates*
1 *Mrs. James W. Fair, Tyler*
2 Mrs. Stewart D. Last, Beaumont
   Mrs. A. G. Natwick, Beaumont
3 *Mrs. Uldene Hill, Grand Saline*
5 Mrs. Ben Kanowsky, Dallas
   Mrs. James Biggart, Dallas
6 *Mrs. N. T. Berquist, Lufkin*
7 Mrs. George A. Hayes, Palestine
8 *Mrs. R. W. Kurtz, Houston*
   Mrs. Roland A. Gray, Houston
9 Mrs. D. D. Napeir, Richmond
   Mrs. Sid Farmer, Jr., Galveston
10 *Mrs. Gail Hill, Austin*
11 Mrs. O. W. Hayes, Temple
   Mrs. Chas. G. Edison, Sr., Waco
12 *Mrs. Peggy Floore, Ft. Worth*
13 Mrs. J. C. Man, Jr., Wichita Falls
   Miss M. MacDonald, Wichita Falls
15 *Mrs. Claude Van Renesse, Pharr*
16 Mrs. R. M. Metcalf, El Paso
17 Mrs. G. W. Ewing, Jr. Breckenridge
   Mrs. A. K. Doss, Jr., Abilene
18 Mrs. G.N. McDaniel, Borger
19 Mrs. Gordon Treadaway, Lubbock
20 *Mrs. Joy Carrington, San Antonio*
21 *Mrs. C. F. Browne, Sonora*
   Mrs. V. H. Wright, San Angelo
22 Mrs. J. W. Martin, Houston

1964 (56 TOTAL DELEGATES)

AT LARGE DELEGATES /*Alternates*
Mrs. I. S. Kampmann, San Antonio
Mrs. Richard Bass, Dallas
Mrs. G. N. McDaniel, Borger
Mrs. L. M. Cox, San Antonio

DISTRICT DELEGATES /*Alternates*
2 Mrs. Dale Hager, Beaumont
   Mrs. R. A. Buchanan, Liberty
4 Mrs. Blanche Martin, Denison
5 Mrs. Jo Kanowsky, Dallas
   Mrs. J. F. W. Hannay, Dallas
6 *Mrs. Bill McNutt, Corsicana*

7 Mrs. B. E. Atkinson, Jr.,Lufkin
   Mrs. Walter Haning, Athens
8 Mrs. E. P. Lowe, Baytown
9 Mrs. Helen May, Lake Jackson
   Mrs. Bette Jo Buhler, Victoria
10 Mrs. Malcolm Milburn, Austin
   Mrs. R. C. Barbour, Austin
   Mrs. Billie J. Pratt, Burnet
11 *Mrs. George Emerich, Waco*
   Mrs. William Lee, Waco
12 Mrs. John Howell, Ft. Worth
13 Mrs. J. C. Man, Jr., Wichita Falls
   Mrs. B. Streeter, Wichita Falls
14 Mrs. T. Armstrong, Armstrong
17 Mrs. A. K. Doss, Jr., Abilene
   Mrs. Jack Edison, Weatherford
18 Mrs. Warren Fatheree, Pampa
19 *Mrs. Charles Gibson, Lubbock*
20 Mrs. Edward T. Hill, San Antonio
   Mrs. Baxter R. Grier, San Antonio
21 Mrs Charles F. Browne, Sonora
   Mrs. Gladys Wright, San Angelo
22 Mrs. G. O. Johnstone, Houston

1968 (59 TOTAL DELEGATES)

AT LARGE DELEGATES /*Alternates*
Mrs. Bradley C. Streeter, Wichita Falls
Mrs. Barbara Culver, Midland
Mrs. Tobin Armstrong, Armstrong
Mrs. Ike S. Kampmann, Jr., San Antonio
Mrs. Malcolm Milburn, Austin
Mrs. Edward T. Hill, San Antonio

DISTRICT DELEGATES /*Alternates*
2 Mrs. B. E. Atkinson, Jr. Lufkin
   Mrs. W. L. Rehkop, Athens
3 Mrs. Jo Kanowsky, Dallas
   Mrs. Robert R McCready, Dallas
4 *Mrs. Jack Martin, Denison*
5 Mrs. Richard D. Bass
   Mrs. Godfrey Collins, Dallas
   Mrs. H. K. Herbert, Dallas
6 Mrs. John J. Andujar, Fort Worth
8 Mrs. E. Lindstrom, Channelview
   Mrs. M. Shepherd, Houston
9 Mrs. Dale Hager, Beaumont
   Miss Estelle H. Tartt, Galveston
10 *Mrs. F. X. Bostick, Austin*
   Mrs. Robert Farris, Austin
11 Mrs. Gordon King, McGregor
   Mrs. Charles Hanson, Temple
12 *Mrs. Alton Ray, Jr., Fort Worth*
14 Mrs. Joe N. Pratt, Victoria
   Mrs. Jack Garrett, Danbury

15 Mrs. Richard M. Sowell, McAllen
    Mrs. J. H. Clement, Kingsville
    Mrs. L. V. Mead, McAllen
16 Mrs. J. T. Morehead, El Paso
18 Mrs. G. N. McDaniel, Borger
    Mrs. Warren Fatheree, Pampa
    Mrs. Tom Suits, Petersburg
22 *Mrs. Warren H. Binkley, Houston*
23 Mrs. W. A. Smith, Floresville
    Mrs. Marvin Selig, Seguin

1972 (52 TOTAL DELEGATES)

AT LARGE DELEGATES /*Alternates*
Mrs. Anne Armstrong, Armstrong
Mrs. James F. Biggart, Dallas
Mrs. Richard D. Bass, Dallas
Mrs. Robert C. McArthur, San Antonio

DISTRICT DELEGATES /*Alternates*
 1 Mrs. Walter Judge, Mineola
 2 Mrs. B. E. Atkinson, Lufkin
    Mrs. Beth Jo Tucker, Beaumont
 3 *Mrs. J. Kanowsky, Dallas*
    Mrs. Dewitt Moffett, Dallas
 5 Mrs. James Clayton, Dallas
    Mrs. Charles Foster, Jr., Dallas
 7 Mrs. Nancy Palm, Houston
 8 Miss Ola Dee Koeppel, Houston
 9 Mrs. O. J. Richardson, Nederland
    Mrs. Elmer B. Vogelpohl, Galveston
10 Mrs. Beryl Milburn, Austin
    Mrs. Thomas G. Price, Austin
    Mrs. Lee Briscoe, Eagle Lake
11 *Mrs. Ruel Dixon, Waco*
    Mrs. James F. Wood , Waco
12 Mrs. Alton S. Ray, Jr., Fort Worth
13 *Mrs. Pierce Langford, Wichita Falls*
    Mrs. Ila Jo Hart, Gruver
14 Mrs. George D. Stevens, Corpus Christi
    Mrs. Owen D. Cox, Corpus Christi
15 *Mrs France Lipe, Brownsville*
16 Mrs. Itha Jeudeman, Odessa
    Mrs Edgar Francis, Odessa
    Mrs. John Root, El Paso
18 *Mrs. Lillian B Tilley, Houston*
    Mrs Dorothy Potts, Houston
19 *Mrs. James W. Lacy, Midland*
20 *Mrs. Pearl Cloud, San Antonio*
21 Mrs. Baxter R. Grier, San Antonio
    Mrs. Louis Bohls, San Antonio
22 *Mrs. Toby Blumenthal, Pasadena*
23 Mrs. Marvin Selig, Seguin
    Mrs. Bruce T. Foster, Hondo

24 Mrs. M. G. Burgland, Arlington
    Mrs. Stan Stooksberry, Ft. Worth
    Mrs. I. Ray Dunlap, Dallas

1976 (100 TOTAL DELEGATES)

AT LARGE DELEGATES /*Alternates*
Fran Chiles, Fort Worth

DISTRICT DELEGATES /*Alternates*
 1 Lila Lee Rehkop, Athens
 2 Betty Jo "B. J." Tucker, Beaumont
    Jeanie Turk, Beaumont
 3 Barbara Staff, Dallas
    Lauren D. Hobbs, Dallas
    Iris Snell, Dallas
    Virginia S. Steenson, Richardson
 4 *Betty Anderson, Terrell*
 5 Jean Sommerfield, Garland
    Carlota Phillips, Dallas
    Beth T. Miller, Dallas
    Barbara Carter, Mesquite
    Sherry Allen, Dallas
 6 Betty Andujar, Fort Worth
    Dorothy Smith, Fort Worth
    Irene Cash, Dallas
    Anna Mowery, Fort Worth
    Shirley Black, College Station
 7 Jacqueline Till, Houston
    Billie Whitefield, Houston
    Ruth McGuckin, Houston
    Carol E. Belton, Houston
 8 *Isabelle Gray, Pasadena*
 9 Nancy Canion, League City
    Wilda Lindstrom, Channelview
10 Rhoda Benson, Austin
    Kay Danks, Austin
    Sue Briscoe, Eagle Lake
    Joye Boggs Flanagan, Austin
11 Bette MacRae, Waco
    Dorothy Wood, Waco
    Dorothy F. Crockett, Marble Falls
    Alta Ada Schoner, Brownwood
12 Pat Jacobson, Fort Worth
    Helen Fitzgerald, Fort Worth
    Gwendolyn C. Morrison, Fort Worth
13 Ila Jo Hart, Gruver
    Kathryn McDaniel, Borger
    Nadine Gregg, Amarillo
14 Sylvia Berry, Rockport
    Demarious K. Frey, Corpus Christi
15 *Martha Alworth, Kingsville*
    Wanda Jones, Alamo
    Linda D. Montemayor, Brownsville

16 Sharon Carr, El Paso
   Bette D. Hervey, El Paso
17 *Dorothy H. Hall, Big Spring*
18 Penelope L. Horton, Houston
   Ann Striegler, Houston
   Maxine Shaver, Houston
   Mary Lou Brooks, Houston
19 Barbara Culver, Midland
20 Mary Jackson, San Antonio
   Elsie L. Franson, San Antonio
   Gladys K. Hamilton, San Antonio
   Sue Heacock, San Antonio
   Jean Bensmiller, San Antonio
21 Dorothy Doehne, San Antonio
   Elizabeth J. Rohn, Kerrville
   Helene Randolph Moore, New Braunfels
22 Marguerite Binkley, Houston
   Nancy Boggs, Pasadena
   Dorothy Hudson, Seabrook
23 Annette Matthews, Luling
   Bonnie B. Sunvision, San Antonio
   Marilyn Brien, San Antonio
   Eddy Mae Mosby, San Antonio
   Lorene Lyles, San Antonio
   Wanda Roe, Jourdanton
24 Jane Burgland, Arlington
   Jane T. (Jan) Sutton, Grand Prairie
   Nancy Johnson, Arlington

1980 (80 TOTAL DELEGATES)

AT LARGE DELEGATES /*Alternates*
Kay Danks, Austin
Beverly Rupe, San Antonio
Martha Weisend, Dallas

DISTRICT DELEGATES /*Alternates*
 1 Lila Rehkop, Athens
 2 Jeannie Turk, Sour Lake
 3 Dorothy B. Golden
   Sally McKenzie, Dallas
   Jeanne Tower, Dallas
   Ida Papert, Dallas
 4 *Jody Smith, Denton*
 5 *Laverne Moore, Dallas*
   Irene McCommon, Dallas
 6 Annabelle Farrell, Duncanville
   Ada Gibbs, Fort Worth
   Katherine McNutt, Corsicana
   Betty Getzendaner, Waxahachie
 7 *Barbara Harris, Houston*
   Barbara Patton, Houston
 8 Sue Helbig, Baytown

 9 Gwen Emmett, Kingwood
   Nancy Canion, League City
   Tommie M. Byrd
10 Pamela Findlay, Austin
11 Dottie Young, Round Rock
   Katrina Stone, Corpus Christi
   Helen Rutland, Belton
12 Fran Chiles, Fort Worth
   Barbara Howell, Fort Worth
   Modean Barry, Fort Worth
13 Bobbie Nisbet, Pampa
   Christina Richardson, Amarillo
   Nadine Gregg, Amarillo
   Sybil Daniel, Perryton
14 *Sylvia Berry, Rockport*
15 Delores F. Clark, Brownsville
   Pat Kline, McAllen
   Jean Bensmiller, Whitsett
16 Sara L. Robbins, Odessa
17 *Dottie Scott, Abilene*
   Mary Dulaney, Snyder
18 Naomi Andrews, Houston
   Claire Moore, Houston
19 Rosalind K. Haley, Lubbock
   Janelle Evans, Brownfield
   Corrine E. Weis, Midland
20 Mary M. Jackson, San Antonio
   Marge Kahler, San Antonio
   Sue S. Heacock, San Antonio
   Lois C. White, San Antonio
21 Dorothy Doehne, San Antonio
   Elizabeth Rohn, Kerrville
22 Adele Hedges, Houston
   Becky Orr, Houston
   Margaret Napier, Richmond
22 Florence Bennett, San Antonio
   Annette Mathews, Luling
24 Naomi Laird, Irving
   Wanda Damstra, Grand Prairie
   Jane Bergland, Arlington

1984 (109 TOTAL DELEGATES)

AT LARGE DELEGATES /*Alternates*
Martha Weisend, Dallas
Mary Ann Leche, Dallas
Anne Armstrong, Armstrong
Kris Ann Vogelpohl, Galveston
Penny Butler, Houston
Carolyn Knight, Granite Shoals
Barbara Campbell, Dallas
Ester Yao, Houston
Fran Chiles, Fort Worth
Belinda Dyer, San Antonio

Diana Denman, San Antonio
Esther Buckley, Laredo
Mary Denny, Aubrey
Dorothy McClellan, San Antonio
Nancy Palm, Houston

DISTRICT DELGATES /*Alternates*

1 Lila Lee Rehkop, Athens
   Nancy M. Gordon, Avinger
2 *Lydia Damrel, Vidor*
   Jackie Dillion, Woodville
3 Mabel Burns
   Mary Scruggs, Plano
   June Coe, Dallas
   Virginia Steenson, Richardson
4 Mary W. Whitt, Terrell
   Edith Jester, Whiteright
   Jan Copas, Tyler
5 LaVerne Moore, Dallas
   Ann Collins, Dallas
6 Naomi Godfrey, Fort Worth
   Evelyn Gustafson, Cleburne
   Shirley Rogers, Conroe
7 Kay Shillock, Houston
   Patricia Vanoni, Houston
   Billie Whitefield, Houston
8 Pat Wall, Kingwood
   Jo Helen McGee, Kingwood
   Patti Johnson, Humble
9 Tommie Byrd, Beaumont
   Vicki Hapke, Houston
   Barbara Nowlin, Friendswood
10 Ellen Garwood, Austin
   Annette Matthews, Luling
   Kay Danks, Austin
   Anne Lassiter, Austin
   Holly Decherd, Austin
11 Louise Irby, Killeen
   Audrey Corbett, Salado
   Jackie LaMonte, Copperas Cove
   Sarilee Ferguson, Waco
12 Iona Reed, Azle
   Elise Cole, Fort Worth
   Mary Conner, Fort Worth
13 Jacque Allen, Wichita Falls
   Carolyn Moorhouse, Seymour
   Jane Juett, Amarillo
14 Sylvia Maddox, Victoria
   Lynn Grebe, Bay City
   Anne Ashy, Victoria
   Patricia Leininger, Shiner
15 Peggy Rodgers, Edinburg
   Virginia Armstrong, McAllen

16 Madge Zuloaga, El Paso
17 Kathy Webster, Abilene
   Birdie Morgan, Abilene
18 Mary Jane Smith, Houston
   Martha C. Baird, Houston
   Helen Hanna, Houston
19 Mary Lou Parsons, Odessa
   Johnnye Davis, Odessa
   Janelle Evans, Brownfield
20 Dorothy Doehne, San Antonio
   Diane Rath, San Antonio
   Evelyn Ruks, San Antonio
21 Carolyn Minton, San Angelo
   Margaret Cosby, Boerne
22 Doris Williams, Lake Jackson
   Ann Lee, Houston
   Patricia Black, Houston
23 Katy Evans, San Antonio
   Ann Peden, Hondo
   Elizabeth Plum, San Antonio
   Cynthia Wood, Laredo
   Alicia Cantu, Laredo
24 Dedie Mankin, Duncanville
   Helen Parker, Grand Prairie
   Amanda Hall, Cedar Hill
   Marge Bega, Dallas
25 Anna Claire Rice, Houston
   Gayle West, Pasadena
   Izzy Gray, Pasadena
26 JoAnn Smith, Denton
   Violet Bradel, Arlington
   Vivian Millirons, Burleson
   Mary Louise Dodge, Dallas
27 Delores Price, Kingsville
   Mildred Thodos, Corpus Christi

1988 (III TOTAL DELEGATES)

AT LARGE DELEGATES /*Alternates*
Penny Butler, Houston
Kay Bailey Hutchison, Dallas
Carole Fleming, Sugar Land
Doris Williams, Lake Jackson
Sally McKenzie, Dallas
Nancy Crouch, Houston
Jocelyn L. Straus, San Antonio
Marta Greytok, Taylor Lake Village
Ruth Fox, Austin
Flo Atherton, San Antonio
Ann Quirk, San Antonio
Holly Decherd, Austin
Beth Mahaffey, Dallas
Rita Clements, Dallas
Jeanne Johnson, Dallas

Dot Adler, Richardson
Cynthia A. Garza

DISTRICT DELEGATES / *Alternates*
1 Beth Furrh
2 Betty Joe Tucker, Sour Lake
   Patti Tate, Conroe
3 Betty Doke, Dallas
   Barbara Pinsker, Dallas
   Alma Carter, Plano
4 *Dorothy Banfield, Whitesboro*
   Beverly Thomas, Greenville
5 Lynne Tweedell, Dallas
6 Faye Diamond, Cleburne
   Florace G. Kling, College Station
   Margaret W. Forehand, Fort Worth
7 Dee Coats, Houston
   Claudette Martin, Houston
8 *Jeanette Guttormson, Kingwood*
   Wanda Hudson, Kingwood
9 Lisa Duperier, Beaumont
   Carolyn Smith, Houston
   Janet Farmer, Galveston
   Letha F. Barber, Galveston
10 Mary Teeple, Austin
   Becky Orr, Austin
11 *Otha Taylor, Temple*
   Helen Quiram, Waco
12 Rita Palm, Fort Worth
   Estelle Teague, Hurst
   Elizabeth Diano, Fort Worth
   Kit Sears, Fort Worth
13 Susan Tripplehorn, Pampa
   Jane Juett, Amarillo
   Jacque Allen, Wichita Falls
   Carolyn Nicholas, Wichita Falls
14 Barbara Schoolcraft, Seguin
   Anne Ashy, Victoria
15 *Beth Brady, Edinburg*
16 Patricia D. Bruce, El Paso
   Bernice Peralta, El Paso
   Marcia Waugh, El Paso
17 Anne Bergman, Weatherford
   Lynn Oates, Decatur
   Claire Johnson, Abilene
   Marilyn Patterson, Abilene
18 *Mary Newsome, Houston*
   Alison Smith, Houston
19 Johnnye Davis, Odessa
   Ruth Schiermeyer, Lubbock
   Carolyn Powers, Odessa
   Jane Anne Stinnett, Lubbock

20 Dorothy Doehne, San Antonio
   Mary Wathen-White, San Antonio
   Diane Rath, San Antonio
21 Lou Brown, Midland
   June Deason, San Antonio
   Cindy Brockwell, Boerne
   Alene Treadwell, Ft. McKavett
   Dianne Thompson, Boerne
22 Claudine Spillos, Missouri City
   Jorene Aycock, Lake Jackson
   Marjorie Arsht, Bellaire
   Beverly Kaufman, Houston
23 Theo Wickersham, Universal City
   Carol Eddlemann, San Antonio
   Helen Marie Jones, Eagle Pass
   Elsa Guajardo, Laredo
24 Caroline Fields, Irving
25 Gayle West, Pasadena
   Betsy Lake, Houston
   Margaret Baird, Houston
   Beverly Montera, Houston
   Dorothy Sanders, Houston
26 Mary C. Denny, Aubrey
   Rosa Lopez Terry, Carrollton
   Terry Grisham, Arlington
27 *Leona Knight, Corpus Christi*

SOURCE:
Delegates to the 1948, 1952, 1956, 1960,
and 1964 conventions from Paul Casdorph,
The Republican Party in Texas 1865-1965
(Pemberton Press, 1965). Delegates in 1968,
1972, 1976, 1980, 1984, and 1988 from the
official proceedings of Republican National
Conventions.

APPENDIX 3

Texas Federation of Republican Women Presidents, 1955–1999

1955   Mrs. Robert D. O'Callaghan (Aileen), San Antonio
1957   Mrs. Dick Elam (Maxine), Abilene
1959   Miss Betty Blodgett, Corpus Christi
1961   Mrs. J. C. Man, Jr. (Barbara), Wichita Falls
1963   Mrs. Irene (Cox) Wischer, San Antonio
1965   Mrs. George Pearson (Ginny), Tyler
1967   Mrs. Malcolm Milburn (Beryl), Austin
1969   Mrs. Louis Bohls (Cleo), San Antonio
1971   Mrs. Maurice Angly, Jr. (Surrenden), Austin
1972   Mrs. Robert C. McArthur (Janelle), San Antonio
1973   Mrs. Jim Lewis (Barbara), Kerrville
1975   Mrs. Robert D. Bergman (Anne), Weatherford
1977   Mrs. Jim Carhart (Vera), Houston
1979   Mrs. Henry C. Smyth, Jr. (Cathy), Dallas
1981   Mrs. Winfree L. Brown (Lou), Midland
1983   Mrs. Mark S. Campbell (Barbara), Dallas
1985   Mrs. Mark S. Campbell (Barbara), Dallas
1987   Mrs. Milton Fox (Ruth), Austin
1989   Mrs. Jay Patterson (Jan), Dallas
1991   Mrs. Al Kaufman (Beverly), Houston
1993   Mrs. Terry Saunders (Marcia), Lake Kiowa
1995   Mrs. James Thompson (Dianne), Boerne
1997   Mrs. Don Kennady (Jan), New Braunfels
1999   Mrs. Don Kennady (Jan), New Braunfels

SOURCE:
Texas Federation of Republican Women

APPENDIX 4

Ten Outstanding Republican Women, 1965–1999

1965

Mrs. W. J. Alexander
Mrs. John J. Andujar
Mrs. Dixie Crossman
Mrs. C. F. Hamilton
Mrs. Elmer G. Kreuber
Mrs. Jack Maxfield
Mrs. Malcolm Milburn
Mrs. Patricia Skinner
Mrs. Bill Steger
Mrs. Frank Wedding

1967

Mrs. John Culver
Mrs. Jack Eidson
Mrs. George Irving
Mrs. Gordon King
Mrs. Glen Leland
Mrs. J. P. Mason
Mrs. Violet Mottwiler
Mrs. Bradlee Postell
Mrs. H. J. Roper
Mrs. Loyd Winship

1969

Mrs. William Walker, Jr.
Mrs. Rudy Juedeman
Mrs. Lorraine Dyas
Mrs. Jack Pumphrey
Mrs. Alton Ray
Mrs. Noel Schroller
Mrs. William Dabney
Mrs. Ralph Bruse
Mrs. Robert McArthur
Mrs. George Pearson

1971

Mrs. Robert Black
Mrs. James Cochran
Mrs. Kendall French
Mrs. Baxter Grier
Mrs. Barney Johnson
Mrs. Pierce Langford
Mrs. Cornelius Olcott, Jr.
Mrs. Robert Paxton
Mrs. Adolf Stieler
Mrs. Earl Wischer

1973

Jo Kanowsky
Peggy Dunlap
Jane Burgland
Mary Kirchoff
Juandelle Lacy
Blanche Martin
Carolyn Messenger
Nancy Palm
Ellie Selig
Mildred Staley
Lou Stapleton

1975

Jewel Fleming
Jacque Allen
Lena Taylor
Jeanne Barnes
Patricia Duaine
Dorothy Crockett
Anna Mowery
Allie Jane Davis
Joan Cason
Nancy Elizabeth Judy
Special: Cleo Bohls

1977

Kit Sears
Iris Snell
Leibert Clinkinbeard
Mary Louise Johns
Joyce Pittman
Marguerite Binkley
Adele Luca
Carolyn Knight
Joy Rash
Dorothy Reed

1979

Elizabeth Paterson
Mary Lou Mergele
Myrtis Gibson
Ann Mason
Shirley Green
Dixie Clem
Ruth Potter
Marion Doubleday
Ada Gibbs
Carolyn Huchton

1981

Mary Jane Allen
Bette Hervey
Ann Covert
Jane Juett
Ruth Fox
Ruth Schiermeyer
Audrey Cannon
Barbara Foreman
Penny Butler
Anne Bergman

1983

Patti Clapp
June Deason
Peggy Engelhardt
Beverly Fisher
Kay Bailey Hutchison
Gerry Johnson
Jean Rheudasil
Helen Rutland
Laveta Sealy
Estelle Teague

1985

Martha Weisend
Ruth Tansey
Rickey Thompson
Beulah Childress
Pat Berry
Jan Patterson
Jane Berberich
Gwyn Shea
Fran Chiles
Natalie Sadler Kern

1987

Cindy Brockwell
Shirley Costello
Maxine Grothouse
Barbara Lockard
Florence Neumeyer
Jane Pieper
Marcia Saunders
Claudene Spellios
Nancy Stevens
Jane Yancey

1989

Nancy Boston
Rita Britow
Barbara Campbell
Alma Carter
Laverne Evans
Louise Foster
Ramona Kennedy
Yvonne Kohutek
Shirley McSpedden
Edith Schuler

1991

Harriet Armstrong
Vera Carhart
Jan Crow
Mary Denny
Florence Kling
Dolly Peralta
Margaret Rhea
Carolyn Robertson
Dottie Sanders
Theo Wickersham

1993

Kay Baird
Anna Claire Rice
Betty Strohacker
Jeanne Cotellessee
Rose Farmer
Gerry Hardway
Marjorie Nunn
Carol "Teddy" Peterson
Peggy Hamric
Phyllis Cole

1995

Lou Brown
Beverly Kaufman
Betsy Lake
Gayle West
Jeanne Musselman
Taffy Goldsmith
Sandra Logan
Neomi Godfrey
Patsy Standerfer
Ann Smith

1997

Dona Bruns
Mattie Friedlein
Sandra Halsey
Gladys Jeter
Mary Kochs
Jo Konen
Sonja L. Main
Bonnie Maynard
Peggy McDuff
Marvel K. Sayers

1999

Sue Bradley
Mary Belle Brown
Merri Easterly
Ann Harrington
Annette Hopkins
Barbara Jordan
Willie Lawley
Barbara Nowlin
Dianne Thompson
Kris Anne Vogelpohl

SOURCE:
Texas Federation of
Republican Women

Index

*The Index is for the main text only
and excludes the participants' hometowns.*